Astute Class
Nuclear Submarine

2010 to date

© Haynes Publishing 2018

First published in 2018
Reprinted July 2018 and March 2019

Jonathan Gates has asserted his moral right to be identified as the author of this work.

A catalogue record for this book is available from the British Library.

ISBN 978 178521 071 6

Library of Congress control no. 2018935483

Published by Haynes Publishing,
Sparkford, Yeovil, Somerset BA22 7JJ, UK
Tel: 01963 440635
Int. tel: +44 1963 440635
Website: www.haynes.com

Haynes North America Inc., 859 Lawrence Drive,
Newbury Park, California 91320, USA

This book has been written using published information collected overtly from public domain sources and provided by equipment suppliers. Some information in the public domain may be speculation, contradictory or even misinformation. In selecting the information for presentation the author has applied engineering judgement in the same way that foreign powers analyse data obtained from open sources. While every effort is taken to ensure the accuracy of the information given in this book, no responsibility or liability can be accepted by the Ministry of Defence, the Royal Navy, the author or publishers for any loss, damage or injury caused by errors in, or omissions from, the information given.

Printed in Malaysia.

Dedication

To my granddaughter Maya whose tenacity has been an inspiration during the writing of this book.

Acknowledgements

This book would not have been possible without the assistance of staff from the manufacturers and suppliers involved in the production of the *Astute* class submarines. I should like to acknowledge the many people who provided assistance, information and images used in the book:

Pavel Vacata (Admiralty Model Works); John Atkins (Aish Technologies); Michelle Wilson (Analox); Nicola James (Babcock International); John Hudson, Neil Lauderdale, Dr Bob Moran, Simon Purvis, Dan Simpson, David Weild, (BAE Systems); Hayden Sutton (Covert Shores); Norman Moody (*Florida Today*); Marcel Gowers (Hutchinson); Antoine Bonnet, David Cunningham, Guillaume Dandrieux (iXBlue); Rohan Dearlove (Kelvin Hughes), Matt Pryor (MSI DSL); Tobias Schiffman (MTU); Pauline Weatherall (National Oceanographic Centre); John Patterson (Raytheon); Colin Higham, David Radcliffe (Rolls-Royce): Tim Wix (JP Sauer & Sohns), Daniel Shackleton (Salt Separation Services); Kevin Barnes (MacTaggart Scott); Dr Graham Honeyman (Sheffield Forgemasters International); Matthew Howat, Alan Rae (Thales); Simon Benham (Ultra Electronics)

I am also indebted to Rear Admiral Mark Beverstock and to Professors Paul Wrobel and David Andrews of University College London for their advice. Special thanks go to the photographers mentioned in the captions who have allowed their images to be used. I am indebted to the staff of the Fleet Regional Photographic Unit (North) who took photographs especially for this publication. Many photographs are from official sources and I am grateful to those who helped unearth suitable images: Harland Quarrington (MoD Defence Images); James McPherson (Royal Australian Navy Media); and to the staff of the RN Media Archive.

The book's visual impact has been particularly enhanced by the extremely detailed cutaways supplied by BAE Systems; the specially commissioned and meticulously drawn cutaways by Charles Gatward and the impressions of HMS *Astute* by Tvrtko Kapetanović. I am very grateful to them all. I should also like to thank Mischa Campen for the illustrations comparing the various submarines.

On a more general note, I owe a great deal professionally to Peter Chamberlain FEng RCNC and the late Prof Louis Rydill FEng RCNC who acted as mentors throughout my career and who selflessly imparted their knowledge, wisdom and an enthusiasm for warship design.

Astute Class Nuclear Submarine

2010 to date

Owners' Workshop Manual

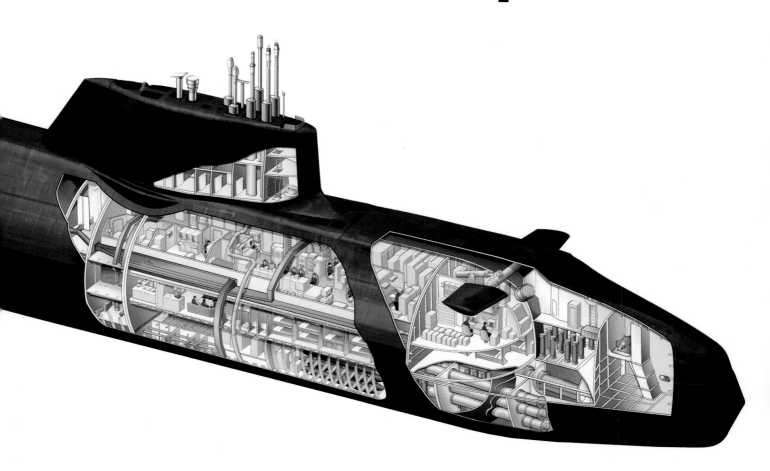

Insights into the design, construction and operation of the most advanced attack submarine ever operated by the Royal Navy

Jonathan Gates

Contents

LEFT HMS *Astute* after her launch at the shipbuilder's yard in Barrow-in-Furness. *(Crown Copyright/Mike Vallance)*

RIGHT HMS *Astute* in transit on the river Clyde on her way to her home base. *(Crown Copyright/LA(Phot) Jonathan 'JJ' Massey)*

Chapter One

Background and history of the *Astute* project

In 2010 HMS *Astute* entered service with the Royal Navy as the first of a new class of seven stealthy, highly capable fleet submarines. She is nuclear-powered and can carry up to 38 weapons, a mixture of Tomahawk land-attack missiles (TLAM) and Spearfish heavyweight torpedoes (HWT). At 7,400T the boats of the *Astute* class are much larger than their immediate predecessor, the *Trafalgar* class submarines. They have been designed to provide the capabilities necessary for the evolving role of nuclear submarines in the 21st century.

OPPOSITE **Two *Astute* class submarines at sea together for the first time off the west coast of Scotland.** (Crown Copyright/LA(Phot) Will Haigh)

7

S119 HMS *Astute*

Laid down	31/01/2001
Launched	08/06/2007
Commissioned	28/08/2010
Operational	25/04/2013

S120 HMS *Ambush*

Laid down	22/10/2003
Launched	06/01/2011
Commissioned	01/03/2013
Operational	26/06/2013

S121 HMS *Artful*

Laid down	11/03/2005
Launched	19/05/2014
Commissioned	18/03/2016
Operational	In service

S122 HMS *Audacious*

Laid down	24/03/2009
Launched	28/04/2017
Commissioned	–
Operational	–

S123 HMS *Anson*

Laid down	13/10/2011
Launched	–
Commissioned	–
Operational	–

S124 HMS *Agamemnon*

Laid down	18/07/2013
Launched	–
Commissioned	–
Operational	–

S125 *To be decided*

The path that led, eventually, to the first-of-class, HMS *Astute*'s commissioning was politically, industrially and technically tortuous. This chapter will outline the background to the *Astute* class and its manufacture. The manual will then describe the construction techniques, the elements of the vessel and explain briefly the operational regime of the class.

The types of submarine

Fleet submarines (*Trafalgar* and *Astute* classes) combine qualities of stealth, endurance and flexibility. Operating on a global basis, these high-speed boats are capable of being used by the Royal Navy (RN) for high-intensity missile strikes, anti-submarine and surface unit warfare, surveillance, inshore reconnaissance and beach observation.

There are three main types of submarine. These are conventionally powered submarines (designated SSK), nuclear-powered submarines (SSN) armed with torpedoes (and, sometimes, also equipped with land-attack missiles) and SSBNs: nuclear-powered submarines armed with nuclear-tipped ballistic missiles.

Before the advent of nuclear power, all RN submarines were SSKs and powered by diesel engines. The diesels required air so could only operate while the boat was on the surface or drawing air from the surface when just submerged. The engines were used to charge batteries that provided power to electric motors so the submarine could then dive and operate at depth. Once the power stored in the batteries was depleted then the submarine would have to return to periscope depth or surface to recharge the batteries. Such diesel-electric boats could only operate on battery power at depth for a few days. The RN operated SSKs for almost a century. The last class to enter service (in 1990) was the 2,400T *Upholder* class SSKs that incorporated much of

> **JACKSPEAK**
>
> The first submarine built for the RN, *Holland 1*, was commissioned in 1903. Its length was just under 20m so it was referred to as a 'boat'. Tradition thereafter has been to refer to submarines as 'boats', never ships.

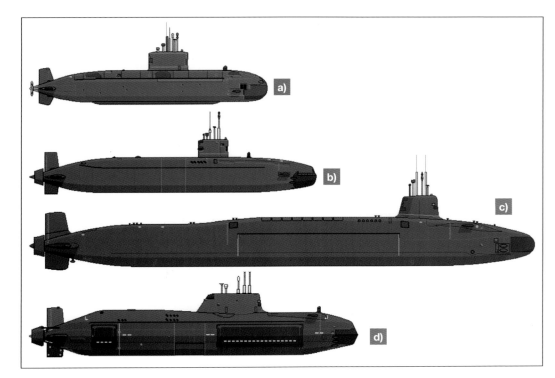

the technology from the nuclear-powered boats and had been designed alongside them. However, in 1994, only a few years after they entered service, the *Upholder* class was paid off and thereafter the RN only operated nuclear-powered submarines. The four *Upholder* boats became the Canadian Navy's *Victoria* class in 2000.

As they do not have to accommodate the nuclear reactor, SSKs are smaller than nuclear-powered boats. They are unable to carry as many weapons as the nuclear boats and have a more limited sensor arrangement. They afford their crew fewer comforts.

In 1955 the first operational nuclear-powered submarine, the SSN USS *Nautilus*, entered service and heralded a step change in submarine technology. The nuclear reactor produced steam to propel the boat and to generate electricity without needing air. Indeed, with the power available, the boat could produce both oxygen and fresh water. USS *Nautilus* showed that a SSN could remain submerged for weeks at a time, the length of the deployment only being limited by the food that could be carried to sustain the boat's complement. The most powerful demonstration of this came three years later when USS *Nautilus* submerged and transited the northern polar region, becoming the first vessel to reach the North Pole.

The first British SSN, HMS *Dreadnought*, was laid down in 1959. She was propelled by a machinery package that was fitted to the American *Skipjack* class boats. This allowed a short design and build period (she was commissioned in 1963). The four-year span for such a novel vessel reflected the importance given to the project and the extensive resources made available.

HMS *Dreadnought* was followed by the *Valiant* class SSNs that were powered by a nuclear reactor designed in the UK. The *Astute* class is the sixth class of SSNs developed for the RN, with HMS *Astute* being the twentieth SSN.

The final, and largest, type of submarine operated by the RN is the SSBN — nuclear-powered submarines carrying intercontinental ballistic missiles with nuclear warheads. HMS

JACKSPEAK

Initially Britain's independent nuclear deterrent was deployed by the RAF from Vulcan bombers. In 1968, the main deterrent was vested in Polaris submarine-launched ballistic missiles deployed on *Resolution* class SSBNs. The SSBNs (and, subsequently their replacement *Vanguard* class SSBNs) became known as 'bombers'.

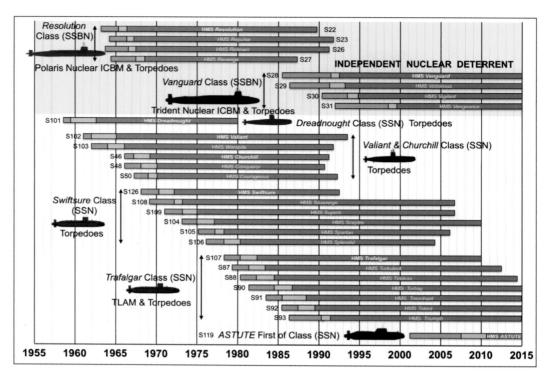

Resolution, the first of a class of four SSBNs, was commissioned in 1967 and was armed with Polaris missiles. These SSBNs were similar to SSNs and their propulsion arrangements were alike, based on the pressurised water reactor (PWR). Their beam was close to that of the contemporary SSNs but they were much longer in order to accommodate a central section with vertical Polaris missile tubes. This *Resolution* class was replaced from 1994 by four larger-diameter *Vanguard*-class SSBNs armed with Trident missiles.

Since 1968, one of the RN's four SSBNs has been on task somewhere in the world's oceans deploying the continuous at-sea deterrent. They carry nuclear-armed intercontinental ballistic missiles that could be launched against an aggressor perpetrating a pre-emptive nuclear strike. The difficulty of locating submarines means that they are an ideal platform for the

COMPARISON OF CHARACTERISTICS OF SUBMARINE TYPES			
	HMS *Vanguard* SSBN	**HMS *Astute* SSN**	**HMCS *Victoria* SSK**
Length	149.9m	97.0m	70.3m
Beam	12.8m	11.3m	7.8m
Draught	12.0m	10.0m	5.5m
Displacement	15,900T submerged	7,400T submerged	2,439T submerged
Propulsion	PWR2 nuclear reactor 2 diesel generators	PWR2 nuclear reactor 2 diesel generators	2 diesel electric 2 motor generators
Range	Worldwide	Worldwide	19,000km
Submerged	90 days	90 days	3 days; 4kts
Complement	135	98	53
Missile tubes	16	0	0
Ballistic missiles	8 × Trident D5		
Launch-tubes	4 × 533mm	6 × 533mm	6 × 533mm
Conventional weapons	Spearfish torpedoes	TLAM and Spearfish torpedoes	Mk 48 torpedoes
Surface sensor	Electro-optical CM010	Electro-optical CM010	Search and attack periscopes
Speed	> 25kts (46km/h)	≈30kts (59km/h)	≈12kts (37km/h)

national deterrent and protecting the nation's security in this way.

The roles of nuclear-powered submarines

Nuclear-powered submarines are not only covert, being very difficult to detect when submerged, but also independent. As they can remain submerged for long periods – for weeks at a time – they are able to roam the oceans virtually unnoticed. Indeed, they are able to completely circumnavigate the world underwater so can deploy rapidly and covertly to any area of the globe. They can also sustain much greater speeds than diesel submarines and do not need to be continually refuelled. As a consequence, they can fulfil roles not open to SSKs or surface ships.

In the Cold War the SSN's primary role was to stalk an adversary's submarines, particularly SSBNs armed with nuclear-tipped ballistic missiles. At the declaration of war they would destroy hostile submarines, limiting the damage that they could inflict. They also had the potential to attack enemy surface ships, thereby denying them the use of an area of sea and eroding their offensive capability. To carry out this role the submarines carry HWTs that can attack both submarines at depth and surface ships.

Since the requirement for the *Astute* class SSN was first drawn up at the end of the Cold War, the operational scenarios in which UK Royal Navy submarines were expected to operate changed significantly. Operations in the littoral were becoming far more commonplace, and commensurately there was less emphasis on deep-water anti-submarine warfare. The traditional roles of gathering intelligence, the insertion of Special Forces and supporting other clandestine operations also increased in importance.

In all roles stealth is at the heart of the SSNs' operations. Against targets at sea they can strike unannounced. Not only can the enemy be unaware of the submarine's presence but also it is equally difficult to ascertain if the threat no longer exists. It has been said, 'You do not know that a stealthy submarine is there, but equally, you cannot be sure that it is not there.' For instance, during the Falklands Conflict of 1982, HMS *Conqueror* became the first SSN to

sink a surface ship in anger. The ARA *General Belgrano* was torpedoed while the Argentinian Navy had only suspected that RN submarines were in the area. Because of the threat of further submarine attacks, the whole Argentinian fleet (with the exception of one SSK) retired to port and no longer participated in the conflict. HMS *Conqueror* remained on task until the Falkland Islands were recaptured, but her action had successfully tipped the balance of naval power and the threat alone would have remained even had she been deployed elsewhere. Submarines are consequently often considered as an asymmetric threat as their impact is much greater than the forces they confront.

SSNs of the *Astute* class and its predecessor, the *Trafalgar* class, have the capability of launching, when submerged, cruise missiles that can attack land targets with high precision. The SSN's ability to strike unannounced at sea has now been extended far inland. *Trafalgar* class boats firing Tomahawk land-attack missiles (TLAM) against land targets played a critical role both in the psychological shock-and-awe campaign in Afghanistan and Iraq in support of the ground assault. More recently, UK SSNs fired TLAMs against critical targets in Libya.

The provision of TLAM on *Trafalgar* and *Astute* class submarines means that they now

ABOVE ***Astute*-class SSN (background) and predecessor, *Trafalgar*-class SSN.** (*Crown Copyright/HMS* Gannet)

have a clear contribution to make to power projection operations ashore. Importantly they can do so in the critical, initial stages of a political crisis and of any military operation. Being covert, they can gain intelligence in the military theatre very early on. The combination of SSN and TLAM acts as an enabling agent for other assets, particularly aircraft and air-delivered ordnance. TLAM can be employed against a wide variety of operational and tactical targets, as part of war-fighting activities and not merely the coercive purpose envisaged originally. TLAM gives the SSNs the ability to reach inland at distance – even into land-locked countries – with the same scale, pace and volume as the land operation itself. Equipped with TLAMs, the RN's Submarine Service has made a potent contribution to US-led coalition operations.

The submarine design challenge

Submarines are extremely valuable assets for naval operations and are able to undertake unique tasks. However, submarines, in particular nuclear-powered ones, are among the most technologically complex and financially demanding of vessels.

Submarines have many of the design requirements that apply to surface warships, such as continuing to be watertight, remaining manoeuvrable, providing a safe environment to carry weapons, retaining sufficient stability to fire weapons and, of course, providing a habitable environment for their officers and sailors. The extra complexity of nuclear-powered submarines concerns the intricacy and safety constraints of both the reactor and maintaining watertight integrity under the considerable pressure of seawater at depth. Features unique to submarine design are the systems of hydrostatics and control that allow it to function in its 3-D world while also being able to operate on the surface. In addition, they need to operate independently of external air and remain undetected. Like any warship, submarines carry weapons containing high-explosives and propellant with the attendant concerns about safety.

The expression 'the devil is in the detail' certainly applies to the exacting principles that concern nuclear submarine design. Apart from

the stringent safety regime, the sheer density of equipment – three or four times that of a surface ship – demands much greater control of the layout. Furthermore, the submarine must remain close to neutrally buoyant (so that it may submerge and resurface), consequently there is a need to maintain equally tight control of the submarine's weight not only on build but also across the boat's life cycle. During design and development there is extremely limited scope for change in weight and space (termed margins). Even small increases or decreases of equipment weight or space have major impacts and are expensive to implement. Consequently establishing accurate predictions early in the design is vital.

The environment in which the submarine operates means that there is little room for error in their design, building or operation, as any mistakes can have major and tragic consequences.

As an indication of the complexity of the *Astute* class submarines, the plan identifies:

- 2,800 contractual requirements in the System Requirements Document
- 7,100 working drawings generated from the computer-aided design system
- 29,000 activities to be undertaken to build the boat
- 96,000 items that need to be installed within the hull
- 10,000 devices to be set to work and tested.

The complexity and technical sophistication of the completed submarine is comparable to the most demanding engineering projects, for instance, the space shuttle.

The *Swiftsure* class of SSNs were intended to be a radical departure from its predecessors. During the initial design investigation, the replacement was termed SSN0X (the letter X being associated with any novel or 'Xperimental' project). Consequently the initial designs for the *Trafalgar* class were named SSN0Y and the follow-on to that class, SSN0Z.

Precursors of the Astute class submarines

The submarines to succeed the *Trafalgar* class, termed SSN0Z, were initially developed in the late 1970s and were led by an in-house MoD design team. This design was a 'clean-sheet' concept that featured the 'next-generation' all-British nuclear propulsion plant being developed at the time – PWR2 – and an improved combat system with a new integrated sonar suite. There was also a desire to incorporate further signature reduction measures to counter increased effectiveness of the sensors deployed by potential adversaries.

The process of design begins with work on a concept design exploring how the very high-level requirements can be met. Options for technical solutions are then examined at both whole boat and major system level. In general the user has a desire for a new boat that is faster, deeper-diving, quieter – and for less money. Accordingly, the capabilities sought may have to be curtailed to meet budgetary constraints – there is a balance between the competing pressures of cost, capability and project risk. Decisions made at this stage have a major impact on the outcome of the project. The output of the conceptual work is an outline design and the development of a requirements document that describes the desired capability.

In 1980 it was announced that a new SSBN (subsequently named the *Vanguard* class) was required for the national deterrent. *Vanguard* would absorb all the nation's submarine design, development and construction effort for the next several years. The SSN0Z design was postponed and the small SSN0Z design team formed the nucleus of the new SSBN design section.

Comparison of space shuttle and HMS *Astute*		
	SPACE SHUTTLE	**HMS *ASTUTE***
Length, diameter	38m, 7m	97m, 10.7m
Weight	78T	7,400T
Propulsion	3 main engines	Nuclear reactor 2 diesel generators
Components	368km of cable 1,060 valves	148km of cable 5,000 valves 23,000 pipes missiles and torpedoes
Coating	27,000 thermal tiles	39,000 acoustic tiles
Crew	5–7	98
Mission duration	5–16 days	> 90 days
Design life	100 missions	25 years
Environment	560km above sea level	At least 250m below sea level Corrosive
Pressure gradient	1kPa	Up to at least 2,450kPa
Speed	7,800m/s	> 10m/s

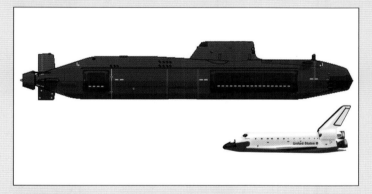

ABOVE HMS *Astute* compared with the space shuttle. *(Mischa Campen)*

BELOW Pie chart of typical submarine weight and space breakdown. *(Author after R. Burcher and L.J. Rydill)*

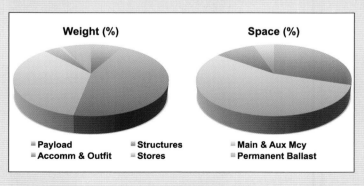

Weight (%) — Space (%)

- Payload
- Accomm & Outfit
- Structures
- Stores
- Main & Aux Mcy
- Permanent Ballast

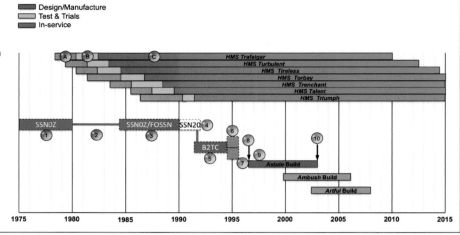

Astute's predecessors. *(Author)*

Legend:
- Design/Manufacture
- Test & Trials
- In-service

1 Concept design SSN0Z
2 Postponement during *Vanguard* design
3 Further design, modified requirements
4 Beginning of full design and build for SSN20
5 Design of *Trafalgar* class derivative B2TC
6 Bidding by two consortia
7 Price negotiation
8 Contract award
9 Design and drawing production for *Astute*
10 Delivery date proposed in GEC bid

In 1984 work restarted on SSN0Z – now called Follow-On SSN (FOSSN). In 1986, the MoD approved the Outline Staff Target and the start of formal feasibility studies. The co-located MoD project team included engineers of all disciplines, reflecting the policy of 'total project responsibility'.

The project team contracted the UK's only submarine manufacturer, Vickers Shipbuilding and Engineering Ltd (VSEL), to undertake studies on specific systems to assess the impact on the overall size and cost of the submarine, and to prepare for the future detailed design. VSEL and their subcontractors were largely unfamiliar with investigative feasibility work, so the MoD provided guidance about policies and standards, operational performance, safety aspects and interfaces with both weapons and the propulsion plant. In 1989, the project moved to a 'Full Design and Build' phase. This started with a more detailed design exercise for the first submarine of the class, now referred to as SSN20. However, towards the end of that year the Soviet Union collapsed. A defence review in light of the perceived end of the Cold War resulted in the SSN20 project being abandoned. All the documentation, including that from industry, was archived.

Beginnings of the *Astute* class project: 'Batch 2 *Trafalgar* class'

Studies for a new, less ambitious, Batch 2 *Trafalgar* class (B2TC) submarine began in June 1991 with preparation of a Naval Staff Requirement. The Treasury believed that purchasing the new class off-the-shelf from the USA would yield significant savings even though this would inevitably result in technical and operational difficulties. In the event, it was shown that this would cost roughly twice as much as designing and building the submarines in the UK. The government of the time desired the UK to retain a sustainable competitive base for the design, build and support of nuclear submarines.

Although the technical requirements and timescale for the next French SSN were likely to be very different from the UK's, it was rumoured that some discussions were undertaken on a joint programme. Both governments wished to retain their own nuclear propulsion plant but there was thought to be potential to adopt a common fore-end. Given the different operational approaches and significantly disparate requirements for the two nations' sonars, this had technical difficulties. Soon the political imperative waned and the discussions ceased.

Initial design studies for B2TC were undertaken by an industrial group formed from the four companies who expressed interest in taking part in the programme: VSEL, GEC-Marconi, British Aerospace (BAe) and Rolls-Royce. This industry team built on the work done for SSN0Z/FOSSN, but recognised the need to constrain the aspirations of the users. A few major decisions were taken but, at this early stage, there was still enormous uncertainty over the details of the final design. In 1993 a single preferred concept was selected as a 'reference design'. This matched a set of performance

In order to accommodate the bigger PWR2 reactor, the B2TC reference design had a larger-diameter bulge amidships. It became known, rather unflatteringly, as the 'pregnant worm'.

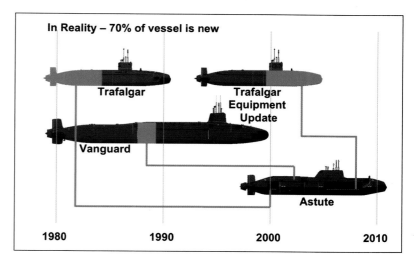

ABOVE **Provenance of *Astute* design elements.** *(Author, using BAE Systems information)*

requirements developed in parallel by a small MoD project team. The design incorporated ways to significantly reduce the cost of the SSN20 design while still improving on the operational performance compared to existing submarines (for instance, the capability in the littoral).

Technologically, B2TC was intended to be a derivative of the preceding *Trafalgar* class, as its designation indicates. The reference design comprised versions of the *Trafalgar* class propulsion system, the *Vanguard* class reactor and the new, state-of-the-art combat system recently developed as an upgrade for the *Swiftsure* and *Trafalgar* classes. The PWR2 nuclear-power plant was, at the time, being fitted to the four much larger *Vanguard* class SSBNs. PWR2 incorporated improved safety features over PWR1 and had the potential to use more advance nuclear cores with longer lives thereby avoiding expensive and time-consuming refuelling during the life of the submarines. However, because PWR2 was larger, the reactor compartment required a greater hull diameter and that had a major impact on the new SSN's size.

As the design progressed, especially in the early years of the contract, additional capabilities were added, changes applied to ease manufacturing,

support issues addressed and the complement reduced. These all led to 'requirements creep' that extended the design process and resulted in pressures to increase the cost.

Competitive bidding

Using the B2TC reference design, the MoD developed performance requirements for the new class. These requirements were 'illustrated but not necessarily met' by the reference design. In accordance with its policy to procure defence equipment by competition, in mid-1994 the MoD invited tenders for a prime contractor to complete the B2TC design and to build the submarines that would become the *Astute* class.

The placing of a contract with a prime contractor was a departure from the normal submarine procurement practice. It would require the contractor to take responsibility to design one

Comparison of in-service HMS *Trafalgar* and HMS *Astute*		
	HMS *TRAFALGAR*	**HMS *ASTUTE***
Length	85.4m	97m
Beam	9.8m	11.3m
Draught	9.5m	10.0m
Displacement	5,300T Submerged	7,400T Submerged
Propulsion	PWR1 nuclear reactor 2 diesel generators	PWR2 nuclear reactor 2 diesel generators
Complement	130	98
Launch-tubes	5 × 533mm	6 × 533mm
Armament	30 weapons	38 weapons
Weapons	TLAM and Spearfish torpedoes	TLAM and Spearfish torpedoes Special Forces payload bay

of the most complex engineering entities before building the finished product. Furthermore, they would be responsible for the performance and associated risks of a vessel that was required to operate a nuclear reactor and weapons hundreds of metres beneath the sea's surface. A prime contractor is a more common approach for aircraft procurement, but in that case several prototypes are built and tested to give confidence in the final version to be manufactured. The prototypes are generally discarded.

In order to take on the challenge, the prime contractor must possess significant and sound financial resources as well as technical and project management experience. The only prospective British companies that were considered by the MoD as having sufficient resources were GEC and BAe. Rolls-Royce & Associates were the nominated single-source subcontractor for the overall propulsion systems and nuclear plant for all bids.

VSEL had built, or were building, 24 of the RN's 27 nuclear submarines. The company saw itself as the natural manufacturing facility for the SSNs and were keen to replenish their order books. As a consequence VSEL teamed with Lockheed-Martin and BaeSEMA. BaeSEMA was, itself, a joint venture, 50% owned by British Aerospace, which could provide the design capabilities that VSEL lacked.

VSEL developed a low-risk response based closely on the reference design. This concentrated on ease of production, and was founded on the performance characteristics of the *Trafalgar* update. A multi-dimensional cost model was produced and used to drive such major decisions as whether to install whole-deck modules. The resulting layout aimed to produce a submarine that was better than *Trafalgar* at a substantially lower cost. The design that emerged had a number of novel features based on a larger-diameter parallel pressure hull (allowing a fully modular approach to construction) with improved signatures and shock protection. It also allowed a much larger weapons stowage compartment with the potential for a 50% increase in weapons load.

As BAe decided not to compete, VSEL was competing against only one other bidder, GEC-Marconi. They bid with an industrial team that had clearly defined responsibilities. It comprised GEC-Marconi (combat system contractor), BMT Defence Services (submarine design), AMEC (submarine production) and, again, they nominated Rolls-Royce as overall propulsion system contractors. All the associated companies had robust defence pedigrees with the exception of AMEC. AMEC, however, could contribute project management skills demonstrated on offshore rig construction. In particular their estimating tools were judged the best in the marine industry. The Swedish company Kockums joined the team to bolster the submarine build expertise, albeit their experience was with SSKs rather than the more complex SSNs.

GEC-Marconi believed that a technical and commercial approach, novel for defence contracts, could be beneficial, centred around bringing the subsidiary design authorities such as GEC-Marconi combat team and Rolls-Royce and into a co-located design and production team with adequate cost models to support and challenge design proposals.

While the GEC-Marconi team considered they had a real possibility of winning the bid, they recognised that it carried risks at GEC corporate level. They also suspected that they might be a 'stalking-horse' intended to secure more competitive prices from VSEL. In order to ensure that no bidder should be disadvantaged by investing in a bid that was primarily intended to satisfy the MoD's desire for competition, GEC requested that the MoD fund both bids. In return the MoD would be offered greater visibility of the emerging design. In the event VSEL declined funding, presumably to guard their proprietary position and to retain control of their actions.

Takeover of VSEL

VSEL did not have a diverse product portfolio and their future relied heavily on winning the contract. Their main order at the time was for four *Vanguard* class SSBNs with the third vessel about to be delivered.

At the beginning of October 1994, during the bidding period, BAe offered to acquire VSEL but GEC countered the offer two weeks later. Because of VSEL's pivotal role in the UK defence industry and because GEC already owned a large warship shipyard, both acquisitions were referred to the Monopolies and Mergers Commission. The commission's conclusion was to recommend the approval of BAe's acquisition as GEC's ownership was likely to 'operate against the public interest'. Unusually, the government overruled the recommendation and permitted GEC to proceed with the acquisition. The consequence would mean that, in future, the MoD would be dealing with a national monopoly. Ultimately GEC revised the offer that was accepted by VSEL, so both bidders for the submarine came under a single owner.

The MoD advice regarding the acquisition of VSEL was that certain conditions should be imposed. For instance, the submarine competition would run its course with the original VSEL and GEC-Marconi teams remaining separate and that they would be prevented from communicating until after the bids had been evaluated. In addition, GEC provided an initial commitment regarding the potential contract including the price.

The two bids were submitted in June 1995. Indeed, it was the VSEL Board's last independent act to approve the submission although, in recognition of their purchase, their price provided 'an adequate negotiating margin for the new owners to agree an acceptable price with the Customer'. Having bought VSEL for a considerable sum of money, GEC must have been tempted not to submit their bid; however, they would then forfeit the payment for bidding agreed earlier by the MoD. GEC-Marconi submitted a bid but it was rumoured that their price was much greater than VSEL's, even taking into account the latter's negotiating margin.

Contract award

A thorough assessment of the bids was undertaken by the MoD, which showed a clear preference for the GEC-Marconi tender. For some reason, their technical solution was submitted without the customary GEC Final Phase Review. Nevertheless the technical offering was largely compliant. Even the in-service date of 2002 was compliant, despite representing an almost unfeasibly rapid programme for a project of such complexity.

GEC were selected as prime contractor in December 1995, subject to final agreement on

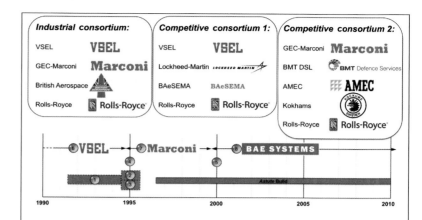

Companies involved in the competition for, and early build of, the *Astute* class. *(Author)*

1 Industrial consortium prepares batch 2 *Trafalgar* class design
2 Competitive consortium 1 prepares *Astute* class bid
3 Competitive consortium 2 prepares *Astute* class bid
4 GEC buys Vickers Shipbuilding & Engineering Ltd and absorbs it into Marconi Marine
5 GEC-Marconi merges with British Aerospace to form BAE Systems
6 Vickers Shipbuilding & Engineering Ltd. owner of Barrow Submarine Facilities 1984–1995
7 Marconi Marine owner of Barrow Submarine Facilities 1994–1999
8 BAE Systems ultimate owner of Barrow Submarine Facilities 1999–present

price. However, the GEC purchase of VSEL in June 1995 to form GEC-Marine created huge uncertainties within the GEC submarine team and led to Rolls-Royce and AMEC withdrawing. This problem was compounded by the difficulty that the MoD faced in finalising and obtaining government approval for a contract for such a large and complex project, the contract not being placed until almost two years after the bid was made. The doubts conspired to disperse much of the original industry team as experienced people left for other projects and companies.

The project heralded a new era for large defence projects. For some time the MoD had dogmatically followed the policy of using competition to reduce procurement costs. In conjunction with this they were favouring fewer, larger contracts. The consequence of these two factors was that defence companies regularly failed to win contracts that would secure their future. This forced many out of business or to leave the defence sector altogether. The natural consolidation of the companies in the defence sector had forced the MoD (the monopsony buyer of large defence equipment) to negotiate with a monopoly supplier of warships. Karl

Marx was correct to predict: 'the end result of competition is the end of competition'. In these circumstances the MoD negotiated on the basis of a 'no agreed price, no contract' procedure, designed to ensure that the MoD obtained value for money from a contract which they were unable to place by competition.

Both the MoD and GEC-Marine wanted to encourage risk-sharing using the best of their joint capabilities. After an all-night negotiation, an order for three boats (*Astute*, *Ambush* and *Artful*) was negotiated and the contract placed just hours before the 'contract freeze' period imposed by the announcement of the general election in March 1997. A £2.8 billion target cost incentive fee contract to design and build the first three *Astute* class submarines was awarded to GEC-Marine as prime contractor and design authority. To incentivise industry, if the final costs were less than the target fee, then the savings would be shared between the contractor and the MoD. Because of delays in negotiating the contract and the commercial effects of the VSEL acquisition (and some degree of realism), the in-service date in the contract was extended to June 2005. The risks in passing design responsibility for an SSN to industry for the first time were clearly large. However, neither the MoD nor GEC-Marine had a clear process or policy that identified the division of responsibilities. While management of project risks were appreciated, this was not the case with the less well-understood additional risks associated with prime contracting.

The initial contract included the first eight boat-years (4½ calendar years) of in-service support in order to encourage proper attention to supportability during design. This was intended to be an extension of the Integrated Logistic Support technique being used in all MoD projects, and the growing use of Contractor Logistic Support by the Naval Support Command.

The final design featured many advances and upgrades on the preceding *Trafalgar* class. Some of the novel equipment, such as the

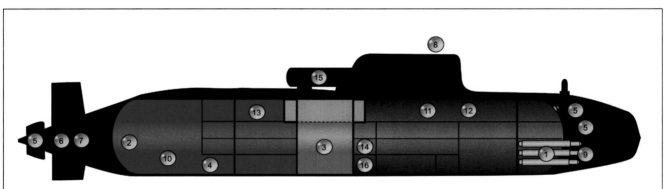

Advances for *Astute* class when compared with *Trafalgar* class. *(Author)*

1 Greater weapons stowage and more launch-tubes than *Trafalgar* class
2 Gearbox improved for acoustic energy reduction
3 PWR2 reactor plant with new core that obviates the need for refuelling
4 Reverse osmosis plant for fresh-water production
5 Use of composite material for hydroplanes, rudder and the propulsor shroud
6 Split aft hydroplanes which increases reliability and manoeuvrability
7 External hydroplane and rudder actuation that reduces the number of hull penetrations
8 Non-hull-penetrating optronics masts that have many operational advantages as well as avoiding a large hull-penetration of the optical periscopes that they replace
9 Air turbine pump for quieter and more controlled weapon launch

10 Electronic main static converters to replace reversible motor generators reducing the space required, the maintenance load and emitted acoustic energy
11 Combat management system improvements to software, consoles and computers
12 Sonar 2076 fully integrated suite of sonar sensors and processors is a leap forward in sonar capability and sensitivity
13 Integrated platform management system increases automation and allows distributed control and instrumentation
14 Atmospheric control system features improved electrolysers and carbon dioxide scrubbers
15 Special Forces capability including the Special Forces payload bay
16 No overboard discharge of garbage – processed, packaged and stored on board for duration of patrol to meet current regulations

Sonar 2076 improvements, would be fitted first to a *Trafalgar* boat and others, having been demonstrated on *Astute*, were planned for back-fit on existing *Trafalgar* submarines.

Prime Contract Office's (PCO) engineering design challenge

GEC-Marine established a subsidiary for the contract, *Astute* Class Ltd, to act as PCO in Frimley, Surrey, that gave them easy access to the few remaining submarine designers, most of whom were established in the south of England, as well as to equipment manufacturers. A submarine is a highly integrated product, both functionally and physically, so there is a need for highly integrated design development involving all disciplines. The PCO was also responsible for the supply chain, in particular first-tier subcontractors for the construction and assembly, the reactor and propulsion system, the platform control system and the combat system. The subcontractors were based throughout the UK. Such geographical dispersion was common for such a complex project, but the PCO sought to alleviate problems by installing a common computer system linking the main sites and that of the customer in Bristol.

The original intent was for little design change from the *Trafalgar*-like B2TC to *Astute*; however, in reality, there were a large number of design modifications, ranging from small equipment upgrades through to major changes. Some of the alterations incorporated in the design period were a result of no longer being able to source legacy equipment, revisions in standards or legislation and the MoD trying to encourage improvements that would meet emerging operational needs. All design changes required assessment to confirm that the original design intent had been maintained and that there were no integration issues. When completed, over 70% of *Astute*, including the nuclear plant, was new equipment, albeit with much being derived from existing boats.

At the highest level, the design was based on nine Key User Requirements (KUR): weapon

system effectiveness, sonar performance, hull strength (survivability), top speed, endurance, acoustic signature, complement, land-attack capability and Special Forces capability.

A nuclear submarine is a complex product for a unique and challenging environment, so requires specialist skills and expertise within the design team. Unlike surface ships there are few third-party design rules or standards and no certifying body such as Lloyd's Register. It follows that it is necessary to design from first principles using a rigorous and integrated engineering process. The PCO was to continue the work of the concept studies from the GEC bid to a much greater level of detail, requiring a step change in personnel. A major concern during the design (and one that reappeared during commissioning) was the lack of suitably qualified and experienced personnel available in the UK, given that *Astute* was the first submarine to be designed in a decade. The hiatus in the UK's submarine-building programme in the 1990s resulted in a haemorrhaging of skilled resources, leading to a lack of continuity and experience in critical disciplines. Much of the former VSEL's design submarine expertise had been lost since HMS *Vanguard* had been launched in 1992.

During the first three years of the project the PCO was to be responsible for refining the boat's size, shape and stability using increasingly accurate estimates of equipment weights and

LEFT Main sites of *Astute*-class activities.
(Author)

1   Prime Contract Office, Frimley, Surrey
2   MoD customer offices, Abbey Wood, Bristol
3   Shipyard, Barrow-in-Furness, Cumbria
4   Submarine Systems Integration & Support Centre, Ash Vale, Surrey
5   Rolls-Royce Neptune test reactor, Raynesway, Derby
6   HMS *Vulcan* Naval Reactor Test Establishment, Dounreay, Caithness
7   Thales Underwater Systems, Templecombe, Somerset (Sonar 2076)
8   Thales, Glasgow (optronics masts)

spatial arrangement. During this phase, weight and space budgets were allocated to the propulsion and platform systems. In addition it was confirmed that key characteristics such as speed and diving depth could be achieved. A major aspect of the project management role was risk management. There were some uncertainties that would diminish as the design became more mature, but others would persist until the boat had been built and trials undertaken. The PCO tracked these risks, devised risk mitigation strategies and ensured that the uncertainty could be tolerated.

The contract included 14,500 requirements that would inform the acceptance process. This requirements set was not complete, consistent or coherent so part of the design process was to generate a System Requirements Document of 2,800 requirements that was logically configured and could be used throughout the remainder of the project.

As the design progressed the spatial and manufacturing detail was developed in a new computer-aided design (CAD) system that had previously been piloted by VSEL for HMS *Ocean*, an amphibious assault ship commissioned in 1998. Manufacturing began at Barrow-in-Furness in parallel with the design activities and the first steel was cut at the end of 1999.

During the first 30 months or so of the contract the *Astute* team slowly began to make some progress with both the design and managerial arrangements. However, they were unprepared for the further industrial hiatus that was to occur at the close of the millennium.

The *Astute* project under BAE Systems

Having acquired VSEL just before the contract award, GEC set about consolidating its defence businesses. During this exercise they came to the conclusion that GEC's future lay outside the defence industry. BAe had been poised to merge with its European partners in the Airbus consortium but found the GEC-Marconi defence concern more attractive because of its American activities. In November 1999, BAE Systems (BAE) was formed when BAe and GEC-Marconi 'merged'. In reality this was a takeover and few GEC-

Marconi senior staff joined the new company.

During the first year under BAE, the *Astute* project continued with design work being performed by the PCO in Frimley. A successful critical systems design review was held with the customer in May 2001. In parallel, CAD production of manufacturing drawings and fabrication of major steelwork was being undertaken in Barrow-in-Furness. The two organisations were managed, and reported, separately. Progress on the detailed CAD definition was very slow with lack of output threatening the fabrication programme. With progress on *Astute* slowing, fabrication of *Ambush* started in August 2001.

By 2002, work on *Astute* and *Ambush* was reduced pending a review of the transition phase from design to production. On examination, the extent of the problem was seen to be more serious than first thought. All fabrication work on HMS *Ambush* was suspended in February 2003, although her ceremonial laying-down ceremony was conducted a few months later in October – an act purely for publicity purposes.

In 2002 BAE decided to form a Sea Systems Group to oversee its naval operations. The group audited the *Astute* project and discovered there was no integrated master plan to design and build the submarine. Without this plan there were disconnects in the design process that resulted in the decision to start building before the design was fully mature. Furthermore, the project was still using GEC's processes that lacked a system to track progress, so no one really understood what little had been accomplished. The audit discovered that the level of expenditure was excessive compared to the progress made and that there were a number of technical and managerial shortcomings. Some of the overspend was a result of MoD changes to the requirements (such as the additional capabilities to meet evolving operational needs) and some the result of the project's difficulty in finding experienced staff as well as the failings of the CAD system.

Estimating the cost of large defence programmes is fraught with difficulties, especially one as complex as a submarine. Because orders are infrequent, equipment costs are high. There is little historic evidence with which to work, especially as some equipment evolves dramatically between submarine classes. The original estimates failed to appreciate that staff shortages in Barrow-in-Furness would be exacerbated by contracts (accepted by GEC) for surface ships and the diversion of skilled submarine workers to reactivate four *Upholder* class of SSKs for Canada.

While CAD was expected to increase productivity, in fact there were severe difficulties with the CAD system, CADDS5. Previous submarine designs relied on 2-D design tools, physical models and hundreds of designers generating detailed plans at drawing boards. *Astute* was the first submarine designed using a single consistent 3-D computer model that would print out the drawings. Although CADDS5 was a proven piece of software, suitable for some surface ships, it had never been used on submarines of the size, detail, complexity and densely packed nature of *Astute*. The software supplier extensively customised CADDS5, but the system was still overwhelmed by the task. Compounding the problem was the shortage of knowledgeable submarine designers in the UK with experience in using 3-D CAD tools.

The MoD, knowing it was a maximum-price contract, took an 'eyes-on, hands-off' approach, having limited interaction with the design team and almost no oversight at the shipyard. The MoD believed it had no authority to challenge the steps taken, or not taken, by the prime contractor.

The overall conclusion of the audit was that the project was at least three years behind schedule and overspent by over £700 million.

Realising that recovery of the *Astute* programme would require greater involvement of the MoD, an agreement was reached between the MoD and BAE for a major restructuring of the programme to improve governance, control and assurance. New financial terms were agreed and new schedules set with both MoD and BAE jointly taking risk-based decisions to deal with problems as they arose. There was an increase in contractual funding of around £430 million, whereas BAE provided a contribution of £250 million (through a provision in its accounts). The contract was placed in 2003 with a new in-service date of 2008.

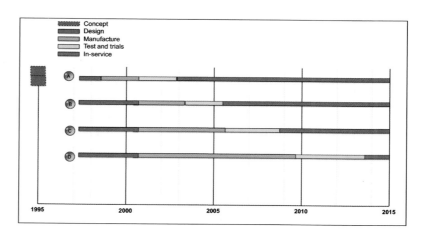

BAE risked disruption to the design activities by relocating the PCO to Barrow-in-Furness and combining it with teams undertaking CAD activities and the manufacturing of the boats. BAE introduced more rigorous project management control, setting clear priorities and ensuring visibility of progress. Key to this was a comprehensive earned value management (EVM) regime already successfully applied to their other naval Prime Contract – for the Type 45 destroyer. EVM allowed a joint MoD/BAE risk and opportunity management programme to be established. Progress was assessed by independent benchmarking undertaken during non-advocate reviews.

To expedite matters, the MoD restored their on-site expertise in Barrow-in-Furness that had been lost with the closure of the Naval Overseeing Service in the 1990s. They also facilitated a small team from US company Electric Boat to provide additional expertise in Barrow-in-Furness and help set up the design tool and establish improved processes. In addition, almost 100 designers at Electric Boat's facility started to develop detailed construction drawings through a secure, classified, high-speed transatlantic data link.

Thanks to these actions, the design of the *Astute* programme started to make progress.

By 2002 the design was sufficiently advanced to reflect on the changes when compared to the original *Trafalgar* class. The most obvious feature was the larger, constant-diameter pressure hull that assisted modular construction that, in turn, reduced integration risk and eased outfit, for instance, of the raft-like floating decks.

ABOVE Evolving *Astute* boat 1 delays. (*Author*)

1 As tendered by GEC
2 As contracted to GEC
3 Revised contract 2003
4 Actual *Astute* programme.

Chapter Two

Building and testing the submarine

HMS *Astute* **and subsequent boats of her class were constructed using a new modular technique that allowed major systems to be set-to-work and tested early in the build, thereby minimising rework later in the process. This was particularly useful for advancing the installation and testing of complex electronic and mechanical systems.**

OPPOSITE *Astute* class boat during build in the Devonshire Dock Hall, Barrow-in-Furness. *(BAE Systems)*

Functional and detailed design

For the first 30 months after contract award in 1997, the project concentrated on the high-level functional design that outlined and balanced the major characteristics of the *Astute* class. This work specified the features proposed at the bidding stage that were documented in the customer requirements. Important aspects were defined such as the operating philosophies for the boat, the build strategy and the means of demonstrating the acceptability of the finished product. Over 300 major equipment procurement specifications began to be developed so that these items could be bought from around 100 suppliers, many through competitive tender.

By 2002 the functional design was frozen and any changes rigorously controlled. This did not mean that there was not a great deal of detailed design work to be done using the CADDS5 system to produce the virtual prototype (3-D product model) from which comprehensive drawings were generated. The model ensured that all pieces fitted together and was the means of communicating data for product development, material ordering, manufacturing and installation. As the difficulties of CADDS5 were overcome, the tool enabled groups of engineers to work simultaneously on design, validation and machining of assemblies.

The aim was to have the electronic product model approximately 80% complete when construction began. Pressure to remain on schedule was resisted to ensure that the design was largely complete, thus reducing the risk of subsequent expensive rework and delay resulting from an immature design. The completed spatial arrangements generated drawings for the build and data for numerically controlled fabrication. Information was also gathered about manufacturing and assembly standards, as well as the means of verifying and validating that the final boat would be fit for purpose and safe to operate. The detailed design was completed and an Initial Certificate of Design issued on 23 October 2003.

Ultimately the outputs of the detailed design process not only produced a complete virtual prototype of *Astute* but also 111,000 drawing sheets as well as details of over a million individual parts, 23,500 pipe spools, 5,000 valves, 240,000m of cable and almost 39,000 acoustic tiles. These outputs were used by over 2,500 people manufacturing *Astute* over a nine-year period and went on to be the basis of the manufacture of subsequent boats of the class.

Two large 3-D stereoscopic theatres were built to project mock-ups from the CAD 3-D virtual models. This visualisation was invaluable for designers to expose any potential clashes between submarine components and assemblies so, if necessary, they could undertake a redesign before building started. It also proved valuable for manufacturing staff, such as welders and pipe fitters, to accurately envisage in 3-D what they were about to physically build.

Because submarines are cylindrical, a 3-D representation provides more information than 2-D drawings and is less ambiguous. The virtual prototype gives a more accurate model of pipe and cable runs and also allows more accurate representation of space around equipment that is needed for installation and maintenance. A simple example is the space needed to open the doors of a cabinet so the maintainer can access the internal components. The prototype can also examine whether there is sufficient clearance to disassemble complex mechanical items. In the same way it can confirm that the layout of equipment allows all items to be shipped into the submarine and installed during production. It can also be used to check the removal routes should faulty equipment need to be exchanged once the pressure hull is fully assembled.

The design process also examines if changes need to be made to improve the efficiency of refit activities. In the past, nuclear refuelling activities had dominated any refit as it required cutting of the hull, decontamination, insertion of new fuel rods and resealing the hull. As *Astute* class submarines are fuelled for life, other tasks dominate the refit critical path. For instance, previously vast effort has been required to remove air bottles, inspecting them ashore and then refitting them – a process that may now lengthen a refit. The CAD system enabled the bottles to be re-sited to allow access for inspection equipment to recertify them *in situ*.

Shipyard facilities

The Barrow-in-Furness shipyard had enjoyed considerable investment for the *Vanguard* class programme, including the main facility later used to build the *Astute* class – the Devonshire Dock Hall (DDH). Built in 1986, the DDH is the second largest undercover shipbuilding construction complex of its kind in Europe. It can accommodate three *Astute* class submarines side by side.

The DDH is used to assemble the construction units, install their modules, weld the units together, complete integration and begin tests and trials. It provides a controlled protective working environment for these activities and also prevents satellites from photographing secret technologies involved. It has a footprint over 250m long and almost 60m wide and is 17 storeys high. The doors allowing the submarines to leave DDH are 22m wide.

JACKSPEAK

DDH was colloquially known as 'Maggie's Farm' after Margaret Thatcher, whose government were funding the upgrading of submarine facilities for the introduction of the Trident deterrent and their associated *Vanguard* class SSBNs.

ABOVE Barrow-in-Furness shipyard from the air. *(BAE Systems)*

BELOW Devonshire Dock Hall. *(Martin Millar)*

LEFT Three *Astute* class submarines in build: *Artful* (left), *Anson* (centre), *Audacious* (right). *(BAE Systems)*

The submarine, once fully assembled, can be rolled out of the DDH on to a ship-lift. A ship-lift is simply a large elevator, 162m long by 22m wide, which is able to lower vessels into the water and can also raise them out for work ashore. The advantage of ship-lifts is that vessels can be constructed on the flat; this increases alignment accuracy and is easier than an inclined slipway.

The adjacent Wet Dock Quay is allocated for testing and trials before submarines leave for sea trials.

The ship-lift is capable of handling vessels as long and as heavy as the *Vanguard* class submarines. Pairs of parallel rail tracks are fitted to the top of the ship-lift and three longitudinal sets of tracks are embedded in the DDH floor. The centre set aligns with the ship-lift tracks, with the others forming the north and south build lines. Transverse tracks allow boats to be moved from the build lines to the centre track. Further tracks extend to the North Quay. The

submarines are supported on cradles every 3m along the boat. Each end of the cradle rests on an electrically driven four-wheel transfer car on the pairs of tracks. The cars have hydraulic lifts rated at 220T.

It was necessary to build new facilities (or refurbish existing ones) to assemble and test specific elements of the boat:

- **New Assembly Shop (NAS)** in which to undertake the steelwork welding and initial outfit of construction units
- **Submarine Machinery Installation and Test Establishment (SMITE)** to test, assemble and outfit the engine modules. This had been used for both the *Trafalgar* and *Vanguard* class submarines and refurbished for the *Astute* programme.
- **Nuclear Build Facility (NBF)** (part of Rolls-Royce's delegated authority) for the manufacture and initial testing of the new PWR2 reactor and its associated steam-

BELOW **Plan of the
Devonshire Dock Hall,
quays and ship-lift.**
(Author)

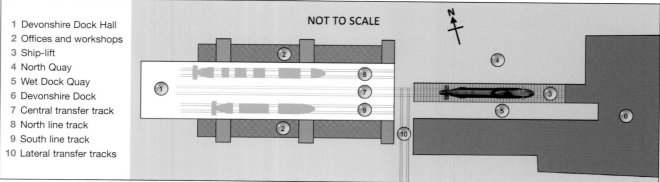

1 Devonshire Dock Hall
2 Offices and workshops
3 Ship-lift
4 North Quay
5 Wet Dock Quay
6 Devonshire Dock
7 Central transfer track
8 North line track
9 South line track
10 Lateral transfer tracks

NOT TO SCALE

N

raising plant. Work began on the NBF in 2004 to create a purpose-built facility that brought together all activities associated with the submarine's nuclear steam-raising plant. The movement around the site of related material, such as pieces of pipework that had been brought from the pipe shop during previous submarine builds, was reduced considerably. When assembling nuclear-related equipment cleanliness is critical. The facility has four enclosed work areas, allowing conditions to be carefully controlled. Each area is dedicated to a specific build item:

◆ reactor pressure-vessel
◆ main coolant pumps and reactor pressure-vessel internals
◆ primary circuit loops, and
◆ reactor pressure-vessel head.

The NBF can simultaneously assemble two submarine reactors.

■ **Warspite Facility** for the manufacture and initial testing of the Command Deck Module.

In addition to these shipyard facilities a **Submarine Systems Integration and Support Centre** (SSISC) was built in Ash Vale, Surrey, to integrate the combat system and test its fabrication and assembly.

An important part of any detailed design is the production of a build philosophy specifying how the boat will be manufactured in manageable elements and how these will be assembled into the finished submarine. The philosophy leads to a build schedule enabling workflow to be managed and for equipment, components and commodities to be ordered in good time.

The basis of the philosophy was to fabricate the pressure hull and outer hull from

construction units that varied in length from about 7m to 14m.

Once the construction units have been joined and the submarine closed, the boat would become an extremely confined working environment of approximately 7,850m^3 with only small access hatches. The philosophy therefore allowed for the construction of a number of equipment modules that would be assembled in parallel with the construction units. The use of modules maximises the amount of work that can be performed off the vessel in a workshop environment, allowing concurrent working with all round access. This not only permits a greater number of tradesmen to work on the module at one time but also allows extensive testing before fitting the module into the pressure hull, thus reducing programme risk.

The key to assembling the submarine from a series of construction units containing large modules is dimensional accuracy and control. The interfaces were defined and maintained

ABOVE Submarine Machinery Installation and Test Establishment from Walney Channel.
(Martin Millar)

BELOW Diagram of construction units.
(Author, using BAE Systems information)

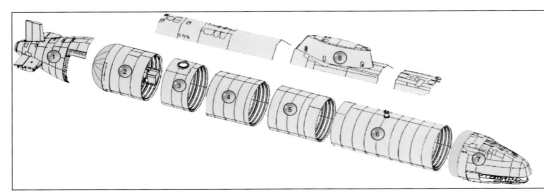

1 Aft end construction (AEC)
2 Units 1 and 2
3 Unit 3
4 Unit 4
5 Unit 5
6 Units 6 and 7
7 Unit 8 and fore end construction (FEC)
8 Bridge fin

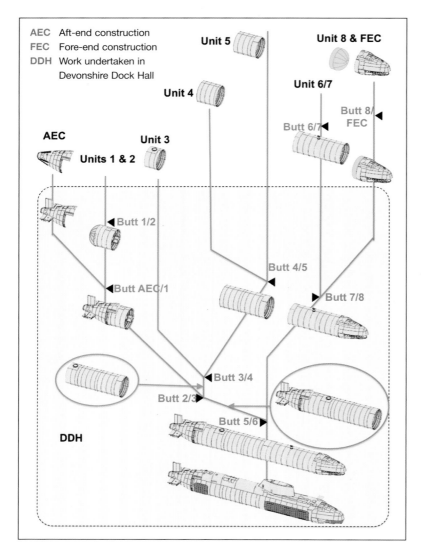

AEC Aft-end construction
FEC Fore-end construction
DDH Work undertaken in
     Devonshire Dock Hall

Unit 5

Unit 8 & FEC

Unit 6/7

Unit 4

Butt 8/
FEC

Butt 6/7

AEC

Unit 3

Units 1 & 2

Butt 1/2

Butt 4/5

Butt AEC/1

Butt 7/8

Butt 3/4

Butt 2/3

Butt 5/6

DDH

LEFT Diagram of construction units and how they are assembled into an *Astute* class submarine. *(Author, using BAE Systems information)*

throughout the evolving design. A 3-D infrared laser theodolite was used to measure the 'as-built' dimensions by relating the positions of plastic trafolite datum pads attached throughout the submarine. The pads have an infrared target recessed into the surface that allow for 3-D co-ordinates to be obtained to within 100μm. After further analysis in the CADDS5 system, minor adjustment of the interfaces was made where necessary before installation of modules and joining of units.

An example of the benefits was first seen with the outfit of the weapons stowage compartment. In the past every piece of equipment for this area had to be shipped in through the small weapons embarkation hatch after the forward end construction had been joined to the unit accommodating the weapons stowage compartment. On *Astute* this was the first compartment to be completely fitted out through an open butt, permitting large assemblies to be installed. The 3-D measurement allowed the equipment to be installed precisely and ensured that the butts fitted together accurately.

All the construction units were fabricated in the NAS. The process for most units was for thick rectangles of steel (about 3m × 1m) to be rolled in order to introduce a curve of the radius of the hull. The normal method of forming high-strength steel into the curved plates of a pressure hull was by rolling at ambient temperatures (cold-work). For areas where the diameter of the bend was small compared to the plate thickness, it was necessary to perform the operations at temperatures between 1,000°C and 1,150°C (hot-work). The surfaces of the steel must be scrupulously clean before hot-working and afterwards the steel must be quenched and tempered.

Both sides of the T-joint are welded

LEFT New Assembly Shop showing single cylinder sub-unit before assembled with others into a construction unit. *(BAE Systems)*

simultaneously with the welding heads remaining stationary while the T-segments are rotated.

Increased productivity was achieved compared with previous submarines by the welding of longer block lengths and increased arc time, using mechanised gas-shielded flux-cored arc welding to weld circumferential butt-joints. As with previous practice, all major butt-welds completely penetrate the joint, but weld time was cut by about 40% with no compromise on weld quality. Instead of the previous semi-automated system using 2.4mm-diameter wire that was only capable of half a weld pass – and with considerable manual intervention – welding machines were used. The two bespoke column-and-boom machines were 4.5m high with a 12m boom and had the capability to use 3.2mm wire. The welding heads (mounted at either end of the boom) completed two passes fully automatically.

Correct welding of the pressure hull components is vital to the safety of the submarine. To achieve the highest standards the welders are highly trained and skilled. As mentioned earlier the pressure hull is fabricated in a number of sections that are welded to produce the final pressure hull. These hull circumferential butt-welds are crucial and challenging, requiring the most experienced welders who operate under conditions that ensure required levels of quality are always maintained. Careful monitoring assures the correct preparation of the butt, the preheating area, the inter-pass temperature, the heat input range and the choice of welding. When the welds are complete, then they are fully checked over their whole length using non-destructive examination (NDE) techniques. This began with a simple visual inspection of surface condition followed by radiographic and ultrasonic examinations that allowed the whole depth of the weld to be examined.

Traditionally, pressure hull external hull welds have been dressed to produce a smooth finish. For the crucial pressure hull this removed excess material that could mask defects during NDE by ultrasonic probes and X-rays. A new automatic ultrasound technique was introduced that penetrated the undressed weld without having to travel over the surface of the cap, so defect detection was unaffected by excess

ABOVE Mechanised welding. (BAE Systems)

BELOW Undressed weld. (BBC)

material. The outer hull of the boats still required dressing as a smooth surface is required to allow the application of acoustic tiles.

The fabrication in the NAS included a great deal of hot-work. Deck and tank collars and both major and minor seats were welded in place as were welded attachments for pipes and hangers for cables and ventilation ducting. The fabrication included the cutting and reinforcement of hull penetrations, the positioning of bulkhead seats and the addition of castings. Paint and insulation was applied to the inner surfaces of the construction unit. Hot-work to fabricate the tank and deck structures was also carried out in the NAS before they moved to the DDH for pre-outfitting, testing and the installation in their relevant units.

Construction units of later boats of the class were partially outfitted while in the vertical

ABOVE Rotation of a construction unit. *(BAE Systems)*

RIGHT AND BELOW **Sequence of rotation of Unit 4:** *(BAE Systems)*

a Unit as fabricated.
b Unit being rotated.
c Unit approaching build orientation.

position but, for *Astute*, they were transported to the DDH without significant outfitting. The smaller units were transported vertically then turned to the horizontal orientation in the DDH. The first steel for *Astute* was cut in October 1999. The formal 'keel laying' ceremony was not performed until 31 January 2001, when a construction unit was unveiled in the DDH. This ceremony represents the start of the manufacture and dates back to the time when surface ships and early submarines were constructed from the keel upwards – however, it is now largely symbolic. The ceremony for *Astute* was almost exactly 100 years to the day after the keel of *Holland 1*, the first RN submarine, was laid at the same yard in Barrow-in-Furness.

Progressively, over several months, completed construction units were transported to the DDH where they were positioned on temporary supports in the sequence in which they would be joined to form the submarine.

RIGHT Keel-laying ceremony for *Ambush*, the second *Astute* class submarine. *(BAE Systems)*

RIGHT Transport of stern dome (Unit 1).
(Jill Hempsall)

Units 6 and 7 were joined together in the NAS before this 800T assembly was moved to the DDH. The unit was transported on a multi-axle self-propelled Scheuerle vehicle that was also used for the Main Propulsion Machinery Package (MPMP) module and the second largest unit, the 500T Unit 5 that would accommodate the nuclear reactor and the main diesel fuel tanks.

Shortly after the units arrived in the DDH, it was necessary to complete installation of equipment and services in areas that, once tank and deck structures were installed, would become difficult to access. Once the decks and tanks were in place the services and equipment on the higher decks could be completed. Butt-joints were made to assemble Units 1/2, Units 4/5 and Unit 8/forward end construction. The units and assemblies were separated by considerable gaps to allow installation of major modules and other pre-assembled modules.

Installation of modules

In parallel with the construction of the hull, modules were being built in special facilities and the NAS. Each module was tested once fabrication was complete so the module could be transported to the DDH and slid into place within the hull.

ABOVE Transport of aft-end construction.
(Jill Hempsall)

LEFT Transport of 800T Units 6/7.
(BAE Systems)

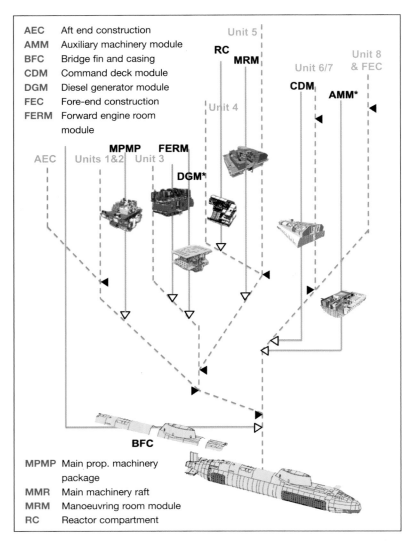

AEC	Aft end construction	
AMM	Auxiliary machinery module	
BFC	Bridge fin and casing	
CDM	Command deck module	
DGM	Diesel generator module	
FEC	Fore-end construction	
FERM	Forward engine room module	

MPMP Main prop. machinery package
MMR Main machinery raft
MRM Manoeuvring room module
RC Reactor compartment

ABOVE Diagram of key construction modules and the sequence of their installation. *(Author, using BAE Systems information)*

LEFT Forward engine room module waiting to be fleeted into Unit 3. *(BAE Systems)*

Manoeuvring Room Module (MRM)

The MRM was the first module to be installed, on 30 October 2004. It was one of the smaller modules, weighing 76T during transport, but housed the centralised control console, the main switchboards and other facilities for monitoring and controlling the reactor, propulsion plant and auxiliary systems. The module was roughly 8.5m long by 8.2m wide. It was installed on 2-deck in Units 4/5 and was two decks high, with the switchboards on its lower deck and the manoeuvring room on its upper deck. The module contained roughly 17km of cabling that was subsequently routed throughout the boat. It was shipped and installed on its acoustic-isolating raft.

The module was lowered on to the shipment rails aft of the Units 4/5. Specially designed hydraulic jacks enabled the module to be fleeted into the hull over the course of about five hours. At the point of shipping, the module was about 50% complete. Once in place, cabling, piping and heating, ventilation and air conditioning ducting were completed and connected. Painting was undertaken and checks carried out to assure that the few items yet to be installed would have access once Units 3/4 butt was completed. As the first module installed, several lessons were learned that changed the details of later stages of the construction.

Forward Engine Room Module (FERM)

After fabrication and testing, the three-deck-high FERM was transported to the DDH on 14 November 2004. This engine room is particularly densely packed with equipment such as plant for heating, ventilation, air conditioning, air purification, water treatment and air pressurisation. Each of these systems has a vast number of associated pipes and cables. Also on the lower deck of the module were the main feed pumps and high-pressure bilge pump. By building this module outside the submarine, access for assembly and testing was improved. Compared with previous submarines (where installation was performed in the cramped space of the submarine hull) installation time was saved.

On 14 November 2004 the FERM was moved on to a frame alongside Unit 3, supported by rails. Hydraulic rams slowly forced the module into Unit 3. Once in position it was secured and connections made to the services already installed around the periphery of the pressure hull.

Main Propulsion Machinery Package (MPMP)

The MPMP included the turbines, gearbox, shaft and turbo-generators and contained 1,263 pipes and 11.5km of cable. It took 56 months to build and test in the SMITE facility. On the submarine, steam to power the turbo-generators is provided by the nuclear steam-raising plant. To test the MPMP, SMITE has its own oil boilers and steam generators to produce steam.

During trials the boilers used 3,105T of fuel oil. Over 1,000,000m^3 of seawater was pumped through the main condensers. During the trials the propulsion shaft turned 1,693,832 revolutions and was load-tested using the facility's dynamometer. The trials replicated the submarine travelling 14,000km – the equivalent of travelling one-third of the way around the globe. During the trials the power generated by the turbo-generators supplied the National Grid. After testing, the MPMP was manoeuvred into its shipping cradle and the 350T module transported to the DDH on 10 June 2005 and, later, eased into position in Unit 2 by hydraulic rams.

Command Deck Module (CDM)

Work to assemble the combat system equipment began at the SSISC. This facility, which took a year to build, was begun in late 2002 in Surrey, close to most of the equipment suppliers. The facility was used to integrate the *Astute* command management system with both the Tomahawk weapon control system and the submarine weapon interface manager (SWIM) to demonstrate that the systems worked together and communicated correctly. Testing was also carried out on the crucial links between *Astute*'s external communication system and the other major combat system equipment.

ABOVE **The SMITE control room during testing of the main propulsion machinery.** *(BAE Systems)*

ABOVE AND BELOW **(a) MPMP being pushed into place.**
(b) MPMP installation complete. *(BAE Systems)*

ABOVE CDM being fabricated in the New Assembly Shop. *(BAE Systems)*

BELOW Equipment being lowered into CDM in Warspite. *(BAE Systems)*

The testing extended to the antennas that would provide the submarine's link with the outside world, with 'over the air' tests of satellite transmissions to the operator workstation. On previous classes of submarine the external communications system would not have been tested to this extent until the boat was at sea. The facility significantly reduced risks to the programme associated with the integration and setting to work of the combat system.

The SSISC had an additional role as a reference site for the combat system allowing problem solving for in-service boats and as a test bed to prove sequential advances as they were made for later boats of the class.

In Barrow-in-Furness, an annexe to the NAS was chosen as the site for the new Warspite facility, which was purpose built during 2004, to construct operational CDMs. Fabrication started in Warspite's equipment preparation area, where the individual combat system elements were assembled and tested. Meanwhile, in the NAS adjacent to Warspite the two-deck-high CDM framework was fabricated. Later, also in Warspite, the 80T framework was outfitted with the complex command deck on its upper deck and, on its lower deck, mess facilities, galley, laundry, wardroom and accommodation spaces. Warspite has space for two CDMs so that a module for a second *Astute* class boat could be begun before the first was completed. The CDM equipment was installed, set-to-work, tested and commissioned in workshop conditions with easy access. To support these activities a purpose-built chilled water plant cooled the CDM's equipment just as it would be on board the boat.

The CDM is a major module containing complex combat system equipment. Construction off-boat gave the significant advantage of reducing the risk of issues only being discovered late in the programme. In addition it was easier to install, set-to-work and test equipment – for instance cabinets could be lowered into the CDM, instead of the traditional method of manhandling them into place within a cramped hull. Pre-outfitting of the CDM shortened *Astute*'s combat system critical path by

LEFT CDM commissioning in Warspite. *(BAE Systems)*

ABOVE **CDM leaving Warspite to its way to the DDH.** *(BAE Systems)*

ABOVE **CDM on rails about to be inserted into Units 6/7.**
(BAE Systems)

RIGHT
(a) **CDM prior to insertion.**
(b) **CDM partially within Units 6/7.**
(c) **CDM installation complete.**
(BAE Systems)

six months, primarily by allowing extensive testing and system commissioning before the CDM was confined to the submarine's hull where remedial action is extremely difficult. The commissioning completed with a combat system-installation trial – a series of submarine operational scenarios enabling the combat system to be demonstrated as a functioning arrangement. This benefit could only be achieved if the cleanliness of the CDM met exacting standards. It involved meticulous cleaning of the module and the Warspite facility, plus regular humidity, temperature and air quality checks, along with the installation of a protective air curtain across the delivery entrance.

The 200T CDM, which is 22m long, was transported to the DDH for subsequent installation in the hull construction unit assembly 6/7. Subsequently, on 5 November 2005, it was moved on to a frame alongside Unit 6, supported by rails. Hydraulic rams slowly forced the module into Unit 6. At times the clearance between the CDM and the pressure hull was just 10mm – the width of a finger. Once in position it was secured and connections made to the services already installed around the periphery of the pressure hull.

Closed boat

Once the CDM was in place, the final butt closure between Units 7 and 8 could be made. Joining the circular butt-weld of two units entails 1,000m of welding and normally takes 28 days; however, a new shipyard record time was set with the 5/6 butt to close the boat, the work being completed in just 11 days. The team of 16 welders was double the number usually involved, working in pairs 'two to the arc' in two 12-hour shifts. Standard procedures only enabled a welder to work for an hour before being forced to stop because of the extreme heat. Pairing the welders meant that when one stopped his partner was ready to take over, thereby allowing continuous welding for the whole 11 days. The welders were supported by a team that provided the right lighting and fume extraction. That team also ensured heating elements raised the temperature of the steel to the optimum temperature for welding and made certain that the joined sections were correctly aligned. To complete the process, the whole length of weld was ultrasonically tested to ensure the integrity of the join. On *Astute*, defect repair was required on only 150mm of the weld.

The joining of Units 7/8 allowed services and cabling to be pulled across the butt so that the boat's switchboard in Unit 4 could be energised. This brought the vessel to life at the beginning of 2006, thereby allowing systems engineers and combat system experts to begin outfitting the boat and start system testing and commissioning before launch.

The bridge fin had been shipped from the NAS during October 2005 and installed six months earlier than originally programmed. The early fin installation involved considerable reorganisation of work plans and required the schedule of painting, tiling and outfitting being condensed into eight weeks rather than the originally planned eight months. Temporary set-ups had been used to operate and check the diesel generators (DGs). Now the permanent air supply and exhaust arrangements could be used, thereby circumventing the rechecks normally needed when the temporary arrangements were later removed.

Once the casing was attached, the physical structure of the submarine was complete, allowing the third and final build stage to begin with the outfit of the closed boat in the DDH before launch.

About 39,000 plastic acoustic tiles were fitted to make the boats less detectable to a potential enemy. The tiles were attached to the hull after its steel surface had been carefully cleaned and prepared with an epoxy primer. Once this primer had cured, a specially formulated epoxy adhesive was used to glue the tiles into place using a process in which the plastic coating was formed on the side of the submarine using a closed machine. A durable bond between the tiles and the hull was created and is intended to last the lifetime of the boat.

In earlier classes the tiles were standardised and, while suitable for most of the outer hull that had a gently curving surface, additional stress was apparent in regions of greater curvature or even double curvature. These areas were covered with new conformal tiles manufactured to follow the contours of the boat.

Temporary enclosures within the DDH were erected around unit-sized parts of the boat in order to control temperature and humidity for more effective curing. Hoses supported on moveable platforms provided local exhaust ventilation from the enclosures; these hoses fed trunks leading to one or more of the 32 extraction points in the DDH that vented to atmosphere. The extraction

BELOW Installation of bridge fin.
(BAE Systems)

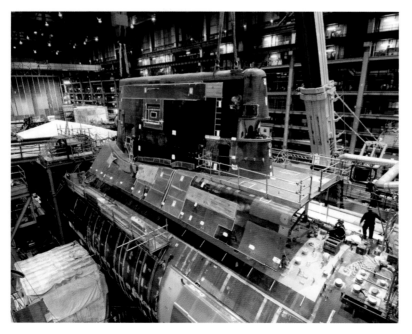

points include filters for particulate matter but there is no abatement of volatile organic compounds. Such exhaust ventilation enclosures are also used in areas where painting takes place and glass-reinforced plastic (GRP) is formed.

Because of its shape, applying tiles to the bridge fin was very challenging. Traditional moulding skills made a comeback to create the full-scale mock-up of the curved bridge fin. The mock-up was covered in GRP, on to which the run of tiling was applied for practice.

During the pre-launch period, the fitting and testing of the sonar flank arrays and bow array were completed and the boat moved from the blocks on which it had rested to a series of wheeled cradles.

Nuclear facilities and licensing

*A*stute's PWR2 is both more complex than most nuclear power stations and has more restrictions placed upon it. It must be engineered and operated in the knowledge that almost 100 people live and work in close proximity – the submarine commander sleeps less than 10m away from the nuclear core – and the submarine not only operates in a challenging environment but is also expected to go in harm's way.

Since 1990 the Barrow-in-Furness site has had a nuclear licence that allows nuclear submarines to be built. The Office for Nuclear Regulation (an agency of the Health and Safety Executive) issues the licence that requires that the site be suitably protected, operated by suitably qualified and experienced personnel and has appropriate operational procedures and contingency arrangements in place. In addition to site regulation, the MoD's Defence Nuclear Safety Regulator issues approval of submarine safety aspects. Regulatory approval was required for all new events, such as the testing and commissioning of the reactor. Careful planning and risk assessment for the activities has to be demonstrated. The storage, transport and disposal of nuclear material is also carefully controlled.

Long-lead items for the nuclear steam-raising plant were ordered at the very beginning of the project. The reactor primary shield tank and pipework assemblies were built alongside the construction units. Following the reactor pressure-vessel build in the NBF, the combination of the reactor and its shielding were shipped to the DDH for installation in Unit 5, after which the primary circuit was completed. Once the boat had been closed, the reactor had its initial fill of coolant for the first cold and hot operation and steam testing. The core was then loaded and incrementally filled before the launch event.

RIGHT *Astute*
roll-out. *(Crown
Copyright/CPOA(Phot)
Colin Burden)*

BELOW *Astute* on
ship-lift. *(Crown
Copyright/LA(Phot)
Jonathan 'JJ' Massey)*

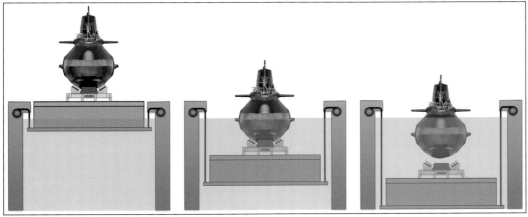

Roll-out and launch

On 8 June 2007 *Astute* was rolled out of the DDH and presented to the world. About 10,000 visitors and dockyard staff witnessed the event as the boat slowly moved (at about 60m/h) on to the flat ship-lift on the dockside in front of the DDH. There was cheering as *Astute*'s patron, HRH Camilla, the Duchess of Rothesay (using her Scottish title), formally named the boat *Astute* by breaking over the bow a bottle of beer brewed by her crew.

Traditionally warships are launched down an inclined slipway into the water immediately after the naming ceremony. Nuclear submarines, however, are launched by using a ship-lift to lower them into the water. *Astute* remained out

of the water for several days while adjustments were made to the ship-lift.

The steel platform of the ship-lift that supports the vessel is raised and lowered by electrically controlled hoists and wire rope cables. Fixed structures and marine piling driven into bedrock support the hoists. Cables immersed in water require special wire-rope dressing that provides a highly water-resistant and long-lasting lubricating film.

BELOW Astute launch celebrations. *(Crown Copyright/LA(Phot) Jonathan 'JJ' Massey)*

JACKSPEAK

The two small muscular tugs that helped to manoeuvre the *Astute* submarine off the ship-lift after launch are known as the 'Pushycats'.

Low-pressure permanent magnet motors, known for their very smooth control and quick response, are used to control the hoists, and all of the electrical motors are activated from a central point.

Basin trials

The different systems on the submarine all have to be integrated and the combined systems demonstrated by a relevant test path. In the nine months leading up to the launch, the test and commissioning team had to complete a total of 2,200 test paths on the *Astute*. First-of-class trials were planned to be undertaken on a methodical basis and would take several years. The first series of trials after launch were performed in the basin in front of the ship-lift and alongside the adjacent dock wall.

When the ship-lift lowered *Astute* into the water, the ability of the boat to float had been demonstrated. Subsequently tests and commissioning activities that could only be done with the boat in the water were undertaken alongside the dock. In late October 2007 initial submerged trials were performed to confirm the dive characteristics of *Astute*. Safety-critical systems such as the hydraulic and electrical systems were tested, as were the vital escape hatches. At this time 22 RN personnel moved on to the submarine in order to become familiar with the boat's operation and to assist with the dives. An initial trim and inclining test (known as a trim dive) was then undertaken – the first opportunity for naval architects to determine the submarine's precise weight and centre of gravity. About 16T of lead were taken on board for the trial and distributed between four wheeled trolleys. The boat dived to 15m in the dock basin and spent seven hours underwater while the weight trolleys were moved across the width of the submarine and measurements of the angle of the boat were taken. These measurements were used to calculate the boat's characteristics, so had to be accurate to the nearest millimetre. A further basin dive was made on the following day.

Engineering and operations teams began further engineering and commissioned work in early November 2007. It was originally intended to start the next phase of testing – the sea trials – at the end of July 2008. However, a range of emergent first-of-class issues conspired to delay the programme.

ABOVE *Astute* inclining experiment during basin trials showing containers of lead on casing used during the experiment. *(BAE Systems)*

LEFT

(a) *Astute* class submarine (*Artful*) prepares for trim dive.

(b) *Artful* venting tanks for trim dive.

(c) *Artful* surfaces after trim dive.

(BAE Systems)

Following the successful basin dives and test and commissioning activities, *Astute* returned to the DDH for remedial work and further build activities. Once more in the dock, *Astute* undertook combat systems trials where the RN personnel ran through a series of scenarios that simulated searching for targets and engaging these with weapons. The trials included a weapons discharge trial.

Fuelling

The fuelling of *Astute* was the first such operation since *Vengeance* (also powered by a PWR2 reactor) was fuelled in 1998. Additional checks were planned for the *Astute* class to guarantee that the operation met new safety regulations added since that date. To ensure that the team had the required skills, a special core-loading training facility was established to deliver an externally verified training programme.

Not only was the team out of practice with fuelling but in an exercise in July 2007 the site failed to demonstrate adequate emergency arrangements based on a possible (but unlikely) nuclear accident. This demonstration (required

before *Astute*'s active nuclear commissioning could start), satisfactorily took place in January 2008. Having achieved regulatory approval, the core-load refuelling process was carried out by a team of 40 trained people, working 12-hour shifts. With no contamination issues and zero weld-defects, *Astute* was loaded safely with the nuclear fuel that would power her for life.

In October 2008 *Astute* was preparing to be relaunched from the ship-lift to begin the nuclear commissioning process. In the unlikely event of a nuclear incident, iodine tablets and warnings were issued to residents of Barrow-in-Furness and nearby areas well before the nuclear reactor was started up. The residents are familiar with the precautions as *Astute* was the 25th nuclear submarine to have reactor tests in the town over a 50-year period.

The nuclear regulatory bodies must inspect the reactor and sanction each of its active commissioning events before they may begin. There was an initial hold-point on activities associated with initial reactor criticality, when the chain reaction of the nuclear fuel becomes (just) self-sustaining for the first time and is able to generate power – although the power is negligible at this stage. Associated with this is physics testing and analysis to confirm the expected performance of the fuel system and core, and power range testing in the course of which the reactor is tested in a number of controlled sequences that ultimately involve full power operation.

There was a further hold-point for 'fast cruise', during which the reactor and propulsion systems are tested at high power for a sustained period that provides pre-sea trials training for the crew.

Active commissioning of the reactor, power range testing was performed in the dock over a two-week period from 5 September 2009 and demonstrated that the submarine's nuclear propulsion plant was safe and operational. This meant that sea trials could start.

Following safety checks, the reactor control rods were slowly withdrawn over a period of 12 hours so that the reactor approached criticality. It was then shut down so that the measurements could be assessed. Over the next few days, as the systems were shown to be operational and as measurements indicated

RIGHT The exit route taken by submarines from the BAE Systems yard. *(Author, map Google Earth)*

1 Devonshire Dock Hall
2 Ship-lift
3 Wet Dock Quay
4 Devonshire Dock
5 Michaelson Road high-
   level bridge
6 Buccleuch Dock
7 Ramsden Dock

8 Anchor basin
9 Lock gate
10 Dock basin
11 Sea lock gate

A Barrow Island
B Walney Channel
C Biggar Sands

satisfactory performance, the reactor power was increased with excursions representing operational conditions.

Astute at sea

By late 2009, with all outstanding defects cleared, *Astute* was ready to leave Barrow-in-Furness for the open sea. The route to the sea taken by *Astute* on 14 November 2009 was under the raised Michaelson Road bridge, through Buccleuch Dock and into Ramsden Dock. The departure had been delayed as the Basin Dock seaward gate, weighing 320T, could not be raised in an earlier check. The Basin Dock acts as a lock and its operation was essential if *Astute* were to enter the shallow Walney Channel at high tide. The 20-year-old gate had to be removed and repaired. Once the

BELOW LEFT ***Astute*-class submarine, assisted by tugs, moving from Devonshire Dock through the open Michaelson Road bridge to Ramsden Dock.** *(BAE Systems)*

BELOW ***Astute* finally at sea accompanied by tugs, 15 November 2009.** *(BAE Systems)*

43

Basin Dock had been filled with water, *Astute* entered it. At the next high tide, she was able to exit the dock and enter the channel and the open sea.

The Walney Channel had been dredged in summer 2006 in anticipation of *Astute*'s departure the following year. Three years later a trailing suction hopper dredger cleared 13km of the channel.

Despite leaving the shipyard, the boat still belonged to the shipbuilder until contractor's sea trials had demonstrated its satisfactory performance at sea and it had been accepted by the MoD. Although the shipbuilder remained responsible for safety, they had no qualified submarine commanders. Custom and practice dictated that the commanding officer was not just in charge of the RN complement on board but was employed by the shipbuilders to be their pilot on the boat – for which he was paid the princely sum of a guinea (£1.05). For the Walney Channel there is a local pilot who comes aboard and acts in an advisory capacity, but even then the ultimate responsibility rests with the commanding officer. Having cleared the channel, *Astute* could proceed, on the surface, on her five-day passage north to her home base of HMNB Clyde. Tighter rules on new nuclear submarines at Barrow-in-Furness meant that, having left the shipyard, it was not intended that she return to clear any defects. Instead, any work would be undertaken at HMNB.

HMNB Clyde had been home to the SSBN fleet but was being expanded to accept *Trafalgar* and *Astute* class submarines. The base was equipped with a covered ship-lift and was scheduled to have a new submarine jetty in 2009 to equip it as the single UK submarine operating base. The 44,000T Valiant jetty was designed to berth and maintain up to six of any type of submarine, including the *Astute*

class, and, with a 50-year life, to accommodate subsequent classes. To give easy access to the boats at all times, the jetty was designed to float up and down with the tide but it is secured to the loch bottom by four giant piles, each one as tall as Nelson's Column. Although delivered in May 2009 there were significant installation difficulties and the jetty did not pass its trials until 2013.

As the jetty was not functional in 2009, *Astute* and later *Ambush*, used RFA *Diligence*,

ABOVE *Astute* arrives at its permanent base, HMNB Clyde, for the first time on 20 November 2009 ahead of sea trials. *(Crown Copyright/LA(Phot) Jonathan 'JJ' Massey)*

moored off HMNB. RFA *Diligence* was a sophisticated, multi-purpose forward support ship, fitted with a wide range of workshops for hull and machinery repairs, as well as facilities for supplying electricity, water, fuel, air, steam, cranes and stores to other ships

BELOW Covered ship-lift and maintenance space, HMNB Clyde, Faslane. *(Crown Copyright/CPOA(Phot) Thomas 'Tam' McDonald)*

ABOVE *Ambush* alongside forward support vessel RFA *Diligence*, Gareloch, HMNB Clyde, Faslane. *(Crown Copyright/CPOA(Phot) Thomas 'Tam' McDonald)*

ABOVE RIGHT Valiant jetty delivery to HMNB Clyde, Faslane, May 2009. *(Crown Copyright/LA(Phot) Stuart 'Stu' Hill)*

BELOW Valiant jetty, HMNB Clyde, *Ambush* alongside. *(Crown Copyright/LA(Phot) Will Haigh)*

and submarines. Once the Valiant jetty was functional, RFA *Diligence* returned to her role of sustaining warships away from UK base ports.

Contractor's sea trials (CST)

Building a nuclear submarine is a huge challenge and demands the highest standards to ensure she can safely perform her demanding duties. To prepare *Astute* for handover to the RN, it was necessary for extensive and exhaustive CST to be performed to demonstrate that these standards had been achieved. Sea trials are necessary because the boat needs to be tested to its design limitations and not all systems can be fully tested alongside. All platforms have discrete characteristics that need to be understood and, where necessary, normalised. In the case of *Astute*, as the first-of-class, the evaluation included a great deal of equipment being used at sea for the first time. Once demonstrated and approved for operational use, less detailed equipment trials could be employed and her later sister boats completed their tests in one-quarter of the time.

The safety of the boat and its operational effectiveness is not just about the equipment – the complement is a vital element of the mix and sea trials offer a period of crew familiarisation and opportunity to hone the operational procedures.

During the next few months the boat was subjected to a series of demanding CST. These were followed by periods of defect rectification in order to find and resolve potential problems. *Astute* was essentially a prototype – albeit one destined to enter service. As might be expected of such a high-technology first-of-class vessel, trials revealed a number of minor problems. Demanding safety standards often required the boat to return to base for rectification of the defects.

In order not to compromise the assurance programme used to demonstrate the correct functioning of all aspects of the boat, the shipbuilder's test group was separate to those who were striving to deliver the submarine. The trials group – some 150 commissioning engineers and a management team of 20 shipbuilder staff – used formally authorised trial instructions and completed over 700 test forms.

CST were a joint undertaking by the on-board RN complement and the contractor's test group. The commanding officer had overriding responsibility for submarine safety and, in particular, nuclear safety. The senior firm's representative assumed overall responsibility for the conduct of all trials within the contractual sea trials programme.

On 16 February 2010 *Astute* left Faslane for nearly two weeks of initial CST. Two days later, having proved the hydraulic systems, she dived for the first time. These initial trials proved the boat's capabilities as a submarine (the propulsion system, dive ability, manoeuvrability, communication facilities and capability to navigate safely). Furthermore, they demonstrated the potential of the new submarine class and the significant improvement in performance that it represented.

After a brief period of maintenance, *Astute* sailed again for further CST starting with surface trials, shallow dive trials in the Sound of Gigha and, finally, the first intermediate depth trials. These continued with a series of independent exercises and basic sea safety training. This part of CST was completed with the first deep-water dive and full-power trial. The boat had now demonstrated that she was a seagoing submarine capable of operating at full power at its design depth.

	Period 1 Contractor's sea trials Platform proving/training
UK based	Alongside
	Leave
	Period 2 Contractor's sea trials Performance trials
	Alongside
US based	Period 3 Combat system capability
	Period 4 Tomahawk
	Period 5A Additional capability
	Period 5B Deperm

LEFT Typical nuclear submarine sea trials programme. *(Author, using BAE Systems information)*

ABOVE *Astute* dives during contractor's sea trials. *(BAE Systems)*

BELOW *Astute* surfaces during contractor's sea trials. *(BAE Systems)*

Before commencing further CST, *Astute* undertook a number of activities including a visit to Southampton in April 2011 where a tragic event took place. A junior rating went on the rampage with a SA80 automatic rifle, during which he killed the weapons engineering officer, Lieutenant Commander Ian Molyneux RN and wounded another officer. The rating is now serving a prison sentence of 25 years for the murder.

The second phase of CST focused on *Astute*'s capabilities as a war-fighting platform – testing its ability to detect targets, its signature performance and its ability to fire weapons. The CST continued with tests with the clip-on towed-array, a second deep-dive trial, atmospheric tests and weapons handling in reduced-manning circumstances.

The remainder of the CST involved measurement and evaluation of characteristics that were carried out at a number of ranges and facilities in Scottish waters:

■ **Loch Goil** provides a 0.5km^2 open water area with a depth of about 80m for trials that require the vessel to be moored between a four-point mooring. It is primarily a static range, where hydrophones are located on the seabed and spaced evenly around the vessel. The acoustic signatures of *Astute* and the performance of her active and passive sonar equipment were measured and electromagnetic signatures assessed.

■ **British Underwater Test and Evaluation Centre (BUTEC)** is a tracking range about 10km long and 4km wide, with water 175–200m deep. It provides real-time tracking in three dimensions of above-water and sub-surface units, weapons and targets. Fishermen are restricted from fishing in the area when tests are under way because their nets may snag underwater equipment. The centre can declare an air danger area, which covers the entire test range, and extends to a height of 500m. The range was used to measure *Astute*'s target echo strength, assessed weapon system performance and ability to fire weapons.

At BUTEC in July 2011 *Astute* successfully fired Spearfish torpedoes for the first time. The trial marked an important milestone towards full operational capability for the submarine and proved the design for future submarines of the class. Over two days four trials-variant (without live warhead) torpedoes were discharged against a variety of targets, proving the ability of the combat system to detect and prosecute dived and surfaced targets. Firings with live warheads would later be undertaken during operational trials.

■ **Rona Noise Range** is a test area approximately 12km by 4km with water 235m deep located just to the north of BUTEC. Islands and the mainland shelter the range on three sides, thereby screening the range from the acoustic energy of distant shipping characteristic of the open ocean. It is equipped with eight acoustic energy measuring hydrophones and nine underwater tracking hydrophones that it used to perform *Astute*'s dynamic acoustic energy trials, in order to measure the radiated acoustic signature.

After conducting trials at Rona *Astute* was on a surface transit to Kyle on 22 October 2010 but grounded at low speed on an ebb tide while undertaking a boat transfer. Tugs were unable to free *Astute* and soon the tide

BELOW UK trials facilities employed for *Astute*.
(Author, maps NOAA)

1 Gigha Sound
2 Rona
3 British Underwater Test and Evaluation Centre
4 Loch Goil
5 HMNB Clyde
6 Barons Point
7 Northern Fleet Exercise Area.

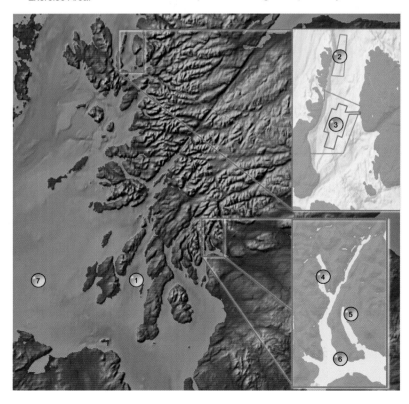

Astute was built to exacting standards and fine tolerances. The programme required an unprecedented attention to detail in design, assembly and testing especially with the extent of the new equipment that the boat incorporates. '*Astute* is like a 7,000-tonne Swiss watch.'

Rear Admiral (later Vice Admiral Sir) Simon Lister RN,
Director of Submarines

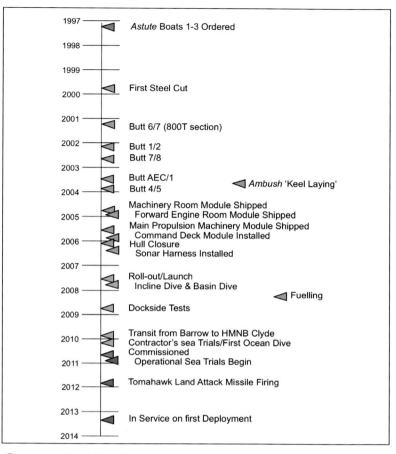

1997	*Astute* Boats 1-3 Ordered
1998	
1999	
2000	First Steel Cut
2001	Butt 6/7 (800T section)
2002	Butt 1/2
	Butt 7/8
2003	Butt AEC/1
2004	Butt 4/5 — *Ambush* 'Keel Laying'
2005	Machinery Room Module Shipped / Forward Engine Room Module Shipped
2006	Main Propulsion Machinery Module Shipped / Command Deck Module Installed / Hull Closure / Sonar Harness Installed
2007	
2008	Roll-out/Launch / Incline Dive & Basin Dive — Fuelling
2009	Dockside Tests
2010	Transit from Barrow to HMNB Clyde / Contractor's sea Trials/First Ocean Dive / Commissioned
2011	Operational Sea Trials Begin
2012	Tomahawk Land Attack Missile Firing
2013	In Service on first Deployment
2014	

ABOVE Timeline for *Astute* design, build and testing. *(Author)*

had fallen too far. The submarine was pulled clear a few hours later on the high tide. A tug towed *Astute* to BUTEC, but unfortunately shortly after arrival the tug collided with *Astute*'s starboard forward hydroplane. This required remedial action in HMNB Clyde that delayed the trials by 50 days. A court martial relieved the CO, Commander Andy Coles RN, of his command.

■ **Barons Point Open Sea Range**
recorded, analysed and adjusted *Astute*'s static magnetic signature. The range is controlled from a shore-based control building that is connected by heavy cables to a large coil lying on the seabed 30m deep. As the subject vessel passes over the coil, the on-board degaussing system is adjusted to reduce the magnetic field inherent in the steel hull and ferrous components of the vessel. The vessel's magnetic signature is then measured, and the process repeated until the desired residual level has been achieved.

Some of *Astute*'s programme delays and tribulations could be traced back to the difficulties with adoption of 3-D CAD. In addition, there had been a several-year hiatus in the submarine programme once the *Vanguard* class had been delivered that contributed to the difficulties of finding experienced staff. Other problems arose from the inherent challenge of any submarine – that the design incorporates as little redundant space as possible.

Nevertheless, in the nine months after *Astute* left Barrow the submarine was tested and successfully proved. The next stage would be for the RN to test her operational capabilities.

Commissioning ceremony

Having successfully completed CST and cleared post-trials defects alongside, *Astute* had demonstrated that she met the contractual requirements and could be accepted by the MoD to begin service in the RN. This would allow the contractor to receive the final cash payment for the building of the boat. The MoD became the approving authority and duty holder for HMS *Astute*, meaning that it adopted full design authority for the in-service submarine. Although accepted into service, *Astute* would not be available for operational duties until she had undertaken a further series of demanding seagoing trials, testing the full range of her capabilities – particularly trials that demonstrated that she could deploy her weapons.

A commissioning ceremony, an important milestone along the road to full operational capability, is held to mark all vessels that become in-service warships. *Astute*'s ceremony

RIGHT Royal Marine
Band starts the
commissioning service
for HMS *Astute* on 27
August 2010. *(Crown
Copyright/LA(Phot)
Stuart 'Stu' Hill)*

BELOW An
overall view of the
commissioning
ceremony of HMS
Astute at HMNB Clyde.
*(Crown Copyright/
LA(Phot) A.J. Macleod)*

was held in HMNB Clyde on 27 August 2010. The boat's patron, Camilla, Duchess of Rothesay, was the guest of honour.

After a short service, a commissioning pennant was raised on the boat. This signified that *Astute* was now formally able to use the prefix 'Her Majesty's Ship' and be referred to as HMS *Astute*. She now sported on her distinctive fin a silver ship's bell, her nameplate and crest.

Operational sea trials (OST)

In October 2011 HMS *Astute* left for an important series of sea trials in the USA, spending 77 days at sea during the 142-day deployment.

Her first port of call was Kings Bay naval submarine base in Georgia, where she visited the Magnetic Silencing Facility. This facility completed the treatment begun at Barons Point to correct the inherent permanent magnetism of the boat. Preparation for treatment entails only the safeguarding of fragile equipment that may be affected by large magnetic fields, after which the boat enters the facility for treatment.

The facility has electrical cables that are suspended permanently overhead as well as

LEFT The commissioning pennant is raised on HMS *Astute*. *(Crown Copyright/LA(Phot) A.J. Macleod)*

beneath the hull. Passing electrical currents from a shore supply through the wires in a controlled manner generates large magnetic fields that reduce the permanent magnetic signature. The process, known as flash deperming, leaves the ship in a stable and predictable magnetic condition.

In Kings Bay HMS *Astute* embarked some Tomahawk missiles and then sailed for the Gulf of Mexico. From the Gulf, in November 2011, she fired four Tomahawk missiles, a mix of older-model Block III and new Block IV missiles. Neither missile type was equipped with a warhead for these tests. The missiles were successfully fired at some shipping containers in a corner of the missile range at Eglin Air Force Base in order to confirm accuracy. Demonstrating the Tomahawk weapon system

ABOVE USN nuclear submarine passing through the magnetic silencing facility at Kings Bay naval submarine base. *(USN photo/Julie Irwin)*

LEFT Tomahawk land-attack missile fired by HMS *Astute* about to transition to its cruise mode. *(Crown Copyright/POA(Phot) Paul Punter)*

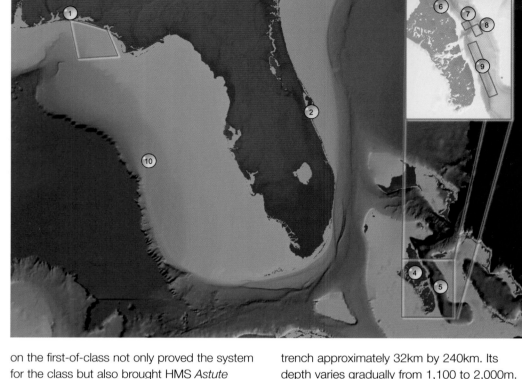

RIGHT US trials facilities employed for HMS *Astute*. *(Author, maps NOAA)*

1 Eglin Air Force Base
2 Port Canaveral
3 Kings Bay Naval Base
4 Andros Island
5 Tongue of the Ocean
6 Atlantic Undersea Test and Evaluation Center
7 Sonar range
8 Acoustic range
9 Weapons range
10 Gulf of Mexico.

BELOW Admiral Sir Mark Stanhope RN, left, and Admiral Jonathan Greenert USN discuss the capabilities of HMS *Astute* with her CO, Commander Breckenridge RN, during the joint Exercise Fellowship, 2012. *(Crown Copyright/POA(Phot) Paul Punter)*

on the first-of-class not only proved the system for the class but also brought HMS *Astute* closer to operational readiness.

The focus of the extensive trials programme then moved to the Atlantic Undersea Test and Evaluation Center (AUTEC), a facility situated off the Bahamas. The USN's AUTEC brochure reveals that the ranges are sited over an underwater feature called the Tongue of the Ocean, a huge deep-water flat-bottomed trench approximately 32km by 240km. Its depth varies gradually from 1,100 to 2,000m. AUTEC's only exposure to the open ocean is at the northern end and numerous peripheral islands, reefs and shoals isolate it from ocean disturbances, particularly high ambient acoustic energy levels that can interfere with undersea evaluations. The semi-tropical climate and sea temperatures of 25°C allow year-round operations.

The trials were principally conducted at AUTEC's deep-water weapons range, which is the largest of the AUTEC ranges – at about 17km wide by 65km long – and is said to be able to track nine objects simultaneously. Crucially, it has reliable and secure two-way digital data communications with submarines operating at speed and depth. Although only operating over a few kilometres' range and data rates of only about 1kbps, the communications adequately support the trials requirements.

Submarine sensor accuracy tests were performed on the weapons range at various keel depths, simulating actual conditions. HMS *Astute* successfully completed final Spearfish deep discharge trials and fired six Spearfish torpedoes, including a salvo. The salvo firing demonstrated the submarine could deploy two teams firing a torpedo at the same time. It was the first salvo firing by an RN submarine for 15 years. Furthermore, the additional capability relating to the Special Forces payload bay was proven and demonstrated.

It is the objective of the trials programme to discover any oversights or errors apparent in the first-of-class in order that they can be rectified and avoided in later boats. Typical 'teething problems' were expected, but were subsequently reported pejoratively in the press during operational trials. There were three categories of problems with the HMS *Astute*: flaws in design that only became apparent when testing started; equipment that broke down too easily; and some problems relating to poor construction at the shipyard.

Having completed its capability demonstrations, in February 2012 HMS *Astute* took part in Exercise Fellowship at AUTEC witnessed by the First Sea Lord, Admiral Sir Mark Stanhope RN, and US Chief of Naval Operations, Admiral Jonathan Greenert USN. HMS *Astute* sparred with a *Virginia* class SSN. Over a two-day period the two contestants tried to outflank, outmanoeuvre and outwit each other.

HMS *Astute*'s CO, Commander Breckenridge RN said:

We met and surpassed every expectation. She is just better than any other submarine I have ever been on. Our sonar is fantastic and I have never before experienced holding a submarine at the range we were holding the USN boat. The Americans were utterly taken aback, blown away with what they were seeing.

HMS *Astute*'s full capability had finally been demonstrated with the submarine, its equipment, its procedures and its complement all operating as smoothly as a Swiss watch.

The boat returned to HMNB Clyde in March 2012 having sailed 26,400km during the trials period. After an extensive base maintenance period, in late 2012 HMS *Astute* returned to AUTEC. This time it was to visit the Fleet Operational Readiness Accuracy Check Site. AUTEC is affiliated to the NATO

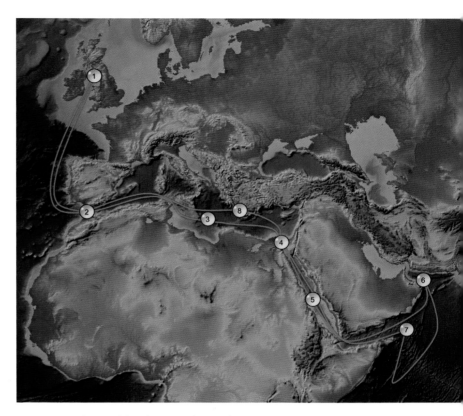

programme for participating member nations to fine-tune submarines ahead of their operational deployment.

Operational handover and operational deployment

On 25 April 2013, HMS *Astute* achieved operational handover and the authority for her scheduling transferred from the naval trials team to the RN. Following a short maintenance period and mandatory operational sea training for RN vessels preparing to deploy, she was available for front-line duties.

HMS *Astute*'s first major deployment spanned eight months of 2014. Her activities were varied:

■ In February 2014 HMS *Astute* was in the Mediterranean, tasked to provide TLAM capability in support of anti-terrorism operations. The boat worked very closely with the USN, regularly taking part in integrated practice strikes – often with the participating units hundreds of kilometres apart.
■ She moved to the Middle East before transiting the Suez Canal into the Red Sea

ABOVE HMS *Astute*'s first major operational deployment. *(Author, maps NOAA)*

1   HMNB Clyde
2   Straits of Gibraltar
3   Mediterranean
4   Suez Canal
5   Red Sea
6   Arabian Gulf
7   Gulf of Oman
8   Souda Bay.

and Gulf of Oman, providing support to anti-smuggling operations. Sea surface temperatures in the Gulf were often recorded in excess of 34°C. This provided an opportunity to demonstrate the boat's satisfactory operation in extreme conditions.

■ HMS *Astute* later exercised with the RFA *Diligence*, HMS *Northumberland* and USS *Annapolis* during which the UK and USA practised their anti-submarine warfare tactics and skills.

■ She returned to the Mediterranean in late August, arriving in Souda Bay (Crete) to replenish. The submarine then sailed for further tasking and an anti-submarine warfare exercise with the USN and the French MN before returning to Souda Bay for a final time in mid-September to restock her supplies.

■ In September HMS *Astute* collected five students for their fourth and final phase of the UK Submarine Command Course that all officers must take prior to serving as an executive officer on board a RN submarine. The four-month course is the first step to commanding a nuclear boat. The candidates would have already completed two phases of training on simulators interposed with a period at sea. This final assessment phase, designed to test potential submarine COs to their limit, enables them to demonstrate their ability to command a submarine unaided during war-like conditions. The course is widely regarded as one of the toughest command courses in the world, with a

historical failure rate of 25%. This was the first course on an *Astute* class submarine and the students had to learn fast how to command the latest boat – a vast leap in technology with several challenging aspects.

HMS *Astute* arrived home on 7 October 2014, having been transformed from a trials platform to a fully operational front-line unit capable of conducting operations to a superior level. HMS *Astute* proved its new equipment and fully assessed it in an operational environment.

Just two days later, HMS *Ambush*, the

BELOW Dolphin badges in glasses of rum with associated cap badges awaiting presentation. *(Crown Copyright/LA(Phot) Will Haigh)*

BELOW RIGHT Submarine dolphins worn with pride on a RN number 1 uniform. *(Crown Copyright/ PO(Phot) Derek 'Des' Wade)*

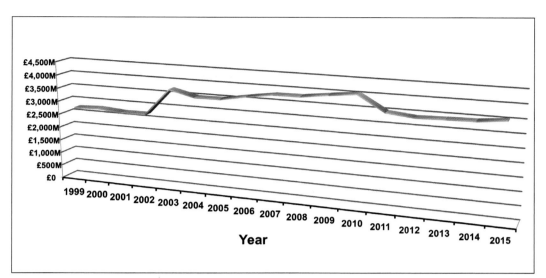

LEFT **Variation with time of forecast costs of Boats 1–3.** *(Author from National Audit Office major projects reports)*

second *Astute* class submarine, also returned to HMNB Clyde after a successful three-and-a-half-month international operational mission to Rio de Janeiro and Kings Bay. On board throughout the deployment were 18 trainees undergoing the 'wet phase' of their training to become fully qualified submariners. Having succeeded, they were presented with their submariner's dolphin badges in a glass of rum. The dolphins are worn with pride, signifying that a submariner was familiar with his boat and was now a member of the elite band of underwater warriors.

Delay and cost overruns

When the contract for boats 1–3 was placed in March 1997, the cost approved was £2,726 million (ignoring £29 million for design and assessment costs). It was anticipated that the delivery of *Astute* would be in 100 months (June 2005). This timescale (and the associated costs) offered by GEC-Marconi reflected the customer's desires rather than a considered and rigorously risk-assessed programme. It actually took 164 months for *Astute* to be delivered. Some of this delay may have been as a result of an unyielding pursuit of safety as a key tenet of the programme in that no short cut warrants reductions in safety standards.

Because of the extreme complexity of the project and factors such as the difficulties of finding sufficient qualified and experienced personnel, *Astute* was not only severely delayed but also over budget. The delays and cost escalation could also be attributed to inevitable

disruption that flowed from the merger of the original prime contractor with BAe, an underestimate of the technical challenges and changes to the requirements during *Astute*'s build. Changes to the fore-end design related to Tomahawk missile capability and improved tactical data link capability (possibly as a result of feedback from the Serbian conflict in 2000) were added early in the programme at a cost of £32 million. When the programme was re-baselined in 2004, equipment that was originally only going to be fitted to *Ambush* was brought forward to *Astute.* An additional £225 million ensured the first three boats would then all have the same equipment. As a consequence, integration and testing of the equipment on *Astute* reduced the trials necessary on *Ambush*.

The lessons learned on HMS *Astute* not only benefited the remaining boats of the class but also formed a key knowledge base for the development of the four *Dreadnought* class SSBNs that were approved in July 2016.

HMS *Astute*, HMS *Ambush* and HMS *Artful* were deployed on operational duties in April 2013, June 2013 and December 2015 respectively. By this time the out-turn cost of producing them was declared as £3,536 million, an increase of £1,303 million. As first-of-class, HMS *Astute* was responsible for much of the overrun, but the experience gained (and process improvements achieved) allowed the two later boats to reduce the eventual bill.

One of the features of long defence programmes is that changes in technology and operational needs often produce pressures to incorporate new equipment. Boats 4 onwards were planned to incorporate additional functionality but it is anticipated that the increased costs will be partially offset from innovations in construction and commissioning. Nevertheless each boat is anticipated to cost about £1,500 million.

Follow-on *Astute* class boats 2 (*Ambush*) and 3 (*Artful*)

For HMS *Astute* the focus had been orientated on schedule and striving to deliver an operational submarine. While a platform with the flexibility of *Astute* provides good value for money, unit costs for nuclear submarines remain high, and the costs and implications of nuclear ownership in conjunction with increasingly stringent nuclear safety regulations means that every effort must be made to constrain costs without compromising safety. With *Ambush* and *Artful* the emphasis shifted to improving affordability through more efficient production processes and design innovations.

Some processes pioneered on *Astute* were honed on *Ambush* and *Artful*. The use of the Warspite facility saved six months on the critical path for *Astute* but saved nine months on later boats.

The traditional method of joining pipework on submarines is welded 'sleeve and socket' joints. There are a total of 5,793 welded sleeves on an *Astute*, each of which is time-consuming to install; they have a high failure rate and require tight alignment tolerances. After welding NDE is undertaken to check for cracks. This uses gamma-ray equipment and takes over six hours.

It was proposed that LOKRING couplings, a permanent mechanical jointing method, replace welded sleeves wherever possible. A total of 4,677 welded sleeves (9,354 welded joints) were suitable for couplings. These were submitted to the full cycle of pressure testing that would form the normal system test path and every one of the 160 connections passed without leakage. Additional tests were undertaken in SMITE; these subjected the couplings to vibration and impulse testing that simulated the whole life of a submarine. After the successful tests, approval was granted for the couplings even for safety-critical piping connections.

On *Ambush* 14% of the suitable welded joints were replaced by couplings with a saving of 2,750 man-hours. On *Artful* all of the 4,677 suitable welded sleeves

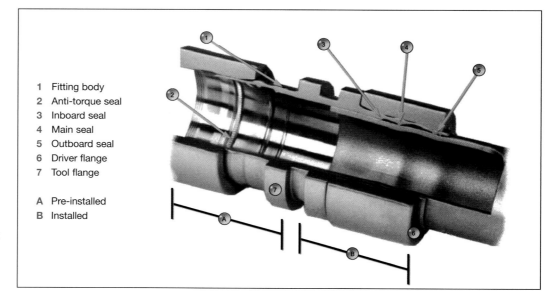

RIGHT LOKRING couplings that replaced welded sleeves. *(Author from LOKRING data)*

1 Fitting body
2 Anti-torque seal
3 Inboard seal
4 Main seal
5 Outboard seal
6 Driver flange
7 Tool flange

A Pre-installed
B Installed

were replaced by couplings, saving 24,449 man-hours.

Another major innovation for *Ambush* and later boats was the outfitting of units vertically before they had been turned ship-wise. This had significant cost and schedule benefits as it increased the work-faces available (which improved access for hull outfitting), avoided overhead welding and allowed sizeable elements (such as large pipe modules) to be lowered into place by crane. Although the technique requires specialised staging and shipping fixtures, outfitting productivity is improved, along with concomitant health and safety improvements.

The intent is to outfit all units in this way (except the reactor compartment) and achieve 85% unit outfit before butt closure.

With the successful use of four prefabricated and partially assembled main modules on *Astute*, the concept had been proved. While the main modules were being installed on *Ambush*, several other elements were installed into the hull units before they were welded together, such as:

Forward dome/bulkhead 26; 1- and 2-deck module	Unit 1
Mini deck outfit bulkhead 74 (aft of reactor compartment)	Unit 4
New diesel generator room module	Unit 4
New battery tank module	Unit 6

In addition, the engine room module was enhanced so more equipment and outfitting was achieved before it was fleeted into place. *Artful* was largely built in the same way as *Ambush*.

Follow-on *Astute* class boat 4 (*Audacious*)

For boats 1–3, whose equipment had been ordered together early in their programme, it had been assumed that many of the parts from the *Vanguard* and *Trafalgar* classes would be used. However, most of this legacy equipment was no longer available as many approved vendors had left the industry when orders stopped or, after the consolidation of the defence industry through the 1990s, suppliers

had focused their businesses elsewhere. Re-establishing suitable vendors and supply lines was time-consuming and was a further cause of delays to HMS *Astute*. By the time that *Audacious* was ordered in May 2007, the MoD was losing its ability to be an intelligent customer while the submarine industrial base was also losing its ability to be an intelligent provider. Skills and expertise had also been lost throughout the vendor base that provided parts and equipment, as they had seen no new UK orders for five years. However, in areas of combat systems and platform management, suppliers had been investing in improvements that would replace HMS *Astute*'s equipment, albeit often with a price that reflected the greater capability. In some cases there were equipment cost savings or integration and installation savings.

The intent with *Audacious* was to achieve an affordable price while initiating technology streams that would reduce risks for both later *Astute* class boats and also the *Dreadnought* SSBNs. In essence, *Audacious* became the first of a new block of *Astute* class submarines that would include *Anson* and *Agamemnon* (ordered in March 2010). However, some new equipment, especially that of the combat system, was also destined to be 'back-fitted' to boats 1–3 to further enhance their capability – in some cases before *Audacious* went to sea.

The major initiatives incorporated on *Audacious* included upgrading electronic systems where recent rapid advances in hardware and software could deliver operational gains thanks to the open architecture nature of the boats' major systems. A total review of the design and manufacturing standards was also undertaken to ensure that the most appropriate standards were still being applied and to determine where cost savings could be made through the greater use of commercial equipment. This also identified where savings in procurement costs could be achieved by refurbishing equipment, such as masts, from decommissioned *Trafalgar* boats as they were replaced by *Astute* boats. An exercise in design rationalisation and simplification addressed areas of complexity, especially where simplification could enhance safety, indicating further savings in manufacturing and equipment costs.

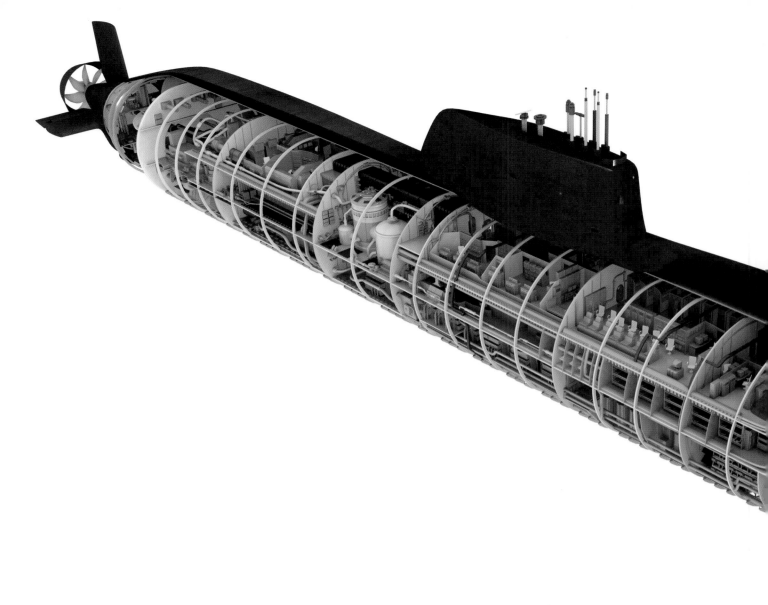
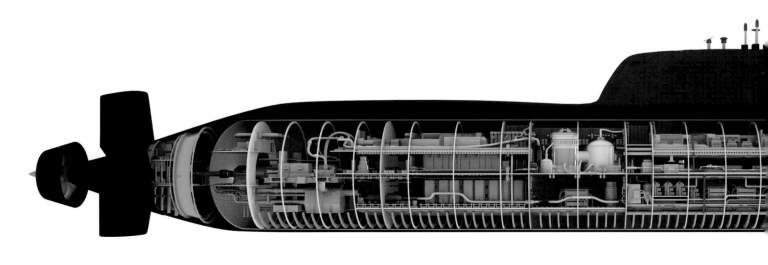

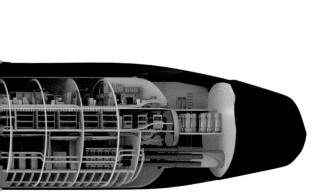

Chapter Three

Anatomy of the hull and boat systems

The cylindrical inner pressure hull is maintained at atmospheric pressure, thereby protecting the boat's complement and vital equipment from the crushing forces exerted by water at depth. The pressure hull is surrounded by the outer hull that is allowed to flood with water. The intervening space is used to accommodate ballast tanks and hydroplane actuators (both necessary for manoeuvring) and sonars.

OPPOSITE Unofficial cutaway diagram generated from information shown on the BBC documentary *How to Build a Nuclear Submarine.* *(Charles Gatward)*

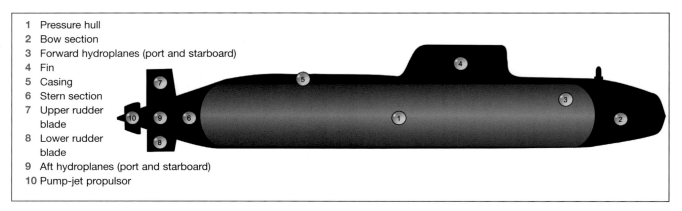

1 Pressure hull
2 Bow section
3 Forward hydroplanes (port and starboard)
4 Fin
5 Casing
6 Stern section
7 Upper rudder blade
8 Lower rudder blade
9 Aft hydroplanes (port and starboard)
10 Pump-jet propulsor

ABOVE Key elements of HMS *Astute*'s hull.
(Author)

Hull arrangement and features

The core of the submarine is the pressure hull, a structure that contains and protects both the boat's complement and its machinery from the pressure of seawater. It is maintained at atmospheric pressure regardless of the external seawater pressure. It comprises steel plates wrapped around circular frames to form a cylinder with rounded ends (a capsule shape).

Surrounding the pressure hull is the streamlined form of the outer hull. The space between the pressure hull and the outer hull is referred to as the free-flood space as it fills with water when the boat dives. It contains items such as the ballast tanks, high-pressure air bottles, the bow sonar and towed-array

BELOW HMS *Astute*'s hull arrangement.
(Author)

sonar winch. These items, unprotected by the pressure hull, are exposed to the full water pressure when the boat is at depth.

The outer hull also supports control surfaces: two rudder blades and horizontal hydroplanes for manoeuvring, diving and surfacing.

The top part of the outer hull – the casing – is an almost-level platform that becomes an operational space when the boat is surfaced. Rising above the casing is the bridge fin that contains the masts for use on the surface or close to the surface. The front of the bridge fin accommodates the bridge (navigational position) from which the boat is controlled when surfaced.

The submarine's complement of at least 98 souls must live and work beneath the surface of the sea for weeks on end, cocooned in the pressure hull that is only just over 60m in length and 11m in diameter. Worse, most of the aft half

1 Forward escape flat
2 Reactor compartment
3 Reactor services compartment/airlocks
4 Lock-in/lock-out chamber
5 Equipment offices
6 Bridge access
7 Control room/sonar room
8 Accommodation

9 Storage
10 Battery tank
11 Forward escape flat/ forward escape truck/ weapons embarkation slot
12 Weapons stowage compartment/ weapons launch tubes

A 1-deck level
B 2-deck level
C 3-deck level
D Containment bulkhead
E Escape bulkhead

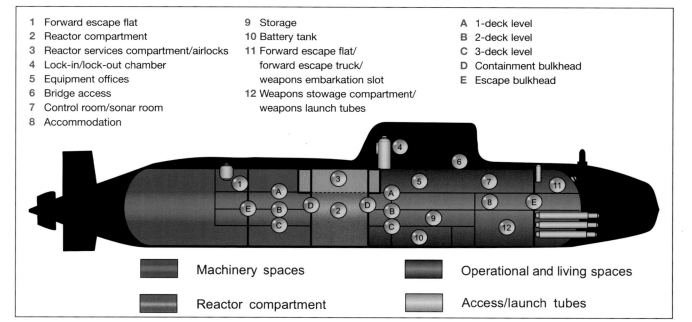

Machinery spaces

Reactor compartment

Operational and living spaces

Access/launch tubes

of the pressure hull is occupied by machinery that renders it an unpleasant hot and noisy working environment. In the centre of the hull is an 8.5m-long nuclear reactor compartment that is too radioactive to be entered. The accommodation space is only 27m by 11m.

The shape that best resists water pressure at depth is a sphere and this is the shape of most scientific vessels that explore the great depths of the ocean (over 10,000m). This, however, is not a practical shape for a vessel that is required to move rapidly through the water; the best shape for this is a teardrop. The compromise is for the pressure hull to be a capsule shape and to surround it by the outer hull that has a more elliptical bow and parabolic-shaped stern allowing the boat to slip through the water more efficiently. The capsule shape combines two configurations that resist the forces of the water pressure – a cylinder and a sphere. There is, however, a potential weakness of sealing either end of the cylinder by a spherical dome, as the join would involve an abrupt change of direction. HMS *Astute* demonstrates a stronger arrangement where the transition is smoothed by adopting a torispherical section dome. The forward and aft domes are sections of a sphere that merge into an annular section that has a much smaller radius.

The pressure hull is similar to many pressure vessels such as boilers but, instead of containing a high pressure, the pressure hull has forces pressing from the outside. In addition, it has also to be able to withstand explosive shock conditions, such as those from mines or torpedoes detonating nearby. Moreover it needs both to protect the nuclear reactor from these forces and, in the event of failure, to contain any radioactive materials.

The long cylindrical part of the pressure hull is made from curved plates strengthened by a series of equally spaced internal circular frames that are fashioned from steel with a T-shaped cross section.

The pressure hull is a totally welded structure fabricated from high-strength steel, a ferrous alloy with small quanitities of nine elements, particularly nickel, chromium and manganese – that is the UK's equivalent to the US HY80 steel. This is more flexible than normal steel, so can withstand greater pressures.

Internal bulkheads are usually attached to the frames and provide additional strengthening to the pressure hull structure. Some bulkheads are watertight and can withstand the full force of water at maximum depth. Watertight bulkheads enable the extreme aft section and extreme forward sections of the pressure hull to be isolated and remain intact even if the rest of the boat is flooded. In the case of a disabled submarine, these fore and aft compartments become escape compartments. They are

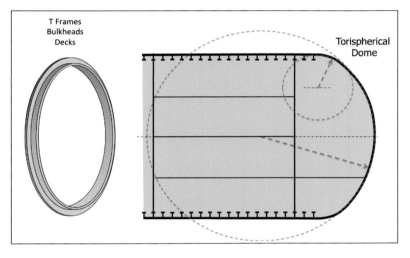

ABOVE Pressure hull structure showing torispherical dome. *(Author)*

BELOW Wrested from Dante's Inferno: first pour of the boat 4 steel castings. *(Sheffield Forgemasters)*

between the forward and aft parts of the boat.
This narrow tunnel-like space has airlocks at
either end so that the forward or aft parts of the
boat are separated at all times.

Forward of the reactor compartment the
submarine has three decks. The highest deck,
1-deck, is reserved for operational activities
whereas accommodation occupies 2-deck. These
spaces take up almost exactly the same area
as the two decks of an Airbus A380 aeroplane.
The number of the first- and business-class
passengers occupying the upper deck of the plane
is about 100, similar to HMS *Astute*'s complement,
yet their period on board the A380 is rarely even a
day, rather than the several weeks that the boat's
personnel have to live and work on board. The
lowest deck, 3-deck, is mainly reserved for heavy
machinery and the heavy batteries.

For strength the pressure hull should be
continuous with no irregularities where stress
can occur and weaken the structure. In
practice, however, there must be access to the
hull and means of firing weapons. Such sealable
holes in the pressure hull are referred to as
penetrations. There are several types allowing:

■ **Access** The main entrance to the boat
is through the watertight accommodation
hatch beneath the fin; this also allows

consequently equipped with life-support
equipment and escape towers for use in an
emergency evacuation of the boat. They are fitted
with power-operated watertight doors that allow
access but can be closed and withstand the
same pressures as the bulkhead. The actuation
systems are capable of operation at all angles of
heel and trim up to 30° in any direction.

Either side of the reactor compartment
are containment bulkheads designed to
contain any radioactive material in the case
of a critical reactor accident. Above the
reactor compartment is the reactor services
compartment that allows personnel to pass

RIGHT Comparison
of HMS *Astute* with
Airbus A380-800, one
of the world's largest
passenger airliners,
with a blue whale
and with the London
Routemaster bus.
(Author/Mischa Campen)

access from the control room to the space under the casing and, through the fin, to the navigational bridge when the boat is surfaced. This is subject to the full water pressure but, as it is not used when submerged, there is no fall-back inner closure. The weapons embarkation hatch is also only used at the surface and so, too, has only a single hatch.

- **Escape** There are two escape trunks that permit escape from the boat if it is disabled. Both have an inner and outer hatch and the latter (which normally experiences the full ambient sea pressure) is not normally open at sea. There are times when it has to be opened, in which case the inner closure experiences the full pressure. The forward escape trunk (FET) allows one person at a time to escape. Its inner (lower) and outer hatches have a diameter of 472mm and 660mm respectively. Both hatches of the logistics escape trunk are larger at 762mm diameter allowing people to escape in pairs. Situated aft, this more generously sized tower is also used for loading stores when in harbour.
- **Operations** The six weapon launch-tubes also have inner and outer doors with the outer one open during operation and the inner door guarding against inundation. The two submarine signal ejectors situated close to the escape towers have a similar arrangement, as does the lock-in/lock-out trunk towards the aft of the fin. The latter is operated when personnel need to leave or enter the boat when it is submerged.
- **Seawater supply** Inlets and outlets allow seawater to circulate for the purposes of cooling – for instance to remove heat from the steam condensers – and for use by systems such as plants producing fresh water and oxygen.

All the penetrations mentioned so far have seals that ensure that no seawater can enter. The main propulsion shaft, because it rotates, has a more complex sealing arrangement. On earlier submarines a similar problem occurred with the periscope. This was a long tube that had to be raised, lowered and rotated, yet its hull penetration had to remain watertight at great depth. These mechanical difficulties have been

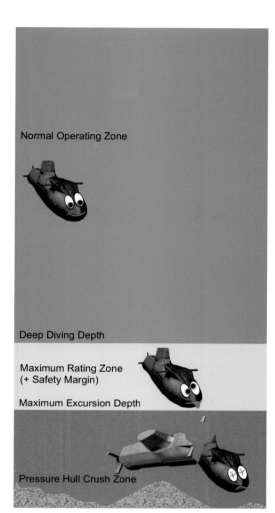

Normal Operating Zone

Deep Diving Depth

Maximum Rating Zone (+ Safety Margin)

Maximum Excursion Depth

Pressure Hull Crush Zone

LEFT Submarine deep diving depth. *(Author)*

overcome on HMS *Astute* by fitting the latest type of periscope – one that does not penetrate the hull. Smaller penetrations that rely on glands for their watertight integrity allow cables and pipes to connect to equipment in the free-flood spaces within the outer hull.

In order to regain the loss of strength that results from the removal of material to form penetrations, the pressure hull around the penetrations is strengthened. Nearly all are circular as these are easiest to reinforce. The reinforcement forms an integral part of the pressure hull and is larger for the bigger-diameter penetrations. It comprises heavier plating welded around each opening. These plates are known as hull inserts.

The maximum depth to which a submarine may be taken intentionally is termed the deep diving depth (DDD). The value of the DDD is highly classified and, officially, the RN will only admit to 'at least 250m'.

1 Pressure hull
2 Free flood volumes
3 Main ballast tank 1
4 Main ballast tank 2
5 Launch-tube water transfer tank
6 Main ballast tank 3
7 Aft main bottle groups
8 Main ballast tank 4

A Sonar bow dome   B Forward main bottle group   C Towed array winch   D Secondary propulsion motor (deployed)

ABOVE Free-flood space equipment.
(Author, based on BAE Systems illustration)

Because emergencies may occur, submarines are designed to survive an occasional excursion below the DDD. However, once the submarine reaches the collapse depth (generally assumed to be 20% below the DDD), the hull is likely to suddenly and catastrophically

BELOW Forward free-flood space.
(Author, based on BAE Systems illustration)

1 Sonar 2076 bow array
2 Number 1 main ballast tank
3 Anchor windlass
4 Anchor cable locker
5 Number 2 main ballast tank
6 High-pressure air blow group cylinders
7 Gemini inflatable raiding craft stowage
8 Air turbine pump
9 Starboard launch-tube bow caps
10 Water transfer tank
11 Weapons embarkation hatch
12 Pressure hull forward dome
13 Forward hydroplane
14 Forward hydroplane hydraulic actuator

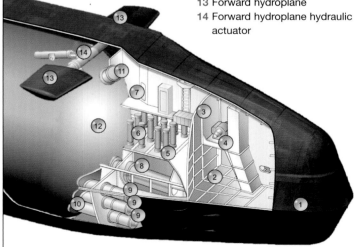

succumb to the pressure of the water. It is irrevocably crushed like someone stamping on a fizzy drinks can.

Outer hull

The streamlined outer hull surrounds the pressure hull and the free-flood space between the two structures that holds equipment that need not be in the pressure hull. HMS *Astute*'s hull has a length to diameter ratio (L/D) of 8.6, indicating that it is slightly fatter for its length than its predecessors (the range of values for the world's SSNs is 8.1–11.0). The hull diameter is larger than HMS *Trafalgar*, primarily in order to accommodate the reactor, but the length is also slightly greater.

The largest free-flood spaces are situated forward and aft of the pressure hull. There are four main ballast tanks (MBTs), two forward and two aft. When the boat is on the surface these tanks contain air that provide buoyancy. To dive, air is released and water floods into the tanks, thus reducing the buoyancy and submerging the boat.

The **forward free-flood** and under-casing spaces are the location for:

■ MBT numbers 1 and 2 and their main bottle group (MBG) – high-pressure (HP) air cylinders that are used to force water from the MBT when the boat surfaces. In an emergency HP air can also be supplied from emergency cylinder groups within the pressure hull.
■ The bow array of sonar 2076.
■ The launch system water tank and the air turbine pump. The pump draws water from this tank to force weapons through the launch-tubes that pass through the free-flood space.

- The actuator mechanisms for the forward hydroplanes.
- The stowed 'Zodiac' inflatable raiding craft – a boat primarily used for over-the-horizon insertion ashore of small clandestine teams of Special Forces troops. This rubber boat can be manhandled from its stowage when the submarine is surfaced and can be inflated in minutes using a CO_2 tank (or even a foot-pump!).

Characteristics of inflatable raiding craft	
Length overall	5.0m
Width overall	1.9m
Payload	1,250kg (includes engine and fuel)
Capacity	10 troops (5 fully laden)
Propulsion	30kW outboard motor
Top speed	37km/h (20kts)
Range	75km at top speed
Stealth propulsion	Paddles

- An anchor must be carried to meet international maritime regulations, even though submarines rarely use them. The anchor is stowed beneath the hull in a depression that allows the flukes of the anchor to present a flat face contiguous with the hull, thereby reducing any turbulence as water flows over it. The anchor and its cable (chain) are held tautly in place by a type of clip called a Blake Slip that prevents these items rattling and producing detectable noise. The anchor can only be released from the free-flood area, so it cannot be used unless the submarine is surfaced. In recognition that there are emergency situations requiring an anchor when the boat is submerged, it is intended to develop a system that allows its release from within the submarine. The anchor is lowered (dropped) and hauled in (weighed) by the winch that is also within the free-flood space.

The **aft free-flood space** tapers towards the shrouded pump-jet propulsor. This shape reduces the hydrodynamic resistance of the hull. The aft free-flood space accommodates:
- MBT numbers 3 and 4 and their MBG of HP air cylinders. As with the forward MBT, in an emergency HP air can also be supplied from emergency cylinder groups within the pressure hull.

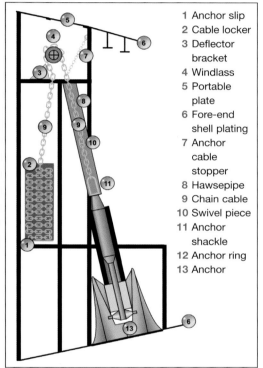

1 Anchor slip
2 Cable locker
3 Deflector bracket
4 Windlass
5 Portable plate
6 Fore-end shell plating
7 Anchor cable stopper
8 Hawsepipe
9 Chain cable
10 Swivel piece
11 Anchor shackle
12 Anchor ring
13 Anchor

ABOVE Inflatable raiding craft Mk 3 used by squadron reconnaissance team of 539 Squadron Royal Marines. *(Crown Copyright/ PO(Phot) Sean Clee)*

LEFT Typical nuclear submarine anchor and chain cable arrangement. *(Author from MoD standard)*

BELOW Aft free-flood space. *(Author, based on BAE Systems illustration)*

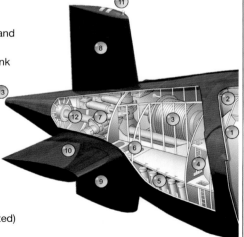

1 Aft pressure dome
2 Main ballast vent system
3 Towed array cable drum and winch
4 Number 3 main ballast tank
5 High-pressure bottles
6 Number 4 main ballast tank
7 Rudder and hydroplane hydraulic actuators
8 Upper rudder segment
9 Lower rudder segment
10 Starboard hydroplane
11 Aft anchor light
12 Propeller shaft
13 Pump-jet propulsor (omitted)

Cutaway drawing of HMS *Astute*.

(BAE Systems)

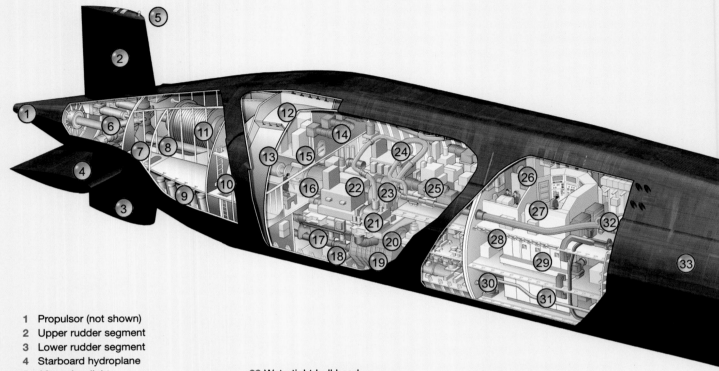

1   Propulsor (not shown)
2   Upper rudder segment
3   Lower rudder segment
4   Starboard hydroplane
5   Aft anchor light
6   Rudder and hydroplane actuators
7   No 4 main ballast tank
8   Propulsor shaft
9   High pressure bottles
10 No 3 main ballast tank
11 Towed array case drum and winch
12 Main ballast vent system
13 Aft pressure dome
14 Air treatment units
15 Naval stores
16 Shaft thrust block and bearing
17 Circulating water transfer pipes
18 Lubricating oil tank
19 Starboard condenser
20 Main machinery mounting raft
21 Turbo-generators (port and starboard)
22 Combining gearbox
23 Main turbines
24 Steam delivery ducting
25 Engine room

26 Watertight bulkhead
27 Manoeuvring room (MR)
28 MR isolated deck mounting
29 Switchboard room
30 Diesel generator room
31 Static converters
32 Main steam valve
33 Reactor section
34 Part of pressure hull
35 Forward airlock
36 Air handling compartment
37 Waste management equipment
38 Conditioned air ducting
39 Galley
40 Isolated deck mountings
41 Batteries
42 Junior Ratings' mess
43 RESM office
44 Commanding Officer's cabin
45 Port side communications office
46 Diesel exhaust mast

47 Snort induction mast
48 SHF/EHF (NEST) mast
49 CESM mast
50 AZL radar mast
51 SatCom mast
52 Integrated communications mast
53 Starboard electro-optronic periscope
54 Port electro-optronic periscope
55 Navigation mast
56 Bridge fin access
57 Junior Ratings' bathroom
58 Senior Ratings' bathroom
59 Battery switch room

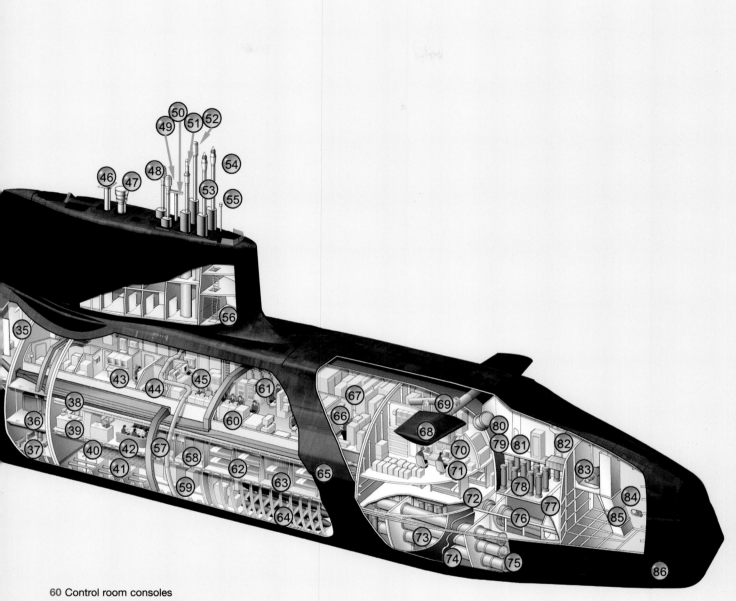

60 Control room consoles
61 Sonar operators' consoles
62 Senior Ratings' bunks
63 Medical berth
64 Weapons stowage and handling
65 Flank sonar array
66 Maintenance workshop
67 Sonar equipment room
68 Forward hydrophone
69 Hydroplane hydraulic actuator
70 Hydroplane hinge mounting

71 Ship's office
72 Junior Ratings' berths
73 Launch tubes
74 Water transfer tank
75 Launch tube muzzle doors
76 Air turbine pump
77 No 2 main ballast tank
78 High pressure air bottles
79 Forward pressure dome

80 Weapons embarkation hatch
81 Inshore raiding craft stowage
82 Hinged fairlead
83 Anchor windlass
84 No 1 main ballast tank
85 Anchor cable locker
86 Bow sonar

- The shrouded pump-jet propulsor that is rotated by the propulsor shaft.
- Secondary propulsion motor (SPM) that provides an alternative source of propulsion.
- The large quantities of seawater needed to be drawn and discharged for cooling the reactor condenser and other services would require large pipes. To avoid sizeable openings in the outer hull, the water is drawn into the pressure hull from the free-flood space through large-diameter circulating water transfer pipes.
- When alongside, the aft free-flood space can be accessed for maintenance and repair of the equipment. First, however, a temporary coffer-dam must be installed around the apertures and inflatable seals employed to prevent leakage from the rudder, hydroplane and propeller shafts. Once this is done, the space may be pumped out. This avoids dry-docking for maintenance of this space.

ABOVE Main bottle group HP air cylinders in fore-end construction.
(Jill Hempsall)

BELOW Casing equipment.
(Author, based on BAE Systems photograph)

- Towed-array cable drum and winch, enabling the linear array of sensors to be streamed and recovered. To avoid the array fouling the propulsor, it is fed through a tube mounted over the propulsor on the starboard side. A similar tube on the port side accommodates a clip-on array.
- Hydraulic actuators for the rudder and the two aft hydroplanes.

Vent-valves located on the casing over the pressure hull allow air to be released from the MBT when the boat dives. The casing is also a free-flood area and contains minor equipment including signal buoys, retractable bollards, fairleads and decoy systems.

When submerged, the outer hull must be as smooth as possible in order to reduce turbulence produced by discontinuities such as apertures and projections. Turbulence reduces

1 Weapons loading hatch	5 Forward escape trunk	11 Aft floodlights	15 Vent main ballast tank 4
2 Vent main ballast tank 1 (port and starboard)	6 Forward floodlights	12 Capstans (port and starboard) and indicator buoy	(port and starboard)
3 Vent main ballast tank 2 (port and starboard)	7 Two bollards		A Fore-planes (port and starboard)
4 Six bollards and indicator buoy	8 Two bollards	13 Six bollards	B Rudder
	9 Two bollards	14 Hinged fairleads (port and starboard)	C After-planes (port and starboard submerged)
	10 Logistics escape trunk		

the ability of the boat to pass effectively through the water and, most importantly, generates acoustic energy that can betray the boat's position. Weapon launch-tubes are covered with shutters except during firing. Apertures for masts also have sliding closures covering them when submerged. Bollards, capstans and fairleads are retracted when not in use. Equipment only deployed occasionally (such as buoys) are stowed behind coverings that ensure that the hull-form is continuous.

The fin and masts

The fin is primarily for use on, or close to, the surface and is a free-flooding space that is integral with the casing. It provides an elevated platform for conning and navigation, as well as housing the masts. So that the boat can surface from beneath sea-ice, the fin is specially strengthened to survive the initial ice breach.

On the surface, the fin is accessed from the pressure hull's accommodation hatch and a short accommodation ladder through the casing. The navigation position is reached by climbing a further 6m inside the front of the fin. When in harbour, the top of the accommodation ladder (and access to the submarine) can be reached from a doorway

ABOVE LEFT Retractable bollards. *(Crown Copyright/CPOA(Phot) Thomas 'Tam' McDonald)*

ABOVE Officer ascending the accommodation ladder on HMS *Ambush*. *(Florida Today/Malcolm 'Denny' Denemark)*

BELOW Fin harbour access door. *(Florida Today/Malcolm 'Denny' Denemark)*

RIGHT **Close-up of HMS *Astute*'s fin with ship's bell, crest and nameplate.** *(Crown Copyright/L(Phot) Stephen 'Stevie' Burke)*

RIGHT **Aft section of the fin that can be removed to accommodate the SFPB.** *(Crown Copyright/LA(Phot) Stuart 'Stu' Hill)*

BELOW **HMS *Astute* mast arrangements.** *(BAE Systems)*

at the base of the fin. There are further access doors further aft on the fin.

Towards the rear of the fin, 8m from the bridge, is a secondary navigation position. When the boat is surfaced this is exposed by sliding open two flaps. They are shut for diving and secured with eight clips and moused to prevent rattling. The aft section of the fin contains the lock-in/lock-out trunk that allows swimmers to leave and enter the pressure hull when the boat is fully submerged but close to the surface. When the Special Forces payload bay is fitted aft of the fin, swimmers can use this to exit to transfer to the swimmer delivery vehicle when this is carried.

The central section of the fin houses a number of masts. A common design used by electronic masts (except the navigation light and radar mast) is the quiet modular mast that extends the masts telescopically from their stowed position within the fin.

All masts experience full water pressure when the submarine is dived. They are enclosed beneath sliding shutters to maintain the smooth lines of boat. When the submarine surfaces, these slide back to allow the masts to be deployed.

The masts are:

■ **Navigation mast** topped by a wind direction indicator that doubles as a flagpole.

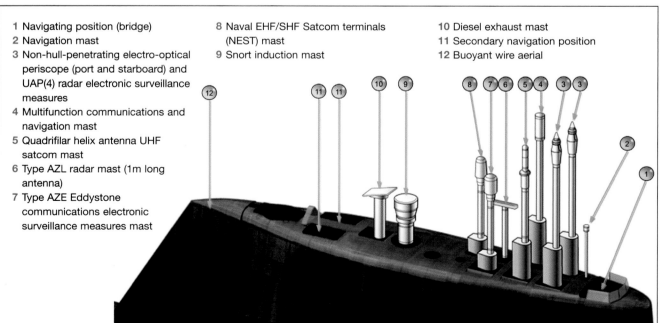

1 Navigating position (bridge)
2 Navigation mast
3 Non-hull-penetrating electro-optical periscope (port and starboard) and UAP(4) radar electronic surveillance measures
4 Multifunction communications and navigation mast
5 Quadrifilar helix antenna UHF satcom mast
6 Type AZL radar mast (1m long antenna)
7 Type AZE Eddystone communications electronic surveillance measures mast

8 Naval EHF/SHF Satcom terminals (NEST) mast
9 Snort induction mast

10 Diesel exhaust mast
11 Secondary navigation position
12 Buoyant wire aerial

ABOVE *Astute* class mast arrangements: HMS *Ambush* commissioning. *(Crown Copyright/WO(Phot) Ian Arthur)*

LEFT Quiet modular mast structural assembly for mast-raising (accommodated within fin). *(MacTaggart Scott)*

BELOW Cross-section of quiet modular mast. *(MacTaggart Scott)*

1	Structural assembly	7	Payload carrier bearings
2	Composite fairing assembly (first lift)	8	Operating cylinder
3	Three-faced fairing bearing	9	Pulley cable space
4	Single-faced fairing bearing	10	Inlet manifold
5	Payload mast (second lift)	11	Electrical connection
6	Payload carrier	12	Cable duct
		13	Cable management

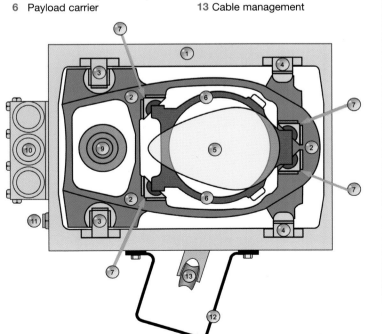

RIGHT Fin mast arrangement with shutters open and navigating position manned. *(Crown Copyright/PO Gavin 'Final' Furlong)*

- ■ **Two non-hull-penetrating electro-optical periscopes** that replace the traditional optical periscopes. Around the top of the electro-optical sensor on each mast are four sensors of the UAP(4) radar electronic support measures equipment. These masts, described in detail later in the book, are raised telescopically from their stowed position within the fin.

- ■ **The multifunction communications and navigation mast** immediately aft of the navigation position on the port side. The housing is 750mm tall and 185mm in diameter and contains three antennas. The first is a discone antenna (a conical antenna

topped by a conductive disc). Above this is a spiral-wound conical GPS antenna, within which there is a monopole antenna for IFF (identification friend or foe) and terrestrial mobile phone communication. The antenna can be used to communicate at the following frequencies:

- ♦ VHF Maritime 156–165MHz
- ♦ UHF Line of Site 225–400MHz
- ♦ UHF Satcom 243–318MHz
- ♦ VHF Tactical 30–88MHz (this is an option and may not be implemented)

The antenna also supports the Joint Tactical Information Distribution System jam-resistant cryptographic digital communication link (96–1215MHz) for data and voice, as well as GPS (1227–1575MHz).

- ■ **A UHF Satcom communications mast**, a high-performance omnidirectional Quadrifilar Helix Antenna 1,680mm tall and 185mm in diameter. It allows uplink (transmit) at 292–318MHz and downlink (receive) at 243–270MHz. UHF Satcom operates at 32k/bits full duplex with demand-assigned multiple access. It has a custom-designed Satcom duplexer and low-noise gallium arsenide field effect transistor pre-amplifier.

- ■ **Type AZL mast** for the surface warning and navigation radar.

- ■ **Type AZE electronic support measures mast** that can receive for analysis communications signals in three frequency groups covering 10kHz–2GHz. Apart from this interception of communications signals for intelligence, it warns of radar signals from airborne radars. The mast may also be used for communications transmission and reception at VHF/UHF (150–400 MHz) that includes the VHF maritime frequencies of 156–165MHz.

    The antenna mounted on a modular mast is 270mm high and 225mm in diameter and contains a conical log spiral-wound antenna with internal dipole and electronics assembly.

- ■ **Naval EHF/SHF Satcom terminal mast**.

- ■ **Snort mast and diesel exhaust mast** mounted aft of the electronic masts mentioned above. These allow the diesel generators to operate when the boat is at periscope depth or surfaced. The snort mast is an air intake enabling fresh air to be

BELOW HMS *Astute* **navigation lights port and starboard (on the forward face of the fin) and a masthead light.** *(BAE Systems)*

sucked into the boat. It can be operated when the fin is almost completely submerged as it has a mechanism that temporarily closes the intake should it become flooded with water from a wave. The fin also supports, on its forward and side faces, underwater communication sonar arrays. Regulation navigation lights are provided for use when travelling on the surface at night.

Surface warning and navigation radar

When the submarine is surfaced, its radar is used to detect surface features for navigation and to provide warning of the presence of aircraft and surface vessels. The radar equipment in the hull is similar to the Type 1007 I-band radar transmitter/receiver used by surface warships. The transmitter generates radar pulses that pass up a vertical waveguide through the pressure hull and up the inside of an antenna mast. The radar pulse is radiated by the rotating antenna; any detected return is passed down the waveguide to the receiver. The transmitter/receiver is sited immediately below the mast so that the waveguide is straight – thereby minimising electrical losses within the waveguide. The mast, topped by a pressure-resistant Type AZL antenna, is telescopic and is retracted into the fin and streamlined by a shutter when the boat is submerged. When the boat surfaces, the shutter can be slid back and the mast and antenna raised. Because of the proximity of their masts, the radar cannot be used when the communications electronic support measures (CESM) mast is raised. When the boat is surfaced, the radar horizon is about 15km. The AZL antenna, the telescopic mast and its waveguide must be able to survive the extreme pressure of the DDD.

From early 2016, an advanced radar began to be rolled out across the fleet in a five-year upgrade with HMS *Artful* as the first submarine to be fitted. The commercial Sharpeye technology was incorporated in a 'downmast' version of the transmitter/receiver fitted within the pressure hull. At 300W this has a much lower power output than the earlier radar (25kW) so is less easily detected by other vessels. Nevertheless its solid-state processor

can detect more targets, earlier and at a longer range. It delivers improvements in sub-clutter visibility of approximately 30dB.

The new radar has been developed to operate with the warship electronic chart display and information system and will include a common maritime data-processing environment.

A secondary (back-up) I-band navigational radar can be manually deployed. The 500mm antenna and 177mm display are secured on the bridge alongside the navigational position using quick-release mounting brackets. No single part of the equipment weighs more than 13kg. It obtains its power (2kW) from a 24V power supply socket. As with the main navigational radar, the secondary radar is capable of operating in adverse environmental conditions, including spray and wave splash.

Control surfaces (rudders and hydroplanes) and hydraulic systems

The submarine's course and depth are controlled by the rudders and hydroplanes. The two vertical rudders control the heading of the submarine. The hydroplanes, two forward and two aft, control the submarine's vertical motion (pitch and depth) under the surface of the water and are essential when diving and surfacing.

ABOVE **HMS *Astute*: two vertical rudder blades, starboard aft hydroplane and, in the distance, starboard forward hydroplane.**
(Christopher Morgan-Jones)

BELOW **HMS *Ambush*'s forward hydroplanes are visible on either side of the hull.** *(Crown Copyright/CPOA(Phot) Thomas 'Tam' McDonald)*

The rudder comprises two mechanically linked blades that are moved together. The rudder has a total height of over 15m and an area of almost 30m^2; its lower blade extends just below the hull, drawing 10.64m at normal surfaced trim. The lower edge of the rudder is fitted with a GRP skeg to streamline it and to provide a buffer against damage from grounding. There are twin hydraulic rudder actuators operating in a push-pull arrangement to share the dynamic loads. Either actuator can be bypassed should faults arise and the remaining actuator can control the rudder, albeit with some performance degradation.

The forward hydroplanes are mounted on the forward hull with actuators in the forward free-flood space. While this position makes them vulnerable to damage from jetties and tugs when the submarine is on the surface, soon after the boat dives, the hydroplanes become submerged so can quickly contribute to the control of the dive. Their position also allows control of pitch and depth independently so that, at low speeds, the boat can remain level when diving. Hydraulic actuators operate both forward hydroplanes in unison on a single shaft.

Unlike earlier classes, the *Astute* class aft hydroplanes are independently actuated providing greater manoeuvrability. The design of aft actuator arrangements is complex as the propulsor shaft passes, centrally, through the space. Plant selection valves controlled from the submarine control console provide a rapid changeover of hydraulic power sources. This increase in integrity avoids the need to employ a completely diverse power source, such as HP air, used on earlier submarine classes. The forward hydroplane actuators are the main item of equipment requiring maintenance in the forward free-flood space, but these are accessible when the boat is alongside as they are completely above the waterline.

Traditionally, submarines operate within the boundaries of a manoeuvring limitation diagram that circumscribes the range of speeds over which the boat can operate at a given depth. This ensures that, in the case of a control surface failure (such as a hydroplane becoming jammed in the full dive position), the boat may safely recover. The increases in reliability from twin rudder actuators, separately actuated aft hydroplanes and duplication of hydraulic supplies have meant that a safe manoeuvring envelope has been introduced for the *Astute* class. In the event of a hydroplane or rudder jam, for instance, then autopilot will compensate by using the remaining available control surfaces to maintain depth control without excessive depth excursions. While the safe manoeuvring envelope uses a similar set of constraints on speed and depth as the manoeuvring limitation diagram, it represents a much wider operating envelope, providing a significant improvement in capability.

Because liquids are almost incompressible, the application of pressure to the confined hydraulic fluid can transmit power along a hydraulic pipe. Harnessing this power can deliver useful work, such as moving an actuator. Hydraulic systems are able to operate remote, heavy and essential items of equipment quietly and efficiently. While a major use is the operation of the rudder and hydroplanes, hydraulic systems power other critical applications including the opening and closing of valves such as MBT vents, hull-valves and HP blow-valves. Further external equipment operated hydraulically includes the SPM, anchor windlass, capstans, weapon launch-tube doors and shutters. Within the pressure hull, hydraulic power is used to operate watertight doors, move weapons in the weapons stowage compartment and to ensure that the machinery raft is isolated to reduce transmitted acoustic energy when operating at low speed.

The submarine employs several separate hydraulic systems with the facility to cross-connect them to ensure continuity of power if one system fails.

Ballast system and compressed air systems

All submarines are fitted with a number of tanks that allow the ballast system to adjust the boat's buoyancy so that it can dive, maintain a level attitude and resurface.

The principal tanks for adjusting buoyancy are MBTs sited forward and aft of the pressure hull. On the surface the boat is buoyant because of the air in its MBT. All MBTs are fitted with hydraulic vent-valves that, when opened, allow air to escape from the tanks. The vents

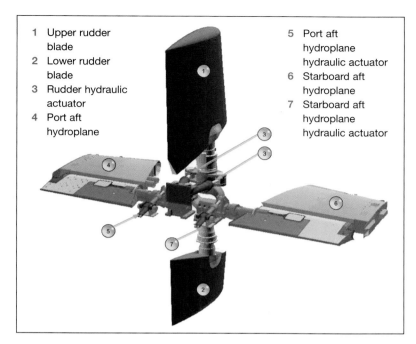

1 Upper rudder blade
2 Lower rudder blade
3 Rudder hydraulic actuator
4 Port aft hydroplane
5 Port aft hydroplane hydraulic actuator
6 Starboard aft hydroplane
7 Starboard aft hydroplane hydraulic actuator

are hydraulically operated from the control room (although with a local backup). The hydraulic fluid is supplied through a Hydel-valve – a solenoid-operated ball valve that controls the supply of hydraulic fluid through a slide valve. This gives a positive fluid flow in either of two directions (opening or closing the vent valve). When the vent is opened air leaves the top of the MBT and seawater enters through free-flood holes located in the bottom of the tanks

ABOVE Rudder and aft hydroplane arrangement. *(BAE Systems)*

BELOW Aft control surface hydraulic actuators. *(BAE Systems)*

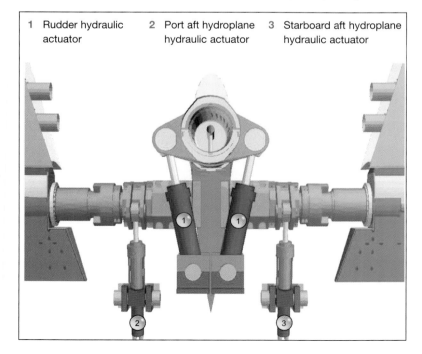

1 Rudder hydraulic actuator
2 Port aft hydroplane hydraulic actuator
3 Starboard aft hydroplane hydraulic actuator

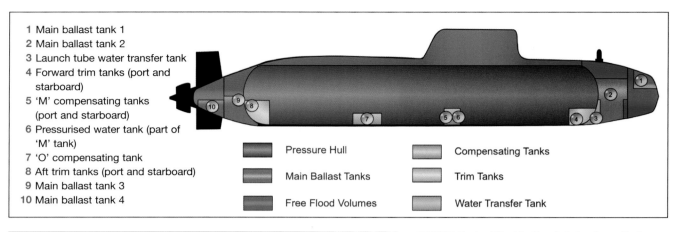

1 Main ballast tank 1
2 Main ballast tank 2
3 Launch tube water transfer tank
4 Forward trim tanks (port and starboard)
5 'M' compensating tanks (port and starboard)
6 Pressurised water tank (part of 'M' tank)
7 'O' compensating tank
8 Aft trim tanks (port and starboard)
9 Main ballast tank 3
10 Main ballast tank 4

Pressure Hull

Main Ballast Tanks

Free Flood Volumes

Compensating Tanks

Trim Tanks

Water Transfer Tank

ABOVE Tanks fitted to the *Astute* class. *(Author from BAE Systems drawing)*

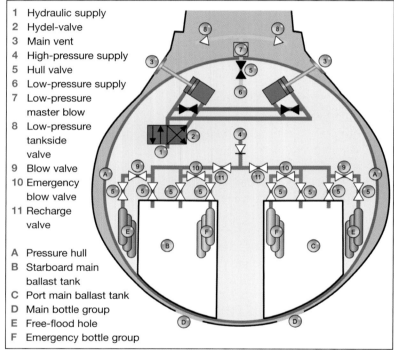

1 Hydraulic supply
2 Hydel-valve
3 Main vent
4 High-pressure supply
5 Hull valve
6 Low-pressure supply
7 Low-pressure master blow
8 Low-pressure tankside valve
9 Blow valve
10 Emergency blow valve
11 Recharge valve

A Pressure hull
B Starboard main ballast tank
C Port main ballast tank
D Main bottle group
E Free-flood hole
F Emergency bottle group

LEFT Schematic of a typical main ballast tank blow system. *(Author)*

near the keel. This decreases the submarine's buoyancy and allows the boat to sink.

To return the submarine to the surface, the seawater is expelled from the MBT by blowing compressed HP air into the tanks. This air is stored in MBG cylinders located in the forward and aft free-flood spaces. When sufficient water has been expelled to restore positive buoyancy, the submarine approaches the surface. When close to the surface, an LP air blower, operating just above atmospheric pressure, is used to bring the submarine to full buoyancy so that it may fully surface. This conserves HP air stored in the cylinders.

Compressed air can also be supplied to the MBT by the emergency blow system – a dedicated reserve of air sufficient to counter the effects of flooding at depth. The system provides adequate reserve of air to ensure that a submarine at DDD, when travelling at the minimum permitted speed, can surface following a 'maximum credible flood'.

The compressors supplying the HP air system recharge the cylinders of the MBG and emergency bottle groups once the boat has surfaced. There are two acoustic energy-reduced compressors that increase air pressure by means of a series of stages. The cylinder

LEFT Air released from main ballast tank vent during basin trials. *(BBC)*

Air compressor characteristics		
	WP5000	WP3232
Type	Radial star	Inline vertical
Pressure	34.5MPa	10MPa
Cooling	Water-cooled	Air-cooled
Stages/cylinders	4/4	3/3
Speed	1,470rpm	1,170rpm
Charging capacity (free air delivery)	145m³/h	11m³/h
Power required	53.0kW	5.3kW
Weight	1.650T	0.291T
Length	1.215m	0.920m
Width	1.095m	0.710m
Height	1,700m	0.970m
Frequency	60Hz	60Hz

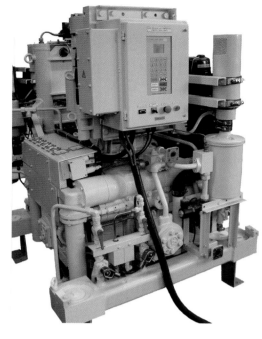

LEFT WP5000, four-stage water-cooled HP air compressor unit. *(J.P. Sauer & Sohn)*

of each stage discharges air into another for further compression. Once the pressure has reached a high value it passes into the distribution system. A smaller 10MPa air-cooled compressor is also carried to supply emergency systems such as emergency air.

The bottle groups, the weapons handing and launch system and the extended-duration breathing apparatus are the principal systems that use HP air directly. Air, once stored, is a source of power – to displace water from tanks, for instance – and requires no further expenditure of energy during operation. HP air is a high-

integrity source of air and power and performs a vital role in controlling the boat's buoyancy. It also supplies several systems, a high proportion of which are used only in emergencies.

Pressure reducing stations allow HP air to be reduced to medium pressure (MP) at 2.8MPa, principally for the auxiliary vent and blow system. MP air is further reduced to LP in order to supply emergency systems including the emergency breathing system operating at 0.7MPa.

When submerged, the aim is to ensure that the submarine's buoyancy matches the weight of the vessel itself, so that it is neutrally buoyant

BELOW Schematic of the aft section of a typical high-pressure air system. *(Author, based on information from Defence Standard)*

1 Main bottle group
2 Hull valve
3 Group isolating valve
4 High-pressure blow
5 Emergency cylinder group
6 Cross connection
7 Services
8 Reactor air services
9 Hydraulic reservoir
10 Integrity non-return valve
11 Watertight bulkhead
12 Bulkhead isolating valve
13 Shore charging connection (not shown)
A Engine room
B Manoeuvring room
C High-pressure air compressor
D To forward part of system
E Emergency bottle group (not shown)

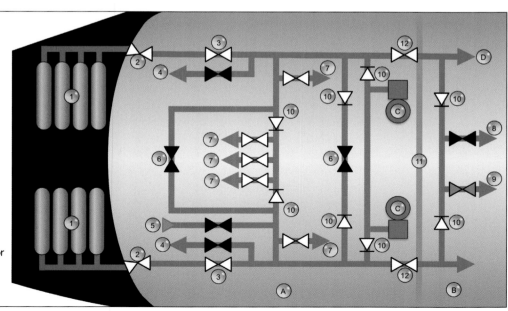

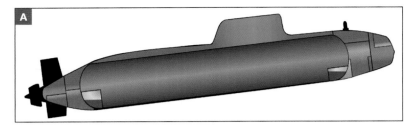

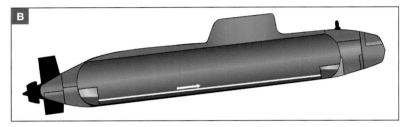

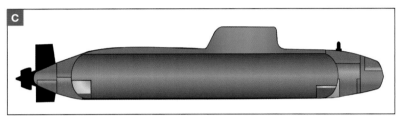

measure of whether the submarine is horizontal – is carefully managed.

If the submarine's weight is greater towards the forward part of the boat then its centre of gravity will be forward of the centre of buoyancy and the boat will incline downwards. Conversely, greater weight to the stern will incline the boat upwards. Adjustment of trim is effected by pumping water between the trim compensation tanks at either end of the pressure hull.

Integrated platform management system (IPMS)

The full-authority IPMS provides screen-based control of the steering, dive control and propulsion system as well as the on-board service and auxiliary systems. It offers a level of automatic monitoring and control not previously possible. Some automated sequences have been introduced as a first stage in reducing the manning levels, although the operator is still in command for most control operations. The IPMS has a safety-justified, distributed architecture that interfaces with both legacy dumb sensors and actuators as well as the increasing number of smart sensors and actuators being introduced on the *Astute* class. The IPMS is a process control system that is specifically tailored for the military environment and includes standard commercial-off-the-shelf (COTS) components from the process industry such as programmable logic controllers and single board computers.

The steering and dive control system within the IPMS is located in the helmsman's submarine control console in the control room. The system provides instrumentation to control course and depth; it includes two autopilots and controllers for trim compensation and hover. There are three modes of control: normal (automatic) mode, manual mode and emergency mode. The system (and its associated hydraulic system) is duplicated to offer a fall-back in both automatic and manual modes of control. The depth and heading is set on the helmsman's panel when the steering and dive control system is in automatic mode;

and neither rises nor sinks. Changes in depth are brought about by using the hydroplanes. Subtle changes of seawater density and the variation of the boat's volume both change the boat's buoyancy. The pressure hull of all submarines is compressed as they dive and experience increased seawater pressure. The *Astute* class is particularly compressible because of the hull's acoustic tiles and the sonar flank arrays. As the boat descends deeper these are squeezed, so reducing their volume, and hence buoyancy, of the submarine.

The trim and compensation system rapidly adjusts the weight of the submarine to accommodate changes in buoyancy. Buoyancy compensation is achieved by pumping water into or out of two compensation tanks within the pressure hull (called 'O' and 'M' compensation tanks). Water can be pumped overboard from 'M' compensation tanks while the boat is at intermediate depths or above. The starboard 'M' compensating tank is fitted with a partition termed the pressurised water tank. This small tank is pressurised by compressed air from the auxiliary vent and blow system to allow rapid ballast reduction down to intermediate depths.

Submarines may experience manoeuvring difficulties unless the trim condition – the

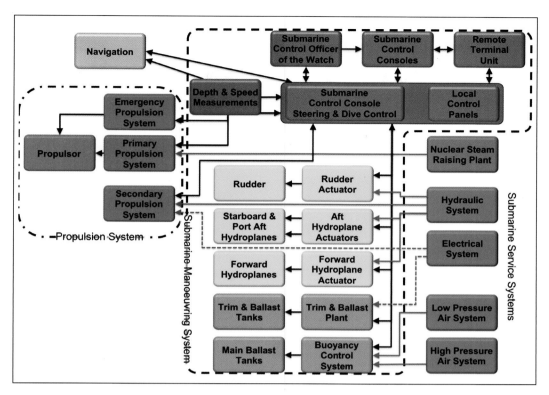

LEFT Schematic of elements of the propulsion and steering and dive control systems. *(Author, from Purvis & Phillips)*

the system ensures that the boat responds to these demands using the closed-loop control and the autopilot steering control algorithms. Depth, pitch and heading are accurately governed by employing multiple rudder options and the split aft hydroplane configuration. Depth is controlled precisely, regardless of ballast and trim errors. At periscope depth stable seakeeping is achieved despite the turbulent conditions that may occur from waves. The autopilot also ensures that there is minimal overshoot when altering depth and reduces the risk of broaching when coming to the surface. The system guarantees that there is minimal hydroplane activity during any manoeuvre and this helps reduce the acoustic energy signature. The two separate autopilots for depth and course can operate either separately or concurrently. This is of considerable value when turning as this manoeuvre makes it difficult to maintain depth.

The steering and dive control system can also incorporate an out-of-trim estimator that calculates the approximate amount of additional water required to maintain trim. This is only an advisory system, and the operator may, for operational reasons (for instance, to avoid the generation of additional acoustic energy which

may jeopardise the security of the boat), decide not to inject more water into the tanks.

Manual control is achieved using a single joystick located at the helmsman's position. When manual mode is selected, the helmsman's mimic displays crucial information relating to the joystick, rudder and planes.

If the IPMS network fails, the closed-loop automatic and manual modes are not available. Instead, the steering and dive control system's hard-wired emergency mode uses rate-control of the actuators.

BELOW Leading seaman at helmsman's position. *(Crown Copyright/L(Phot) Stephen 'Stevie' Burke)*

The watch-keepers' main interface with the IPMS is in the manoeuvring room. Control is through touch screens (avoiding the need for keyboards and pointer devices). In addition to the main control panel there are also remote terminal units distributed throughout the boat.

Acoustic tiles and acoustic signature reduction

More than 39,000 tiles cover the outer hull. They are bonded to the steel with epoxy resin and totally cover the hull except for the acoustically transparent 'windows' that protect the sonar arrays. The tiles reduce the potential for detection by the sonars of other submarines, torpedoes or surface ships. Tiles have a threefold function:

■ They are anechoic, thereby reducing the submarine's target echo strength – the amount of acoustic energy that is reflected when the submarine is illuminated by a sonar pulse from any vessel or torpedo actively searching for the boat. The tiles absorb the incident acoustic energy thereby diminishing that returned to the enemy's sonar.
■ They reduce the radiated acoustic energy signature by attenuating any acoustic energy emitted by the boat that could be detected by passive sonars listening for such signals.
■ They reduce the self-noise interference by attenuating any acoustic energy emitted by the boat that could interfere with the boat's own sonars, which might reduce their effectiveness.

The tiles are made from an elastomeric material filled with small voids giving them the ability to both absorb acoustic waves and to attenuate acoustic energy passing through them. The wavelength of the active sonar transmissions of torpedoes is 50mm (30kHz). To be effective, a simple anechoic material needs to be at least this thickness. Tiles are less effective at the wavelengths used by surface ship active search sonars (150–500mm). Damping at these frequencies relies on the material's internal structure. The challenge is formulating a material with voids that are sufficiently compliant to absorb

If the submarine encounters an emergency, the autopilots are sufficiently sophisticated to manoeuvre the boat to the correct depth, pitch and automatic trim. The autopilot can also control the pitch of the boat and maintain a constant depth with a slight bows-up attitude necessary for discharge of weapons.

To avoid unnecessary inconvenience and delay in making tactical decisions, a subset of ship control information is provided on displays close to the command position in the control room. In addition to the normal information provided to the command (such as depth and depth rate, speed and shaft revolutions) a single display, the ballastometer, represents the submarine's trim-condition and indicates uncertainties and trends.

In addition to the steering and dive control system, the IPMS is also used to control both the electrical and auxiliary systems. The latter include:

■ Compressed air systems
■ Hydraulic system
■ Chilled water system
■ Atmosphere control and monitoring system
■ Heating, ventilation and air-conditioning system
■ Fresh-water systems
■ Bilge and waste-water system
■ Flood alarms.

1 Pressure hull
2 External hull covered in acoustic tiles
3 Active acoustic sonar beam from ship or torpedo
4 Tile absorbs most incident acoustic energy
5 Attenuated sonar beam reflected by submarine

LEFT Acoustic tiles reducing the target echo returned to an active sonar. *(Author)*

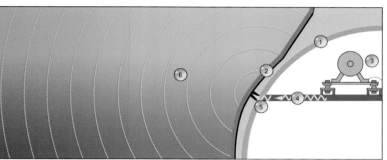

1 Pressure hull
2 External hull covered in acoustic tiles
3 Internal noise source
4 Acoustic transmission path to pressure hull
5 Acoustic transmission path to outer hull
6 Attenuated acoustic emission by submarine

LEFT Acoustic tiles reducing radiated acoustic energy. *(Author)*

BELOW Workers inspecting the hull indicate the scale of acoustic tiles coating the structure. *(BAE Systems)*

the acoustic energy, yet are able to survive the pressures at extreme depth. The massive changes in pressure as the submarine moves up and down in the water cause the tiles to compress and expand. In extremely harsh environmental conditions the adhesive used to hold acoustic tiles in position must be very strong and durable. In the past tiles have been dislodged and boats have returned from missions with several missing. Not only does this degrade the boat's stealth properties, but the composition of tiles is militarily sensitive – no navy would like one to fall into the hands of an adversary.

The tiles are the final stage of a series of measures taken to prevent energy being radiated by the boat. The other measures taken are:

■ Make sure that the acoustic energy produced by equipment is minimised. For rotating machinery this means ensuring that their parts are carefully balanced. For instance, HMS *Astute*'s gearbox is exceptionally well balanced and produces little acoustic energy. It is claimed that one could place a coin on its edge on top of the gearbox, run the gearbox at full power, and the coin would remain upright. Fluids travelling along pipework can generate acoustic energy if their flow is turbulent, so, to maintain smooth flow, the design must avoid constrictive pipes and sharp bends.

■ Containing any acoustic energy generated, major items of machinery are mounted on rafts that reduce the transmission to the submarine's structure and acoustic enclosures are employed to contain airborne

noise. For example, pumps that pass seawater through the steam condensers and the steam turbines are a potential major source of acoustic energy, so they are mounted on rafts. Many pieces of equipment are mounted on shock mounts to protect them from experiencing high accelerations and consequent damage caused by a torpedo or mine exploding nearby. These mounts also isolate acoustic energy from the submarine's structure.

■ Preventing any acoustic energy, in the form of vibration transmitted along pipes or cables, from reaching the submarine's structure. Transmission is attenuated by the addition of flexible sections within pipes and isolation of pipe and cable clips. Even the mechanism that flushes the toilet is designed to ensure that it cannot be detected outside the boat.

Sometimes it is necessary for the submarine to adopt the ultra-quiet silent routine. To ensure that the off-duty personnel make as little detectable noise as possible, for instance by dropping something, they are encouraged to lie in their bunks and are forbidden to run water. All non-essential machinery is stopped.

While the acoustic tiles and other measures reduce the acoustic signature emanating from within the submarine, there are other sources – such as the flow noise over the hull and that emanating from the propulsor. Both of these sources have been addressed in the design

of the *Astute* class; the smooth tiles and the carefully shaped outer hull-form help reduce flow noise resulting from turbulence and eddies and the innovative composite propulsor duct also reduces the emission of acoustic energy.

Overall the *Astute* class is extraordinarily difficult to detect using sonar. Despite operating a nuclear reactor and four turbines capable of generating tens of megawatts, less than 1W of power is radiated into the sea.

Magnetic and other signatures

Although it is challenging to detect a submarine using sonar, it is still the most effective method of location. However, there are other types of signature that can betray a vessel's presence, particularly its magnetic signature. The process of manufacturing the boat causes its steel hull to act as a large magnet – its permanent magnetic signature. The term 'permanent' is, in a way, misleading as it can be reduced by the process of deperming in a magnetic silencing facility such as that used by HMS *Astute* in Kings Bay during trials. This imposes a magnetic field that is equal and opposite to the boat's permanent field, thereby cancelling it out. The effect does not last, however, and the magnetic signature reasserts itself as the boat's structure flexes during successive dives and even on surface passage (particularly in rough weather). Consequently, the deperming process has to be regularly repeated.

There is a second component to the magnetic signature – its induced signature. Whenever a conducting material, such as a submarine's steel hull, moves in the earth's magnetic field, currents are induced in the metal that generate a magnetic field. This is dependent on the strength of the earth's field and it varies across the globe in both magnitude and direction. To counter the resultant induced field, submarines are fitted with three sets of degaussing coils arranged orthogonally.

BELOW Artist's impression of a typical shock and vibration 'X-mount'. *(Stop-Choc)*

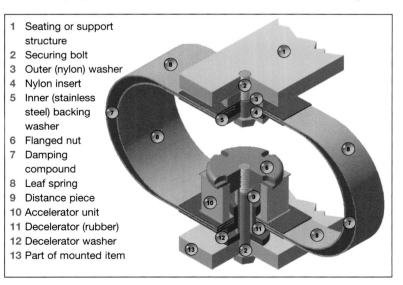

1 Seating or support structure
2 Securing bolt
3 Outer (nylon) washer
4 Nylon insert
5 Inner (stainless steel) backing washer
6 Flanged nut
7 Damping compound
8 Leaf spring
9 Distance piece
10 Accelerator unit
11 Decelerator (rubber)
12 Decelerator washer
13 Part of mounted item

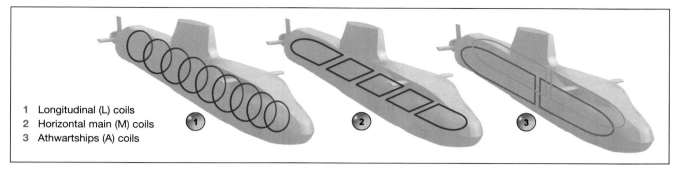

1 Longitudinal (L) coils
2 Horizontal main (M) coils
3 Athwartships (A) coils

The overall induced magnetic field may be represented by three orthogonal components that are (relative to the submarine) vertical, horizontal and athwartships. Passing a measured current through the degaussing coils produces an equal and opposite magnetic field to that of the hull, thereby cancelling out the induced field. Horizontal main (M) coils counter the vertical fields, pairs of athwartship (A) coils counter the athwartship field and longitudinal (L) coils counter the longitudinal field.

The original method of determining the value of the currents necessary to counter induced magnetism was to depend on approximate values of the earth's field for different areas of the world. Modern systems can not only set values that are much more accurate, but the latest closed-loop degaussing system is very effective at reducing a submarine's magnetic signature because it, in effect, measures the actual resultant magnetic field of the boat and adjusts the degaussing compensation accordingly. As a consequence it can counter not only the induced magnetism but also some of the degradation in the permanent magnetism.

Magnetic signatures have been important for many years because of their potential to trigger sea mines that are fitted with magnetic detectors. More recently aircraft have searched for submarines using magnetic anomaly

JACKSPEAK

Reduction of the magnetic field produced by a submarine is called degaussing after the German scientist Carl Gauss, who also gave his name to a unit of magnetic flux density. The prefix 'de' indicates removal and, contrary to some sources, the process is not named after a mythical Frenchman 'de Gauss'!

detectors that are sensitive to the disturbance of the earth's magnetic field by a submarine. A degaussing system, by cancelling the magnetic signature, makes such detection extremely difficult. Nevertheless, close to the vessel the magnetic field is irregular and difficult to cancel exactly, resulting in a small residual magnetic disturbance. This means that magnetic anomaly detectors can locate submarines at very short ranges (about 1km).

In addition to magnetic signatures, electromagnetic signatures play an important role in the detection of submarines and in the fuzing of sophisticated mines. The underwater electrical potential is the electric field associated with the corrosion of the submarine's metallic structure. It is caused by the galvanic potential differences between metals of different types (for instance paint-damaged steel and phosphor-bronze hull fittings) in contact with the seawater. This action causes corrosion of the metal least able to resist corrosion, usually the steel hull. In addition, there is a corrosion-related magnetic field caused by the corrosion-related electric currents flowing in the seawater. These signatures can be reduced by systems intended to lessen corrosion and so maintain a corrosion-free hull, although their use does make signature prediction more complex. These systems are:

■ **Sacrificial anode cathodic protection**, a passive system where blocks of metal (sacrificial anodes) are connected to areas of the hull vulnerable to corrosion. It is the anodes, rather than the hull itself, that are corroded, so the anodes require periodic replacement.

■ **Impressed current cathodic protection**, a custom-built high-technology anti-corrosion system of active anodes and

ABOVE Typical degaussing coil arrangement in a submarine. *(Author)*

reference electrodes made of platinised titanium and silver/silver-chloride respectively. The anodes emit a current into the seawater enabling electrical currents to dissipate over the hull, preventing corrosion and thereby countering the galvanic current. The anodes' current is produced by on-board power supplies and managed by a controller using feedback from the reference electrodes strategically placed around the hull.

Another non-acoustic detection technique with some potential is wake detection. As a submarine advances it pushes seawater aside and this generates a conical wave pattern that spreads out from the bow of the submarine. Where this cone breaks the surface of the sea it manifests itself as a triangular set of low surface waves that can persist for up to 12 hours. In calm water, aircraft use them to detect a submarine's recent track. However, to extract this wake pattern from the complex wave patterns of, say, the northern Atlantic Ocean, requires a great deal of signal processing and is a substantial computational task. Like all signatures, there are difficulties because of interference, not just the complexity of surface waves but also interference of similar signals including those produced by surface ships, whales and shoals of fish. Hydrodynamically efficient hull forms, such as that of HMS *Astute*, reduce the wake signature.

ABOVE Row of active anodes of the impressed current cathodic protection system located on the lower part of the sonar flank array. *(BAE Systems)*

BELOW Diagram of heading, roll, pitch and yaw. *(Author)*

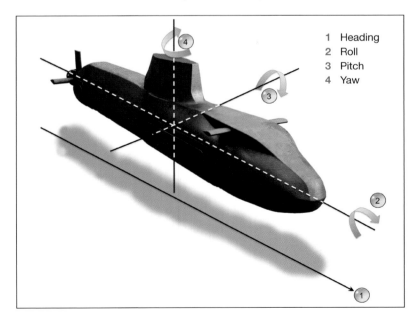

1 Heading
2 Roll
3 Pitch
4 Yaw

Inertial navigation system (INS)

Beneath the sea's surface a submarine has no external navigational aids (such as GPS) to determine her position. Submarines use motion sensors of their duplicated INS to generate positional information: heading (direction of travel) and the attitude (roll, pitch and yaw). These data are used by the helmsman, the IPMS and combat system.

The INS determines the position by measuring the accelerations (and decelerations) from a known position, typically that from which it dives and which will be accurately known from GPS. By measuring the changes in acceleration

Comparison of gyrocompasses		
	Ring-laser Mk 39	**Fibre-optic MARINS 37**
Dimensions (L × W × H)	492 × 465 × 622mm	433 × 324 × 329mm
Weight	–	42kg
Velocity root mean sq	1.1km/h (0.6kts)	1.1km/h (0.6kts)
Positional variation	1nm (1.85km) per 8hrs	1nm (1.85km) per 24hrs

in three orthogonal directions, the position of the boat underwater can be determined. The first three boats of the class were fitted with Mk 39 attitude and heading reference systems, that includes three orthogonal ring-laser gyro compasses (RLG).

Earlier boats may be fitted with MARINS, although a more accurate version is now available. In the fibre-optic gyrocompass (FOG) an external laser produces a beam that, passing through a opto-electronic component, is split into two identical beams that are injected into the ends of a fibre-optic coil. The counter-rotating beams emerging from the coil are then recombined by the same optical component and shone on to a detector that interprets any phase shift between the beams as changes in direction of the boat along the axis of the coil. Again, there are three orthogonal FOG units in the INS. There are no moving parts, which increases the unit's life, makes it perfectly silent and reduces maintenance. The accuracy of the INS is enhanced by the input of data from the boat's log that measures velocity through the

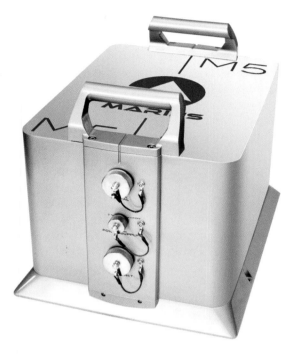

LEFT **MARINS fibre-optic gyrocompass.** *(iXBlue)*

water and the depth information. The position indicated by the INS will deviate slowly over time until it can be corrected by GPS when the boat comes to periscope depth or surfaces.

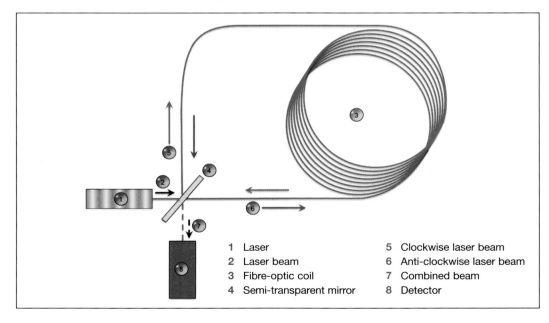

1 Laser	5 Clockwise laser beam
2 Laser beam	6 Anti-clockwise laser beam
3 Fibre-optic coil	7 Combined beam
4 Semi-transparent mirror	8 Detector

LEFT **Diagram of an accelerometer of a fibre-optic gyrocompass.** *(Author, from Vali and Shorthill, Applied Optics, vol. 15 (1976))*

Breathing air and air purification system

A submarine is a sealed environment in which the boat's complement may work and live continuously for periods of up to 90 days. In order to sustain life, the submarine must supply clean, breathable air. Failure to do so can have effects on personnel that are immediate and require more rapid rectification compared to the two other essentials for life – drinking water and food.

Atmospheric air comprises nitrogen, oxygen, trace quantities of other gases and negligible quantities of carbon dioxide. Oxygen, making up 21% of the atmosphere, is needed for humans to survive. Although low oxygen levels of 16% will extinguish a flame, significant physiological responses in healthy individuals are not triggered until 14% is reached. At that point impaired judgement is seen, while at 10% a person would rapidly lapse into unconsciousness and death would occur quickly. Conversely, 50% oxygen levels are tolerated by healthy people indefinitely and 100% oxygen tolerated for at least 12 hours.

Oxygen is consumed at different rates depending on activity, but each person on board requires, on average, about $0.028m^3/h$ of oxygen. At rest a normal adult would consume two-thirds of this but more than eight times if working aerobically (which can only be sustained for short periods). Respiration of oxygen results in the exhalation of carbon dioxide and a build-up of this gas in the boat's confined space is particularly dangerous. Each person will produce approximately $0.025m^3/h$ of carbon dioxide. Concentrations of 10% carbon dioxide is toxic after a few minutes' exposure but even a few hours of breathing only 0.1% concentration affects cognitive abilities.

When the submarine dives its atmosphere is similar to ambient air. Without an attempt to control the atmosphere, the air would rapidly become degraded by respiration and other activities such as operating machinery, cooking and released volatile compounds. As the boat may be submerged for 90 days or more, its atmosphere needs to be carefully managed to limit exposure of the crew to potentially harmful substances and to ensure the atmosphere is capable of supporting life.

Activities that alter the submarine's atmosphere	
Activity	**Products**
Respiration	Oxygen (O_2) reduction and carbon dioxide (CO_2) production
Smoking	Carbon monoxide (CO) and aerosol production
Charging batteries	Hydrogen (H_2) production
Cooking	Production of water vapour (H_2O), carbon monoxide and fumes
Cooling systems	Leakage of refrigerants and volatile organic compounds

To actively manage the on-board atmosphere, air is continuously passed through the air purification system to maintain a breathable, uncontaminated atmosphere by reducing major contaminants and replenishing the oxygen. The dedicated plant comprises:

■ **The local air monitoring system** that uses a number of local sensor modules located around the boat to provide data to the main control panel that displays the submarine-wide situation. Because potentially dangerous chemicals may build up in the continually recycled air, the boat is equipped with a system that continuously monitors the atmosphere for about 40 gases. Of particular interest are hydrogen sulphide, chlorine,

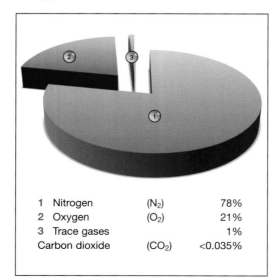

1	Nitrogen	(N_2)	78%
2	Oxygen	(O_2)	21%
3	Trace gases		1%
	Carbon dioxide	(CO_2)	<0.035%

RIGHT Composition of the earth's atmosphere at sea level. *(Author)*

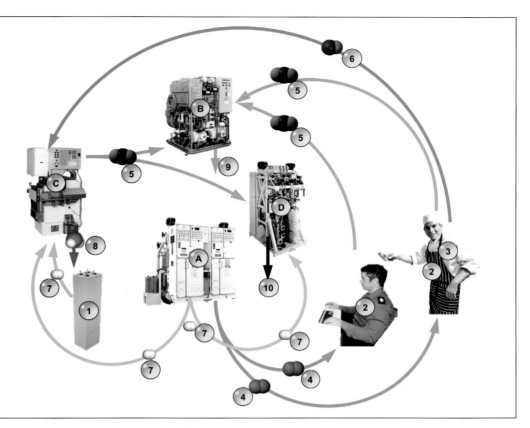

A Low-pressure electrolyser
B Carbon dioxide scrubber
C Carbon monoxide/ hydrogen eliminator
D Gas management plant

1 Battery charging
2 Respiration
3 Cooking
4 Oxygen (O_2)
5 Carbon dioxide (CO_2)
6 Carbon monoxide (CO)
7 Hydrogen (H_2)
8 Water (H_2O) discharge
9 Carbon dioxide discharge/storage
10 Aqueous solution discharge/storage

sulphur dioxide and methane. Each of these gases is examined against maximum permissible concentrations for exposure times of 90 days, 24 hours and 60 minutes.

■ The oxygen generation system

ensures that oxygen is maintained above 18% yet below 20% where there is an increased risk of on-board fire. High oxygen concentrations can accelerate reactions, so normally benign compounds (such as hydrocarbon-based oil) can spontaneously combust. Consequently, oxygen generators must be kept free from hydrocarbon contamination.

Low-pressure electrolysers produce oxygen at ambient pressure by passing an electrical current through demineralised water in a cell stack. The cell stack comprises a Nafion proton exchange membrane typically 305–430µm thick with an integrated electrode structure. Water is continuously supplied to the anode. Under the influence of the DC voltage applied to the cell, hydrogen ions from the water pass through the membrane and collect at the cathode where they form gaseous

hydrogen. At the anode oxygen ions combine to form gaseous oxygen that is swept out with the circulating water and collected for distribution to the ventilation system at 50kPa. The hydrogen, generated at 700kPa, is cooled from its discharge temperature of 55°C and compressed for discharge overboard or passed to the gas management system.

ABOVE Air purification cycle on board a submerged submarine. *(Author, equipment photos TPG Maritime)*

BELOW Schematic of an electrolyser cell. *(Author)*

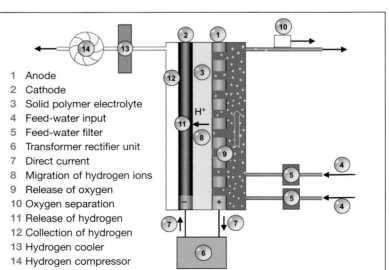

1 Anode
2 Cathode
3 Solid polymer electrolyte
4 Feed-water input
5 Feed-water filter
6 Transformer rectifier unit
7 Direct current
8 Migration of hydrogen ions
9 Release of oxygen
10 Oxygen separation
11 Release of hydrogen
12 Collection of hydrogen
13 Hydrogen cooler
14 Hydrogen compressor

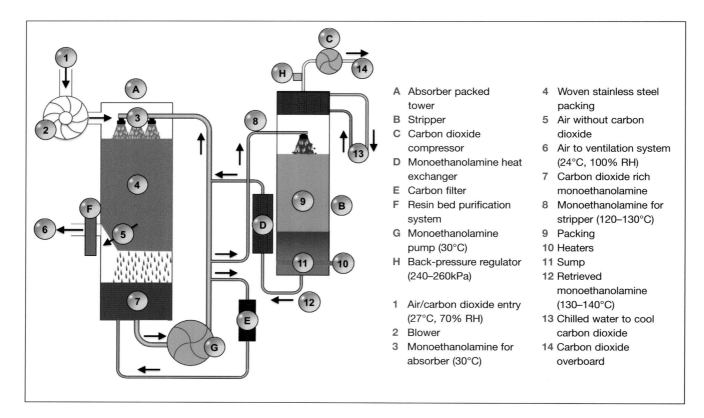

A Absorber packed tower
B Stripper
C Carbon dioxide compressor
D Monoethanolamine heat exchanger
E Carbon filter
F Resin bed purification system
G Monoethanolamine pump (30°C)
H Back-pressure regulator (240–260kPa)

1 Air/carbon dioxide entry (27°C, 70% RH)
2 Blower
3 Monoethanolamine for absorber (30°C)

4 Woven stainless steel packing
5 Air without carbon dioxide
6 Air to ventilation system (24°C, 100% RH)
7 Carbon dioxide rich monoethanolamine
8 Monoethanolamine for stripper (120–130°C)
9 Packing
10 Heaters
11 Sump
12 Retrieved monoethanolamine (130–140°C)
13 Chilled water to cool carbon dioxide
14 Carbon dioxide overboard

ABOVE Schematic of a typical monoethanolamine packed tower carbon dioxide scrubber.
(Author)

■ **Monoethanolamine packed tower carbon dioxide scrubber** uses an absorbent to remove carbon dioxide continuously from the submarine's atmosphere. Air is passed into a packed tower on top of which the absorbent, monoethanolamine (MEA), is sprayed. The absorbent becomes rich in carbon dioxide and air with minimal carbon dioxide is returned to the ventilation system through a resin bed to prevent contamination by the absorbent. The absorbent is then passed through a stripper where it is sprayed into the top of another packed column and allowed to fall to the sump. The sump is heated, boiling off the carbon dioxide and regenerating the MEA absorbent allowing it to be returned to the packed tower after it is cooled in a heat exchanger. A control system maintains the level in the sump by regulating the return of the lean absorbent. The carbon dioxide is compressed for discharge overboard.

■ **Carbon monoxide and hydrogen eliminator** removes carbon monoxide and hydrogen by oxidising them to carbon dioxide and water vapour respectively. Carbon monoxide is produced by incomplete combustion and, like carbon dioxide, is toxic. It can be fatal in doses of only 0.07% and, in the confined space of a submarine, is cumulative in its effects.

Oxidisation of the gases is achieved by heating them to 315°C and forcing them at 845m³/h across a specially formulated oxidising catalyst, Hopcalite®. As Hopcalite® is poisoned by moisture, its operating temperature must be held above 150°C to prevent water vapour, a result of the oxidation, condensing on the catalyst bed.

Refrigerants that have leaked from the cooling plant are treated at 150°C in the eliminator and produce carbon dioxide, hydrochloric acid and hydrogen fluoride. The Montreal Protocol bans refrigerants that deplete the ozone layer; their replacements, however, produce greater quantities of hydrogen fluoride, a very toxic and highly corrosive gas. The eliminator was modified to lower the operating temperature and a segregated bed added. The heated air leaving the catalyst in the segregated bed passes through an absorbent bed of calcium oxide and sodium hydroxide to remove any acid gas.

■ **The gas management plant** combines waste hydrogen from the low-pressure electrolyser with carbon dioxide from the packed tower scrubber to produce an aqueous solution that can be stored. Discharge overboard can thus be delayed to more convenient operational times.

■ **Carbon filters** remove hydrocarbon and organic material not oxidised in the high-temperature catalytic burners. About 90kg of activated carbon is held in units throughout the boat in main carbon beds, and at the ends of trunking where air is drawn through the filters by the fans of the main ventilation system. The inlet to each bed contains a mechanical filter to remove larger aerosol particles from the atmosphere and electrostatic precipitators to protect against finer particles. Precipitators also safeguard the galley filters.

■ **Electrostatic precipitators** remove particulates and aerosols by imparting a positive charge to the particles in an ioniser section. The charged particles migrate to earthed plates where they are collected and removed. The precipitators have mechanical filters on both their inlets and outlets.

Because the boat is a sealed environment and the air is constantly recycled, there are strict rules about the types of oils, soaps and other substances that are allowed and deodorants are banned.

Closely associated with the breathing air and air purification system is the heating, ventilation, air-conditioning and refrigeration systems. The ventilation system is used to circulate and distribute air throughout the submarine and to provide adequate ventilation of the battery space. When the submarine is on, or close to, the surface the snort mast induction system provides air for the on-board diesels. It also supplies a fan-induced fresh air to the ventilation system to replace stale air exhausted from the submarine through the exhaust mast used by the diesels. The LP air blower used to fill the buoyancy tanks as the submarine approaches the surface is also used to flush

1 Air circulation	7 Ventilation return	A Air-conditioning space	E Reactor compartment
2 Precipitation chamber	8 To ventilation exhaust mast	B Air purification space	F Diesel generator space
3 Cooler	9 Valve-controlled air flow	C Battery tank	G Engine room
4 Main circulating pumps	10 Flap valve	D Reactor service compartment	
5 Forward ventilation trunking	11 Filter		
6 Aft ventilation trunking	12 Battery clearance fan		
	13 Hydrogen to boat's air		

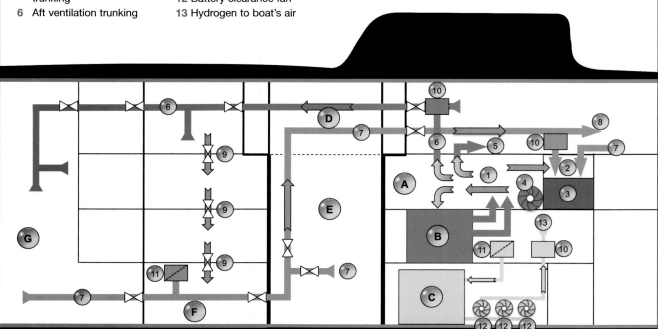

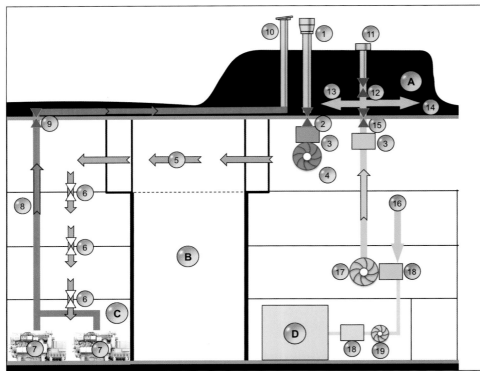

1	Snort induction mast
2	Induction hull valve
3	Emergency flap valve
4	Main supply fan
5	Air flow through submarine
6	Valve-controlled air flow
7	Diesel generator
8	Piped exhaust flow
9	Back-up hull valve
10	Diesel exhaust mast
11	Ventilation exhaust mast
12	Outboard hull valve
13	Low-pressure blow aft
14	Low-pressure blow forward
15	Inboard hull valve
16	Feed from ventilation return
17	Low-pressure blower
18	Flap valve
19	Battery clearance fan
A	Fin
B	Reactor compartment
C	Diesel generator space
D	Battery tank

ABOVE Schematic of the ventilation arrangements when the submarine is surfaced. *(Author)*

out the air supply on the surface in the case of fire. Air conditioning maintains compartment temperatures and humidity to ensure a habitable environment for personnel within the accommodation and control spaces.

Domestic fresh water system

Fresh water is produced by a technique called reverse osmosis whereby seawater is applied under pressure to a semi-permeable membrane; pure fresh water passes through the membrane leaving salt-enhanced seawater on the input side. Fresh water is required not only for domestic purposes but also to replenish the feed water for both the reactor and steam propulsion plants.

The domestic fresh-water system supplies hot and cold fresh water, principally for drinking, washing and other domestic purposes. In the submarine's austere regime each person aboard is allowed about 90 litres every day – an amount that is about half that considered appropriate for surface ships. The fresh water is transferred to two tanks from where it is distributed. The distribution system is pressurised at 200kPa by air from the auxiliary vent and blow system. A further

LEFT Submarine reverse osmosis water purification plant. *(Salt Separation Services Ltd)*

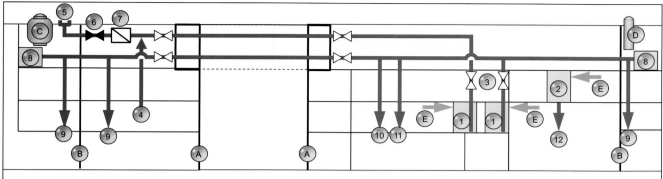

1	Forward fresh-water tank	7 Filter	A Containment bulkhead
2	Weapons spray water tank	8 Emergency storage tank	B Escape bulkhead
3	(Cross-connection omitted)	9 Users	C Logistic escape trunk
4	Fresh-water plant supply	10 Galley and messes	D Forward escape trunk
5	Shore connection	11 Heads and bathrooms	E Auxiliary vent and blow system
6	Locked-shut valve	12 Weapons stowage spray	(pressurisation)

pressurised tank of fresh water is located close to the weapons handling and launch system, where it can supply a spray system in case of fire in the weapons compartment. A shore supply connection can be used to top up the fresh-water tanks when in harbour. The tanks are protected from contamination by a shore supply filter and from pressure-damage by a relief valve set at 250kPa.

Cold fresh water is supplied to the galley, laundry and the sanitary spaces, feeding the hot fresh-water system and drinking water dispensers. Hot drinks are always available in messes from boiling water dispensers. A drinking water dispenser, cooled by the chilled water system is provided in the main machinery space, one of the hottest compartments on board, in order that those using the space do not become dehydrated. Similar dispensers are located in the accommodation spaces to dispense both soft drinks and cooled water. Fresh water is also used to flush the shaft seal and supply the demineralisers (demineralised water is required for special purposes such as battery top-up).

The fresh-water system supplies emergency drinking water storage tanks in both forward and aft escape compartments. Each holds over 4,000 litres of fresh water – sufficient for the entire crew for seven days.

Water from the cold water system pressurises the single hot water system that supplies hot water to the forward part of the boat. The cold water is heated in a calorifier to about 70°C and distributed by a ring main and can supply up to 450 litres per hour. Hot water is not pumped around the ring main but

ABOVE Schematic of typical cold fresh-water system. (Author, from information in Defence Standard)

JACKSPEAK

Dispensers of boiling water located in mess spaces provide instant hot water for drinks. These are technically called Jackson Boilers but, more colloquially, as 'fog lockers'.

LEFT The laundry, featuring a raft-mounted washing machine to reduce the transmission of its acoustic emissions. (BAE Systems)

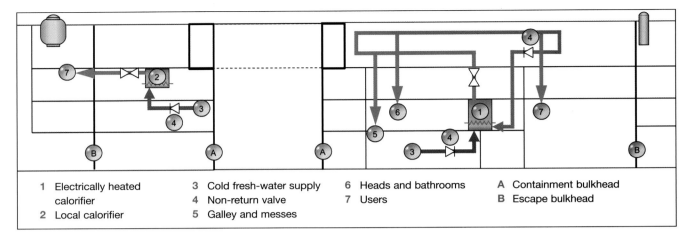

1	Electrically heated calorifier	3	Cold fresh-water supply	6	Heads and bathrooms	A	Containment bulkhead
2	Local calorifier	4	Non-return valve	7	Users	B	Escape bulkhead
		5	Galley and messes				

ABOVE Schematic of typical hot fresh-water system. *(Author)*

BELOW Pressure hull forward of the reactor that contains the control centre (upper deck) and accommodation. *(BAE Systems)*

relies on convection (natural thermosyphon circulation) with hot water flowing from the calorifier and unused cooler water returning to the calorifier through a non-return valve. While hot water is supplied principally to sinks, wash-basins, showers and the galley, it also supplies various bib cocks and is used to wash the electrostatic precipitators. The hot water supply does not penetrate the containment and escape bulkheads so where hot water is required outside the control and accommodation area it is generated by local electric water heaters fed from the cold fresh-water system.

Accommodation

HMS *Astute* has accommodation for her complement of 12 officers and 86 ratings but can accommodate 110 because there is space for a further 12 'riders' that is used at various times by trials staff, trainees and embarked forces.

The conditions on board are austere as space is at a premium. Submarines are, first and foremost, a military asset where comfort is a secondary consideration. The living quarters are tiny with cramped passageways and little headroom. Submariners operate in two

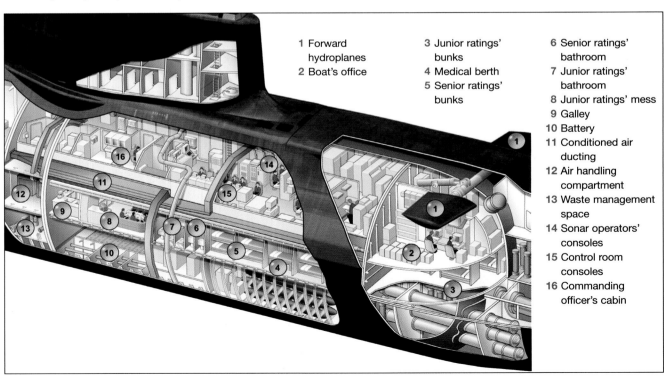

1	Forward hydroplanes	3	Junior ratings' bunks	6	Senior ratings' bathroom
2	Boat's office	4	Medical berth	7	Junior ratings' bathroom
		5	Senior ratings' bunks	8	Junior ratings' mess
				9	Galley
				10	Battery
				11	Conditioned air ducting
				12	Air handling compartment
				13	Waste management space
				14	Sonar operators' consoles
				15	Control room consoles
				16	Commanding officer's cabin

Those on duty aboard a submarine are known as being 'on watch'. Under normal conditions, only part of the complement is on watch at one time, with watches divided into three rotating shifts, each lasting six hours. Each crewmember on watch is assigned specific duties. Under certain conditions (when leaving and entering port, or when the crew is ordered to action stations) everyone on board the submarine will have a watch station, regardless of his position within the three-shift rotation.

or three shifts of six hours. In the past, two submariners on different shifts often had to share the same bunk – a practice known as 'hot bunking'. The *Astute* class will be the first RN submarines in which each member of the crew has their own bunk.

Ratings' berths are in six-person bunk spaces with three bunks stacked either side of a passageway that is barely big enough for two people to pass. The bunks are 1m wide and 2m long – a slight increase on previous standards to allow for the fact that the population is becoming taller. The headroom in the bunk is approximately 800mm and each bunk has

a reading light, air vent and power socket for personal electronic devices. The bunk has a curtain that affords the only privacy available to the rating. Retaining straps and removal side-bars are provided to avoid injuries during violent manoeuvres. Each bunk is allocated a small locker, hanging space for a few items and one of the three drawers situated beneath the bunk; all the ratings' personal and uniform items have to be stowed in these three spaces.

All accommodation (except the CO's) is on 2-deck. The junior ratings' berths are forward and the senior ratings' berths are amidships, arranged in groups of four six-person spaces

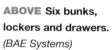
ABOVE Six bunks, lockers and drawers. *(BAE Systems)*

FAR LEFT
Passageway showing limited space and headroom.
(Florida Today/Malcolm 'Denny' Denemark)

LEFT Ratings' six-person bunk space.
(Crown Copyright/ LA(Phot) Jonathan 'JJ' Massey)

ABOVE LEFT Cdr Neil Botting, RN, CO HMS *Astute*, in his cabin. *(Crown Copyright/L(Phot) Stephen 'Stevie' Burke)*

ABOVE Commanding officer's cabin. *(BAE Systems)*

LEFT Officers in the wardroom. *(Crown Copyright/L(Phot) Stephen 'Stevie' Burke)*

BELOW The wardroom. *(BAE Systems)*

end-to-end. While this would normally provide 24 bunks, two of the top bunks are not fitted so that the middle bunk can be used as a medical berth. The additional headroom given by removing the top bunk makes it easier to examine a patient lying on the middle bunk.

Officers' berths are in four- and two-person cabins and there is a nine-person cabin for riders. For easy access to the operations space, the CO's cabin is on 1-deck, just aft of the command space. The CO's cabin is the only private space on board. It contains a wash-basin and a sofa that converts to a bed.

Aft of the berths on 2-deck are three messes where different ranks eat and relax: the wardroom for officers, and messes for both junior and senior ratings. The messes each have a large-screen TV, a PlayStation, an Xbox and a media centre for the entertainment of off-watch personnel.

The messes act as dining halls as well as recreational spaces. Food is served to the ratings from serveries that connect to the galley. Food for the wardroom is prepared and served from the adjacent wardroom pantry.

The submarine's complement is fed by a team of five chefs (one petty officer caterer, one leading chef and three chefs) who

provide a 24-hour service preparing four meals a day including one served at midnight for the night shift. On an average patrol over 30,000 meals will be served – for breakfast alone this will comprise about 18,000 sausages and 4,200 Weetabix.

All the food is prepared in a galley that is just as economical with space as the rest of the boat. Food is very important for morale on board especially as, without external indications of the passage of time, breakfast can be used to indicate the beginning of a new day and the traditional Sunday roast signals a new week. However, it is important to vary the menu so

ABOVE Junior ratings relaxing in their mess. *(Crown Copyright/ L(Phot) Stephen 'Stevie' Burke)*

BELOW Junior ratings' mess. *(BAE Systems)*

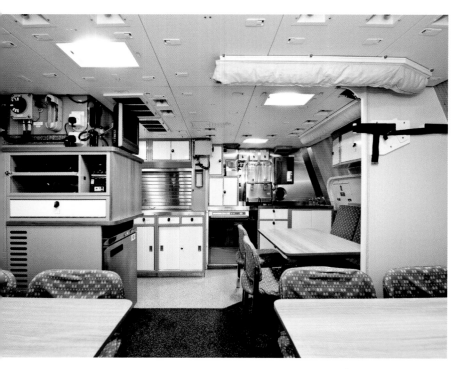

theme nights, such as Mexican nights, are a regular feature.

All food has to be loaded at the beginning of the patrol and brought on board manually. Storing is time-consuming and requires careful planning as the food stowed in tight spaces has to be loaded so that last in is used first. As the boat can make fresh water, dried stores can be loaded to save space. It is a challenge for the chefs to provide appetising meals from the constituents available to them. Perishable goods and frozen food are accommodated on 3-deck in the cold room and the chill room, respectively. Both are cooled by the boat's chilled water system.

For patrols that are anticipated to be longer than usual then more stowage is gained by loading the passageway decks with 200mm high tins of food covered with wooden walkways. This, of course, further reduces the already restricted headroom in the passageway until all the tins are used.

During a patrol, there is an accumulation of food waste and other rubbish. In the past this was compacted and ejected but the *Astute* class boats are the first RN submarines to meet International Convention for the Prevention of Pollution from Ships (MARPOL) regulations.

JACKSPEAK

Rubbish, or items of no value, are referred to as 'gash'.

ABOVE Junior ratings' mess showing part of the serving hatch and the drink-dispensing area. *(BAE Systems)*

RIGHT Petty officer chef admires one of the chefs' handiwork. *(BAE Systems)*

BELOW Chef preparing food in the galley. *(Crown Copyright)*

BELOW Chef arranging food at the servery.
(Crown Copyright/PO(Phot) Owen Cooban)

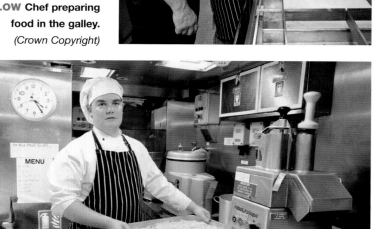

FAR LEFT Cold room for food storage. *(BAE Systems)*

LEFT Senior ratings' wash space. *(BAE Systems)*

Consequently, garbage for the entire patrol has to be stored on board for eventual disposal when in harbour. All empty cans, plastic, cardboard and wrappings are compacted and then placed in special bags in the dry-store stowages as food is consumed. Food waste, once put through a macerator, is sent to its own storage tank.

The whole complement has access to sanitary spaces on board comprising only five showers, five toilets, two urinals and eight wash-basins (the CO has his own wash-basin). Seawater is used to flush toilets and urinals; the resulting 'black water' is stored in an effluent storage tank. Water from the galley, showers and wash-basins, termed 'grey water', can be treated on board before subsequent discharge overboard.

FAR LEFT Junior ratings' wash space showing the shower cubicle. *(BAE Systems)*

BELOW Toilet cubicles ('heads'). *(BAE Systems)*

> **JACKSPEAK**
>
> To use the urinal is referred to as 'draining down the snort mast'.

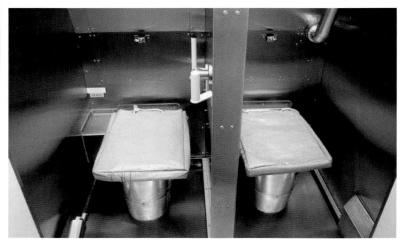

Chapter Four

Anatomy of the nuclear propulsion system

The main power source on the *Astute* class, the nuclear reactor, can create enough energy to power a small city. While submarines in general pose several major engineering challenges, this is doubly so for nuclear-powered ones. The reactor is both more complex and has more regulatory restrictions than a civil nuclear plant. However, it can generate air and water allowing the boat to remain submerged for many weeks and to travel at high speed, so enabling her to access all the world's oceans.

OPPOSITE HMS *Astute* **sails up the Clyde estuary into her home port of Faslane for the first time following the journey from Barrow-in-Furness shipyard.** *(MOD Open Government License)*

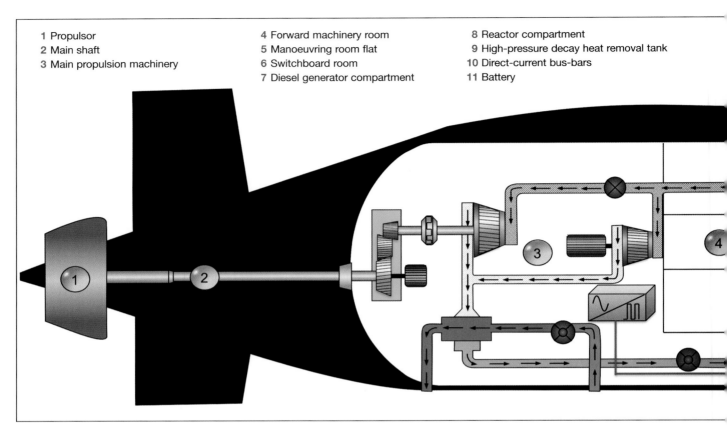

1 Propulsor
2 Main shaft
3 Main propulsion machinery
4 Forward machinery room
5 Manoeuvring room flat
6 Switchboard room
7 Diesel generator compartment
8 Reactor compartment
9 High-pressure decay heat removal tank
10 Direct-current bus-bars
11 Battery

ABOVE Schematic of nuclear submarine pressurised water reactor and propulsion plant. *(Author)*

The submarine's reactor must be operated in the knowledge that about 100 people live and work in close proximity, it is in a vessel that submerges hundreds of metres and that the submarine is specifically designed to sail into harm's way. Ensuring the safe operation of the nuclear plant requires great attention to detail and rigorous testing, both of which impose time and cost overheads throughout the life of the propulsion system.

The function of the propulsion system is to provide a method of propelling the submarine through the water, surfaced or dived, while retaining the ability to remain undetected. Modern submarines do not use propellers to drive them through the water – instead they employ pump-jet propulsors. Like all RN nuclear submarines. The *Astute* class is powered by a PWR. Within the core of the reactor, radioactive material ('the fuel') undergoes nuclear fission that produces a great deal of heat. This heat is transferred to water that is passed through the core. In order to prevent the water from boiling, it is maintained at a high pressure. As it is at a temperature higher than the atmospheric boiling point of water, it is referred to as 'super-heated' water.

The system generating the super-heated steam is referred to as the nuclear steam-raising plant (NSRP). Main turbines driven by the steam rotate the boat's shaft. As the speed of rotation of the main turbines is too great to directly drive the propulsor, a main gearbox reduces the rotational speed by a fixed reduction ratio. This results in an output rotational speed that is within the range appropriate for the propulsor.

Steam from the NSRP is also used to power turbo-generators – the primary source of electrical power for the boat. Through the electrical system the reactor is used to power the boat's equipment, including the vital services that generate a breathable atmosphere and fresh water to sustain life aboard. This means that nuclear submarines are true submarines as they have the ability to submerge for long periods of time.

As mentioned in the first chapter, the RN's first nuclear submarine, HMS *Dreadnought*, was a British submarine design but powered by the latest USN reactor and propulsion plant. She was commissioned in 1963 and was followed three years later by HMS *Valiant* with a nuclear propulsion plant designed in the UK.

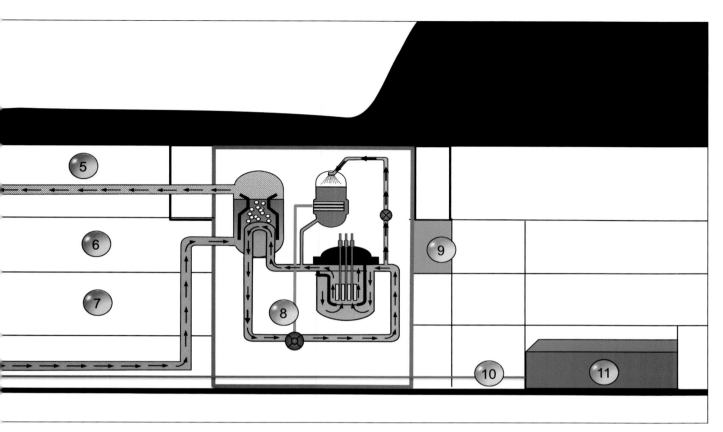

Nuclear fission

In order to explain the nature of the nuclear fission reaction, it is necessary to describe the nuclear structure of elements. There are 98 naturally occurring elements that combine to form all the substances with which we are familiar. A few elements, especially metals, can exist in their pure, or elemental form, but most are predisposed to combine with other elements. Hence iron can exist in a pure form but tends to combine with oxygen from the air to form rust.

An atom is the smallest size particle that still retains the chemical properties of an element. Atoms comprise a central nucleus of positively charged protons and uncharged neutrons surrounded by a cloud of very much smaller negatively charged electrons. It is the number of protons that define an element's chemical properties and when the atom is not electrically charged, the number of electrons equal the number of protons. The naturally occurring elements can be ordered by the number of protons from hydrogen (one proton) to californium

(98 protons). Atoms of the same element but with different numbers of neutrons are termed isotopes of that element. The number of neutrons does not affect the chemical properties of an element but does affect its physical properties, such as the weight of the atom (broadly the sum of the number of protons and neutrons). It will also determine whether or not it is radioactive.

BELOW Diagrammatic representation of the atomic structure of helium. *(Author)*

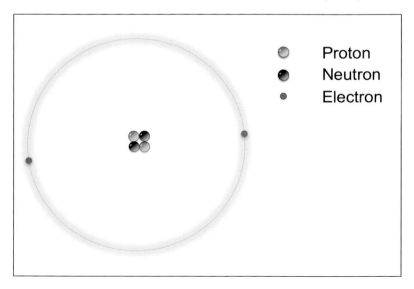

○ Proton
◑ Neutron
• Electron

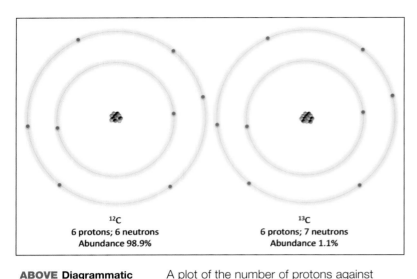

¹²C	¹³C
6 protons; 6 neutrons	6 protons; 7 neutrons
Abundance 98.9%	Abundance 1.1%

ABOVE Diagrammatic representation of two isotopes of carbon. *(Author)*

BELOW Plot of protons against neutrons for naturally occurring elements showing the decay mode of each isotope. *(Brookhaven National Laboratories)*

A plot of the number of protons against neutrons shows the extent of isotopes for each element although some of the isotopes may be very rare. Running approximately diagonally on the graph are the stable isotopes of each element (shown in black). All isotopes on the same horizontal line are of the same element (the same number of protons). Elements above bismuth (83 protons) have no stable isotopes. All but the stable forms of the elements will spontaneously undergo radioactive decay over time, although the rate of decay varies considerably from isotope to isotope. The form of decay also varies; it may involve the ejection of a radioactive particle from the nucleus or a nuclear fission reaction that results in the atom splitting into two smaller elements. All these decay modes involve the transmutation into a different element or elements. A few radioactive isotopes eject a neutron producing a new isotope of the same element. The common feature of all of these decay mechanisms is that there is a small loss of nuclear mass associated with the nuclear reaction. According to Einstein's equation, $E=mc^2$, energy (in the form of heat) is released. Nuclear reactions differ from chemical reactions, such as the burning of coal, where the elements are unchanged and the energy is derived from changes in the molecular bonds between the atoms. Nuclear reactions are far more potent than chemical reactions; for instance a gram of fissionable nuclear material releases the energy equivalent of 2.5T of coal.

The nuclear fuel used in HMS *Astute's* reactor is uranium. Uranium has 92 protons and three naturally occurring isotopes with 142, 143 and 146 neutrons. By convention isotopes are distinguished by the total number of protons and neutrons in the nucleus so these isotopes are given the notation ^{234}U, ^{235}U and ^{238}U respectively. Other isotopes of uranium decay rapidly and only occur fleetingly and ^{234}U occurs in negligible quantities. The most common of uranium's naturally occurring isotopes is ^{238}U that makes up 99.27% of mined uranium ore. Unfortunately the isotope that is most valuable as a nuclear fuel is ^{235}U. As this is only 0.72% of ore, the proportion of this isotope must be increased to produce a viable nuclear fuel.

All uranium isotopes are radioactive and, if left to their own devices, decay slowly by emitting an alpha particle from their nucleus. An alpha particle comprises two protons and two neutrons so, in ejecting this particle, all transmute into isotopes of thorium (90 protons).

In a nuclear reactor the concentrated ^{235}U fuel is bombarded with neutrons to engender a nuclear reaction. If a neutron hits a nucleus of ^{235}U then it is momentarily absorbed to form a highly unstable isotope ^{236}U. This isotope immediately undergoes fission and splits apart to form two different elements, ejecting subatomic particles as it does so. There is a range of nuclear reactions that can occur when ^{236}U splits, so the reaction following neutron absorption by ^{235}U produces a distribution of fission products. A typical fission produces ^{140}xenon (54 protons), ^{94}strontium (38 protons), two neutrons and electromagnetic waves called gamma-rays. The fission products ^{140}Xe are ^{94}Sr are both highly unstable and

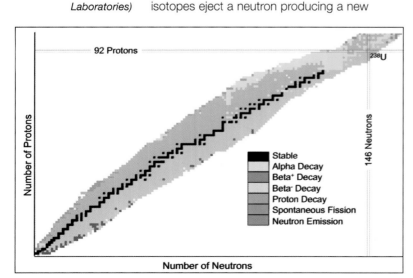

JACKSPEAK

The resulting products of nuclear fission are often referred to as 'fission chips'.

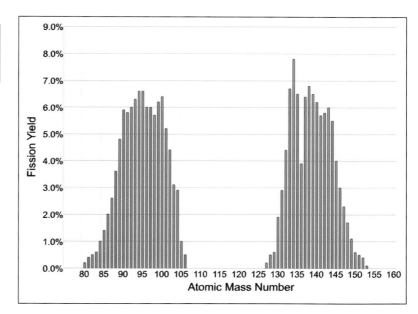

ABOVE The range of fission products from the decay of ^{235}uranium. *(Author)*

undergo further decay until stable elements are produced (in this case caesium and zirconium respectively). Some reactions release two neutrons and some three neutrons but, on average about 2.5 neutrons are produced by the reaction of ^{235}U.

The neutrons released immediately as a result of the nuclear fission (called prompt neutrons) can go on to strike the nucleus of another atom of ^{235}U, thus causing a further fission reaction. However, the probability of striking the nucleus of an atom is very small because most of an atom is empty space – the nucleus of the ^{235}U atom is about 10,000 times smaller than its atom. If this atom were the size of the London Eye then, on the same scale, the nucleus would be half the diameter of a golf ball. The probability of another fission occurring is greater if there is a larger proportion of ^{235}U atoms, hence the need for nuclear fuel to be enriched (by increasing the proportion of ^{235}U). It is also easier for neutrons to impact a nucleus if they are travelling slowly. Prompt neutrons emitted from a fission reaction are high-energy and fast-moving. Nuclear reactors intersperse their uranium fuel with a neutron moderator that slows down the neutrons, allowing them to more easily impact a nucleus and produce another fission reaction.

If, on average, fewer than one ^{235}U fission results in the emission of a neutron then the ^{235}U will remain a piece of radioactive material that is mildly warm. If, however, more than one neutron from the ^{235}U fission strikes another ^{235}U nucleus and causes it to fission, then the reaction will quickly escalate in a chain reaction – with the rapid release of energy leading to an explosion. This type of fission reaction occurs in the atomic bombs invented towards the end of the Second World War.

In a PWR not every neutron emitted during a fission reaction will lead to a further fission because the moderator will absorb some neutrons. To usefully generate energy, nuclear reactors have to maintain the rate of fission at a critical level where the reactions are just self-sustaining, because each fission reaction results

BELOW Schematic of the fission of ^{235}uranium. *(Author)*

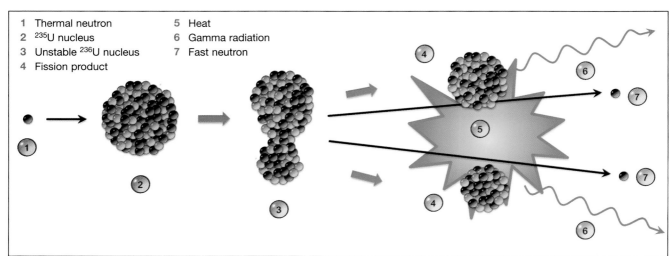

1 Thermal neutron
2 ^{235}U nucleus
3 Unstable ^{236}U nucleus
4 Fission product
5 Heat
6 Gamma radiation
7 Fast neutron

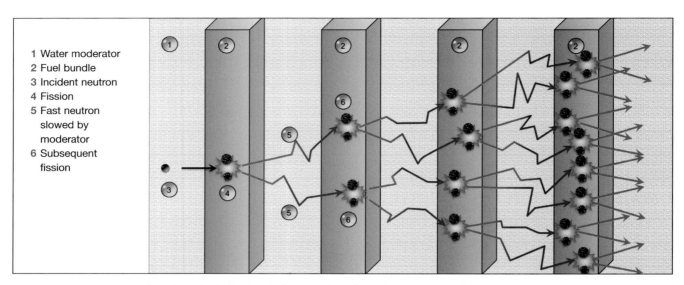

1 Water moderator
2 Fuel bundle
3 Incident neutron
4 Fission
5 Fast neutron slowed by moderator
6 Subsequent fission

ABOVE **A conceptual uncontrolled nuclear chain reaction.** (Author)

in only a single further fission reaction. A nuclear reactor is designed to ensure that this self-sustaining nuclear fission process occurs under controlled conditions and that the resulting energy of the reaction can be harnessed. Control is exercised by means of control rods of neutron-absorbent material that can be lowered into the reactor to quench the reaction or, conversely, raised out of the reactor to increase the reactivity and the energy released.

Pressurised water reactor (PWR)

BELOW **A conceptual controlled nuclear chain reaction.** (Author)

The pressure vessel of a typical PWR is cylindrical with a hemispherical bottom and a hemispherical head at the top. The head is removable to allow for fuel to be placed into the reactor. The coolant passed through the reactor enters and exits through pipes towards the top. The reactor vessel is constructed of manganese molybdenum steel that is thick enough to contain the HP water coolant.

The core barrel is fitted inside the reactor pressure vessel. It creates an annular channel for the incoming coolant and provides radiation attenuation that gives some protection to the reactor vessel. Within the core barrel is the core containing the fuel and control rods. The fuel assemblies rest on a lower core plate at the bottom of the core barrel.

The fuel is enriched uranium dioxide. Enrichment is the physical process that increases the proportion of ^{235}U isotope. The highly enriched fuel is turned into uranium dioxide powder that is then fired in a high-temperature sintering furnace to create hard,

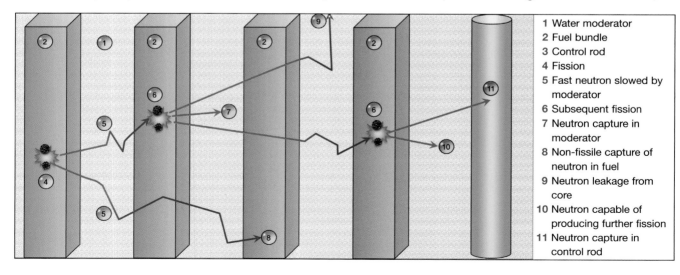

1 Water moderator
2 Fuel bundle
3 Control rod
4 Fission
5 Fast neutron slowed by moderator
6 Subsequent fission
7 Neutron capture in moderator
8 Non-fissile capture of neutron in fuel
9 Neutron leakage from core
10 Neutron capable of producing further fission
11 Neutron capture in control rod

ceramic pellets that are then clad in an alloy. Typically the pellets are filled with helium to aid heat conduction and detect leakages. The alloy is not only corrosion resistant, but has a low absorption cross section for neutrons that does not impede the nuclear reaction. The fuel rods are normally grouped together in bundles and, when loaded into the core, arranged with cruciform gaps between the bundles that provide access for the control rods.

Water at high pressure is used as the primary coolant in a PWR. Water entering the PWR is forced to flow downward in the annulus between the reactor vessel and the core barrel. On reaching the bottom of the vessel, the flow is turned upward through the fuel assemblies. Heat produced by the fission process is passed by thermal conduction through the fuel cladding, producing an elevated water temperature. Despite its high temperature the water remains liquid due to the high pressure at which it is maintained in the PWR. The heated water leaves the PWR through an outlet opposite the inlet and is used to produce the steam to power the submarine.

The coolant water in the PWR performs a second, and vital, role – that of a neutron moderator. A moderator increases the probability of a neutron produced by fission will undergo an interaction with the nuclear fuel and generate a further fission reaction. The coolant allows the neutrons to undergo multiple collisions with the light hydrogen atoms in the water, losing speed in the process. The slowed neutrons are termed thermal neutrons

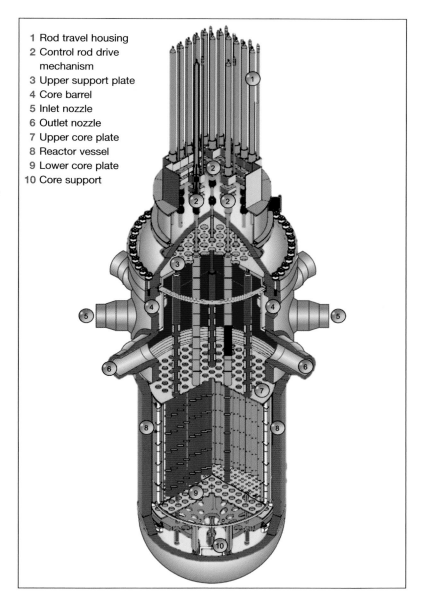

1 Rod travel housing
2 Control rod drive mechanism
3 Upper support plate
4 Core barrel
5 Inlet nozzle
6 Outlet nozzle
7 Upper core plate
8 Reactor vessel
9 Lower core plate
10 Core support

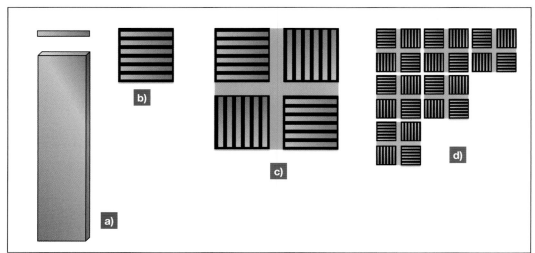

ABOVE Typical Westinghouse pressurised water reactor on which all RN reactors have been based. (Westinghouse/Author)

LEFT Configuration of fuel bundles in the core (a) fuel 'rod', (b) 'bundle' of rods, (c) bundles grouped around control rods and (d) part of fuel core. (Author)

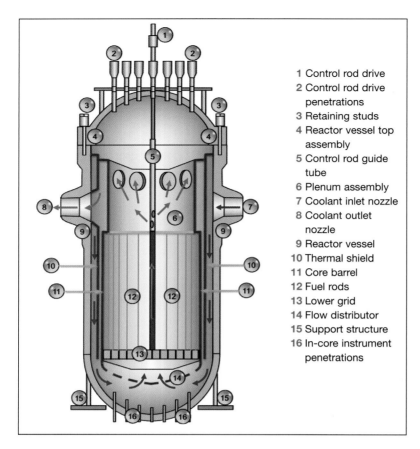

1 Control rod drive
2 Control rod drive
  penetrations
3 Retaining studs
4 Reactor vessel top
  assembly
5 Control rod guide
  tube
6 Plenum assembly
7 Coolant inlet nozzle
8 Coolant outlet
  nozzle
9 Reactor vessel
10 Thermal shield
11 Core barrel
12 Fuel rods
13 Lower grid
14 Flow distributor
15 Support structure
16 In-core instrument
   penetrations

ABOVE Simplified cross section of a pressurised water reactor showing coolant water flow. *(Author)*

BELOW The self-regulation of a pressurised water reactor. *(Author)*

moderating effect. If the reactivity of the PWR increases beyond normal, the overheating of the water reduces its moderation of neutrons and the reaction will slow down, producing less heat. This property, known as the negative temperature coefficient of reactivity, is an important safety feature and makes PWR reactors very stable. The reactor is thus self-regulating as the hotter the coolant becomes, the less reactive the plant becomes, shutting itself down slightly to compensate and vice versa. Thus the plant controls itself around a given temperature set by the position of the control rods.

The control rods determine the power that can be produced by the PWR. The rods contain neutron-absorbent materials that, by reducing the number of neutrons available to produce further fission reactions, reduce the reactivity of the PWR. The control rods penetrate the core between the fuel rods and, when at their lowest extent, they quench the nuclear reaction and the ability of the PWR to generate power. The neutrons available to interact increases as the control rods are raised. Once sufficient neutrons are available the reactor 'goes critical' with a self-sustaining reaction. Withdrawing the rods further allows higher powers to be generated, provided that the coolant removes the heat generated. Below the critical level no power is generated.

The control rods are operated by electric motors that can slowly extract or insert them to gently increase or decrease the reactor's power. Withdrawn, the motors hold them above the reactor's core against two safety features: their own weight and a powerful spring. The failure of the electrical current (or deliberate disconnection) releases the rods to drive them into the reactor core in four seconds or less. By absorbing liberated neutrons the nuclear reaction is rapidly halted. There are additional systems to insert control rods in the event that primary rapid insertion does not promptly or fully actuate.

because they are in thermal equilibrium with the moderator and the fuel. They are 1,000 times more likely to produce a further fission than a prompt neutron.

Water is a better moderator when it is cool as it is more dense (so more collisions will occur). As the water increases in temperature it expands, increasing the space between its molecules thereby reducing the probability of a collision with a neutron and, consequently, its

JACKSPEAK

The sudden shutdown of a nuclear reactor by rapid release of the control rods is termed a 'scram' or 'reactor trip'.

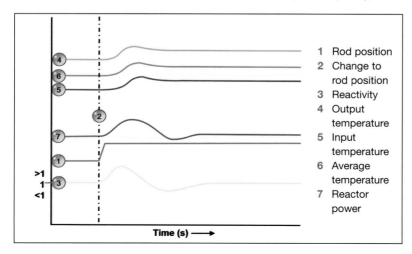

1 Rod position
2 Change to
  rod position
3 Reactivity
4 Output
  temperature
5 Input
  temperature
6 Average
  temperature
7 Reactor
  power

>1
1
<1

Time (s) ⟶

To guide the control rods as they move within the core there are guide columns in the upper internal assembly of the PWR. The force of the coolant flowing through the PWR tends to push the core upwards, but it is held in place by the weight of the assembly resting on top of the core.

When the reactor has been shut down, heat will still be produced by the nuclear decay of fission fragments even though ^{235}U fission has ceased. At the moment of reactor shutdown, decay heat will be about 6.5% of the previous core power if the reactor has had a long and steady power history. The decay heat will continue to slowly decrease over time.

Decay heat is a significant reactor safety concern, especially shortly after normal shutdown or following a loss-of-coolant accident. Failure to remove decay heat may cause the reactor core temperature to rise to dangerous levels and emergency removal of this heat is essential. If the main circulating pumps are not available, emergency cooling is provided by natural circulation of water from an emergency cooling tank. Heat is removed from this tank by seawater.

The power output of nuclear reactors can be unintentionally reduced by the products of corrosion and wear, technically known as crud, that absorb the neutrons that sustain the fission reaction. Crud is mostly composed of nickel and iron leached from the coated stainless steel tubes of the primary circuit. It is a yellowish substance that can be flaky, porous or hard, depending on its chemical make-up. It accumulates on the outer coating of fuel rods and can promote local corrosion that, with time, can cause the cladding to rupture so releasing radioactive fission products into the coolant.

Reactor shielding

Radiation from the fission reaction and the decay of its radioactive products can escape from the reactor. Both thermal and prompt neutrons as well as gamma-rays penetrate the reactor vessel, although its iron construction absorbs some thermal neutrons. The capture reaction, however, results in further gamma-rays. The submarine has shielding

to protect personnel from the detrimental effects of the radiation. The shielding design presents a challenge, as personnel may have to work, eat and sleep within a few metres of the PWR continuously for months at a time. The designers must keep all exposures within prescribed limits. However, the design intent was to further reduce the exposure to a level that is 'as low as reasonably practicable' (ALARP). This is the lowest level achievable without incurring costs that are disproportionate to the benefits gained.

Previously, submarine compartments were assigned one of three different categories according to the radiation dose-rates that would be encountered within them. The higher the dose-rate, then the shorter the time that personnel could spend within the compartment within any 24-hour period. The periods were calculated to ensure that no crewmember would experience exposure that exceeded 50µSv/h. A new approach was used for the *Astute* class with the requirements expressed in terms of the limiting dose to the submarine's personnel to that used by the Health and Safety Executive for civil reactors. The dose-rates must not exceed the basic safety objective. If basic safety limits were exceeded, the design must be justified using ALARP

BELOW Production of heat from decay products after reactor shutdown. *(Author)*

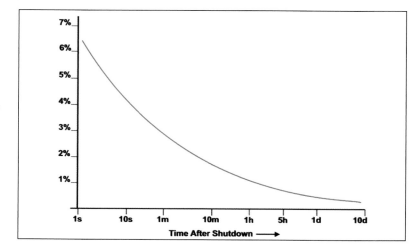

principles. For normal operation of the boat these levels are:

Normal operation	Basic safety limits	Basic safety objective
Annual collective dose	200mSv	20mSv
Annual individual dose	15mSv	2mSv

All personnel wear radiation-monitoring dosimeters as a check on their individual exposure to radiation. Every person on earth is exposed to some radiation, principally cosmic ionising radiation that, on average, is 2.7mSv per year, although this is attenuated by seawater so lower on a submerged submarine. Over 75% of HMS *Astute*'s crew would get a bigger dose from background radiation staying ashore than they would get from the reactor while they were on board. The remainder receive exposures below accepted international standards.

Radiation can be stopped by elements with a high atomic number with lead the preferred choice. Unfortunately, because of its weight, lead can only be used sparingly. It forms a radiation shield of interlocking bricks around the reactor. Antimony is sometimes added to lead to improve its structural strength in applications ashore; however, antimony can generate gamma-rays when bombarded by neutrons so pure lead is used.

Dense hydrogenous materials such as borated polyethylene are the most efficient neutron shields, made from high-density polyethylene with 5% boron content by weight. This material is light and easy to install as it is available in blocks and slabs. Although relatively large volumes are needed, it is suitable for shielding the radiation from the top of the reactor where the weight of more dense material would provide a problem with the submarine's stability.

The primary shielding surrounds the reactor. At lower levels is a shield tank of fresh water outside of which are lead blocks. Blocks of polyethylene over the top plate complete the primary shielding.

Secondary shielding is provided at the reactor compartment boundary itself. Its steel, when enhanced with additional shielding material, captures further neutrons. Also part of this secondary shielding is the reactor compartment bulkheads and the reactor services compartment deck running over the reactor. This deck has an access hatch with an observation porthole of thick lead-glass shielding.

There are multiple barriers to prevent radioactive material escaping in an accident and affecting either the crew or the submarine's external environment. Radiation shielding is provided within the reactor compartment for accident conditions as well as normal operation. Containment structures and systems are designed to operate at various levels to restrict radioactive releases in progressive accident scenarios.

The key elements of the containment are:

- The fuel cladding
- The integrity of the sealed primary circuit, its pipe work and components
- Containment boundaries built into the submarine structure and pressure hull
- Automatic protection systems to isolate pipework that penetrates containment boundaries.

BELOW Reactor primary and secondary shielding. *(Author, from BAE Systems Shield Forum Presentation)*

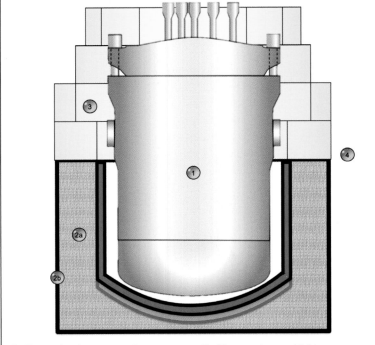

1   Pressurised water reactor
2   Lower primary shield comprising
2a Fresh water tank
2b Lead plate
3   Upper primary shield (polyethylene blocks)
4   Secondary shielding

Development of the second pressurised water reactor (PWR2)

The RN's first nuclear submarine, HMS *Dreadnought*, was powered by a USN reactor and propulsion system. The next 22 nuclear submarines used a UK design of submarine nuclear reactor later termed PWR1. Over time the PWR1 was honed by improvements to the design of the reactor core that yielded increases in power.

It was realised that the reactor of *Trafalgar* class submarines fitted with Core Z represented the ultimate potential development of the PWR1 plant, and that future improvements would require a radically new design of reactor and reactor core. In April 1976, the definition of a new reactor plant, PWR2, started. The MoD required increased margins of safety, reduced plant unit production costs and through-life costs and, in addition, acoustic energy levels lower than for Core Z, even though the power was again to be increased.

In parallel with this design work, a wide range of parametric studies, including work to size the pressuriser and a detailed survey of core performance, was undertaken to optimise the plant and core. In support of the design process experimental work was also carried out. Over the next few years, physics, thermal and hydraulic techniques were further improved, while experimental work continued in the engineering laboratory. A zero-power test reactor was used to conduct experiments on reactor cores in order to validate new calculation methods. Different fuel-loading schemes were also investigated. An innovation for the PWR2 programme was to use a large hydraulic model of the reactor, constructed in Perspex. It represented the whole of the reactor pressure vessel and its internal arrangement. The model was used to improve the accuracy of measurements used in the design analysis and the subsequent safety case. The emphasis on safety reflected public concern over nuclear risks. Tried and proven standards for nuclear vessels, originally defined by the USN and adapted by the RN, were no longer enough. The MoD, as advised by the United Kingdom Atomic Energy Authority, now required nuclear submarines to conform to safety regulations covering international nuclear installations.

An intensive 14-week study concluded that, by making limited design changes to the reactor core and the steam generators, a core with more than 50% greater power than Core Z could safely be achieved. As PWR1 is reported to be rated at about 70MW, this implies that HMS *Astute* has a reactor of over 100MW. The reactor plant proposed by the study required a significantly bigger pressure vessel than PWR1. A larger pressuriser and more powerful main coolant pumps were needed to deliver improved overall performance. Additionally, all plant components would be redesigned for better safety. It was also proposed to use a new digital electronic control and instrumentation system. The new core, designated Core G, would be of similar design to Core Z, but with larger fuel sub-assemblies. PWR2 with Core G was first successfully installed on the *Vanguard* class SSBNs.

In a departure from earlier practice, the first production Core G was installed in a zero-power test reactor so that its performance could be

BELOW The PWR2 prototype plant at its build yard at Barrow-in-Furness.
(Rolls-Royce)

evaluated before delivery to the Shore Test Facility at Dounreay, Scotland. The programme allowed six months for this activity from the spring of 1985. The core underwent initial criticality tests, followed by an extensive experimental programme that delivered extremely valuable information, while at all times generating less power than that required to light a domestic light bulb. The advantage of using the real core was that structural differences present in the Core G mock-up were eliminated when Core G itself was used, removing uncertainty when key design parameters were measured.

In June 1985, the PWR2 prototype construction was completed in the Barrow-in-Furness nuclear licensed yard that builds the RN's submarines. The completed plant, in its containment vessel, was then transported to Dounreay by sea. This radically different manufacturing approach resulted in estimated savings amounting to 10–15% of the total project costs. The reactor unit and its containment, weighing 1,300T, was loaded on to a barge, which together with a similar barge carrying 80T of auxiliary machinery, was floated out into Morecambe Bay. Both barges were shipped on the seagoing vessel *GIANT2* – which was 140m long and 36m wide, for the 500-mile voyage to Scotland, a journey that took three days. The PWR2 prototype was installed in HMS *Vulcan* Naval Reactor Test Establishment on the Dounreay site.

Core G was transported to HMS *Vulcan* after its zero-power reactor trials, and installed in the PWR2 prototype plant. It was taken critical on 25 July 1987. Initial testing of the plant revealed a problem related to the control rod gear operation. This needed rectification before the plant could be fully used as a prototype facility.

CENTRE The PWR2 prototype plant being rolled up the beach in Dounreay. *(Rolls-Royce)*

LEFT The PWR2 prototype plant arriving at the Shore Test Facility. *(Rolls-Royce)*

In March 1997, 18 years after the start of design work on PWR2 and Core G, orders were announced for three submarines of the new *Astute* class, the submarine design for which this power system had originally been intended. During the intervening period work had been undertaken for a new core, Core H, that was destined for the PWR2 reactors of the *Astute* class submarines. PWR2 with Core H is designed to last four times longer than its predecessors, eliminating the need for refuelling during her full 25-year life. By avoiding two expensive reactor-refits during their service life, the submarines have reduced maintenance costs and provided greater availability.

Nuclear steam-raising plant (NSRP)

Within the reactor compartment there are two identical primary circuits, port and starboard. Forced flow is necessary to remove heat from the reactor core so powerful main coolant pumps circulate the pressurised water through the reactor. These pumps are radial motors with an external stator and internal rotor that turns an impeller to circulate the coolant. If necessary, main isolating valves can be used in both circuits to isolate the supply and return to the PWR. These are hydraulically operated gate-valves that can be latched in position.

Water in the primary circuits is maintained at a high pressure to prevent unwanted boiling in the core. A single pressuriser controls the pressure of the reactor and both primary circuits. Electrical heaters within the pressuriser heat the water to generate steam – this

RIGHT HMS *Vulcan,* Naval Reactor Test Establishment Shore Test Facility housing the PWR2 prototype plant that was commissioned on 25 August 1987. *(Rolls-Royce)*

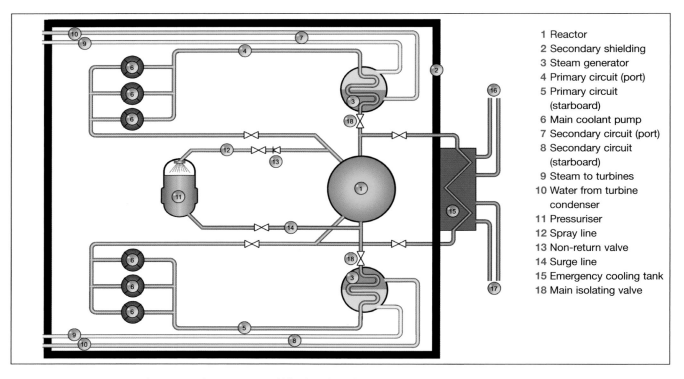

1 Reactor
2 Secondary shielding
3 Steam generator
4 Primary circuit (port)
5 Primary circuit (starboard)
6 Main coolant pump
7 Secondary circuit (port)
8 Secondary circuit (starboard)
9 Steam to turbines
10 Water from turbine condenser
11 Pressuriser
12 Spray line
13 Non-return valve
14 Surge line
15 Emergency cooling tank
18 Main isolating valve

ABOVE Simplified schematic of equipment within the reactor compartment. *(Author)*

BELOW Schematic of typical nuclear steam-raising plant. *(Author)*

1 Nuclear reactor
2 Steam generator
3 Pressuriser
4 Primary circuit
5 Main coolant pump
6 Steam to turbines
7 Water from turbine condenser
8 Electrical supply
9 Containment boundary

increases the pressure within the closed system of reactor and primary circuits. If the pressure becomes too high, then cool water is sprayed into the top of the pressuriser to condense some of the steam, thus reducing the system's pressure. It is important to monitor the pressure of the reactor coolant as too high a pressure can cause leaks and ruptures; conversely, too low a pressure can cause boiling in the core and cavitation in the coolant pumps. The pressuriser is connected to the primary circuit at the reactor outlet through a pipe called the surge line. Cool water to reduce pressure is supplied by a connection to the reactor inlet.

The coolant gains heat as it passes through the reactor core. The primary circuits then deliver coolant through large pipes to their respective steam generators. The pipes, like all components in contact with the coolant, are made of stainless steel in order to minimise corrosion. The primary (and indeed the secondary) coolant water is de-ionised and demineralised to reduce corrosion. The steam generator is a heat exchanger in which the primary coolant flows through hundreds of small tubes. Heat is transferred through the walls of these tubes to the lower-pressure secondary coolant surrounding the tubes.

While the water in the primary circuit is at high pressure, the water in the secondary circuit is at a lower pressure, so evaporates (boils) to produce steam thereby extracting heat from the primary coolant. Even at the secondary circuit pressure, the temperature of steam is well above the boiling point of water at atmospheric pressure (100°C) – a temperature of 275°C is typical of the steam used to turn a steam turbine. The secondary circuit carries saturated steam – a mixture of steam (gaseous water) and some liquid water. Having cooled in the steam generator, the primary coolant is then returned to the reactor to be heated again.

The transfer of heat between the two circuits is accomplished without mixing the two fluids, so preventing the secondary coolant from becoming radioactive. Water in the primary circuit becomes irradiated as it passes through the reactor but the secondary circuit, not irradiated, can leave the heavily shielded reactor compartment and circulate within the machinery spaces that are occupied by the submarine's staff. The secondary circuit does not need to be shielded or decontaminated before repair work is carried out.

Main propulsion machinery

The secondary circuit carries the saturated steam to the aftermost compartment of the pressure hull that contains the main propulsion machinery. Here the steam drives the main turbine and turbo-generators that provide propulsive power and electricity respectively. After passing through the turbines the secondary coolant is cooled in the main condenser. The condenser removes heat from any residual steam and then converts to a liquid so that it can be pumped back into the steam generator in the reactor compartment. The main condenser is cooled by seawater from the main circulating water system; this is drawn from outside the submarine and returns it at a higher temperature. Condensing the steam produces very low pressure at the turbine outlet, increasing the pressure drop across the turbines and maximising the energy extracted in the turbines. The speed of the submarine is adjusted by a throttle that controls the flow of steam to the main turbine, thereby increasing or decreasing the turbine power demand. The propulsor speed is also determined by the amount of steam supplied to the turbines.

The following sequence of events increase the propulsion power:

- The operator opens the throttles of the turbine inlet valves increasing the steam being drawn from the steam generators;
- This causes the secondary circuit temperature to decrease;
- This leads to a similar decrease in the temperature of the primary circuit coolant water that circulates within the reactor;

BELOW Components of secondary circuit and propulsion machinery. (*Author*)

1 Steam feed from reactor	6 Main turbine	11 Shaft seal
2 Main steam valve	7 Condenser	12 Main shaft
3 Circulating pump	8 Clutch	13 Propulsor
4 Turbo-generator	9 Gearbox	14 Secondary propulsion motor
5 Main static converter	10 Emergency propulsion motor	15 Steam return to reactor

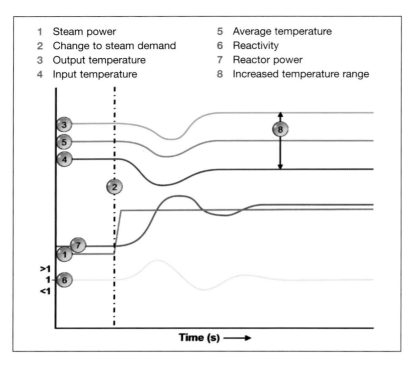

1. Steam power
2. Change to steam demand
3. Output temperature
4. Input temperature
5. Average temperature
6. Reactivity
7. Reactor power
8. Increased temperature range

Time (s) ⟶

ABOVE Load following of the output of a pressurised water reactor. *(Author)*

JACKSPEAK

Boat's staff of the marine engineering specialisation who operate the nuclear propulsion system and other machinery aft of the reactor space are referred to as the 'aftendies'.

the reactor consequently follows the overall power demand of the turbine. This is another manifestation of the stability of the PWR that results from the temperature-induced changes in the moderation of the fission reaction.

At a given reactor operating temperature there is a limited range of powers that can be supplied to the turbines. The reactor's control rods are used to maintain primary system temperature at the desired point for the amount of steam needed for the propulsor. Withdrawing the control rods to raise the temperature of the reactor requires the coolant flow to be augmented by increasing the number and speed of the main coolant pumps deployed.

The speed of rotation of the main turbine is reduced in the gearbox to match that required by the propulsor. The gearbox is a new design, manufactured to extremely high standards to achieve a silent, maintenance-free transmission. Gearboxes are potentially a major source of emitted acoustic energy but HMS *Astute*'s gearbox is recognised as one of the quietest fitted to a nuclear-powered submarine. The gearbox can be isolated from the main turbine using a clutch.

■ The decrease in coolant temperature increases its density and affects its moderator properties leading to more fission events (increasing the reactivity) and providing greater reactor power output;

■ The increase of reactor power will eventually result in primary system temperature returning to a steady-state value.

The converse effects occur if the operator decreases speed by closing the throttles, which leads to a decrease in reactivity and reactor operating temperature. The power output of

If there is an operational need to proceed quietly at slow speed the acoustic energy generated by the boat is minimised by reducing the power of the nuclear plant and disconnecting the main turbine from the gearbox. The clutch of the emergency propulsion motor (EPM) is engaged to turn the propulsor through the gearbox. This motor is powered from the battery, so allows the boat to proceed, albeit slowly. It is an AC variable-speed induction motor-drive system using insulated gate bipolar transistor technology. The EPM is also used if the steam supply or main turbine fails (or if the reactor has to be shut down).

The whole main propulsion machinery is mounted on a raft, a unique innovation introduced with the first British-designed nuclear

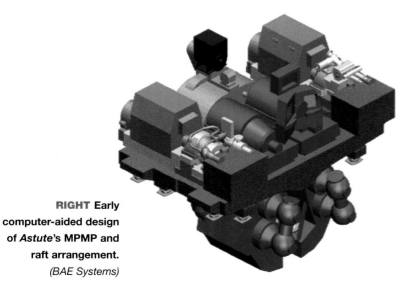

RIGHT Early computer-aided design of *Astute*'s MPMP and raft arrangement. *(BAE Systems)*

MPMP on HMS *Valiant* and subsequently copied by other nations. The primary purpose of the raft is to allow the machinery to be supported on acoustic energy-isolating mounts when the boat is operating at slow speed and acoustic emissions have to be at an absolute minimum. The seats for the raft and machinery (that together weigh over 300T) are supported on the large reserve feed-water tanks. The tanks fulfil multiple roles depending on the situation. They provide a reservoir of water that can be supplied at low pressure to the reactor and an unpressurised discharge container for the water-making plant. In an emergency they can inject water at low pressure into the reactor in the event of a loss-of-coolant accident or act as a source of HP water for the engine room aqueous firefighting foam system.

Shaft, seals, main propulsor and propulsion motors

The gearbox, whether driven by the main turbine or the EPM, rotates the shaft of the main propulsor. The main propulsor used on recent RN submarines is a ducted pump-jet. Its advantage over the traditional propeller is that, for a given speed of rotation, the pump-jet produces the same thrust with a smaller diameter. Consequently, the speed of the blade-tips is slower, which reduces the acoustic energy emitted by the blades. The disadvantage of a pump-jet is that it has poor astern performance when compared to a conventional propeller.

HMS *Astute* features a new generation of pump-jet propulsor compared with her predecessors. This achieves improved efficiency, significant signature reduction and major improvements in shock capability. Pump-jet propulsors have an annular duct that reduces in internal diameter towards the rear (outlet). This duct lessens the acoustic signature as it tends to trap generated acoustic energy while its anechoic covering reduces the reflected acoustic energy. Fixed radial stator vanes help guide the flow of water through the duct, as well as supporting it. Rotor blades turned by the propulsor shaft provide the means

of propulsion. The first submarine pump-jets were 'post-swirl', with the rotor blades ahead of the stator, but these gave way to 'pre-swirl' propulsors where the stator was located ahead of the rotors, giving a smoother hydrodynamic flow through the propulsor.

The *Astute* class propulsor is both lighter (by 11T) and more corrosion-resistant than previous designs, using improved materials and higher-quality casting to deliver significant improvements. Whereas previous designs required significant maintenance work after two years, the new propulsor has a maintenance period equal to that of the boat (25 years). Unlike previous propulsors that had been built as part of the boat, the *Astute*-class propulsors are a complete, fully assembled unit delivered to the shipbuilder ready for installation. It is also installed in a different way that reduces the installation (or replacement) time from ten to just two weeks. The propulsor can be manufactured in 30% less time (27 months) compared with earlier designs.

Of the many materials considered for the vanes, blades and rotor hub, an alloy was selected. The completely new composite duct and fairings are fabricated as a single unit from a marine composite material, glass fibre-reinforced resin. Previous duct designs required metal reinforcement to meet operational loads, but these would not meet the high shock-load requirement of the *Astute* class. They also suffered from corrosion at sea, leading to significant through-life repair costs. The new

BELOW **Diagram of a typical pre-swirl ducted propulsor.** *(Author, after P.M. Vinton, S. Banks and M. West, RINA Warship Conference 8, paper 15, 2005)*

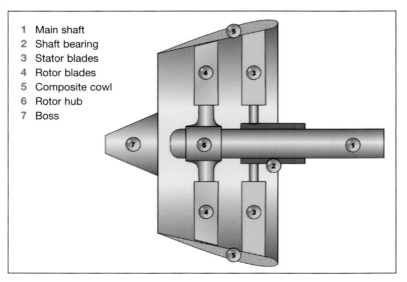

1 Main shaft
2 Shaft bearing
3 Stator blades
4 Rotor blades
5 Composite cowl
6 Rotor hub
7 Boss

RIGHT Cutaway of HMS *Astute*'s aft pressure hull. *(BAE Systems)*

1 Main steam valve
2 Main static converters
3 Diesel generator room
4 Switchboard room
5 Manoeuvring room
6 Watertight bulkhead
7 Engine room
8 Steam delivery ducting
9 Main turbines
10 Starboard turbo-generator
11 Gearbox
12 Starboard condenser
13 Circulating water transfer pipes
14 Propulsor shaft trust block
15 Bearing
16 Naval stores
17 Air treatment unit

corrosion-resistant duct is a one-piece design, with full-length longitudinal ribs to achieve the required shock strength and manoeuvring rigidity. An encapsulated acoustic layer gives the double advantage of exceeding the stringent signature requirements and dispensing with the need for tiles to be bonded to the ducts.

As the propulsor rotates, it generates a forward thrust along the shaft that pushes the boat through the sea. This thrust is applied to the boat's structure through a thrust block located on the shaft within the pressure hull. The other main component related to the shaft is the seal where it passes through the pressure hull.

It is an engineering challenge to seal a large rotating shaft against the demanding deep-sea pressures experienced by a submarine. The bespoke solution is a high-performance inboard sealing system that includes a double sealing arrangement. The seal also meets the requirements of long-life and low-acoustic energy necessary for such a vital component. It is water-lubricated and incorporates both redundancy and emergency packing arrangements.

The SPM is a low-power electrically powered propulsor that is used in the event of the failure of the main propulsor, its main shafting or the loss of the gearbox. It is normally withdrawn within the aft free-flood space. It is constructed with a base plate that is normally flush with the outer hull so that the flow of water over the hull

BELOW Rating ascending ladder from the aft machinery space. *(Crown Copyright/L(Phot) Stephen 'Stevie' Burke)*

BELOW RIGHT Diveguard propulsion shaft seal. *(Wärtsilä)*

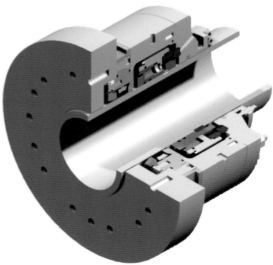

The secondary propulsion motor is known as the 'eggbeater'.

is not disrupted. The SPM can be lowered on a shaft so that it protrudes beneath the hull to provide an alternative electrically driven, albeit modestly powered, source of propulsion for manoeuvring at slow speed or as a 'get you (slowly) home' device. It can be rotated to steer the boat – a feature that is also used when manoeuvring in confined waters.

Manoeuvring room

Reactor control, propulsion control, electrical generation and distribution are managed from the centralised control console located in the manoeuvring room on the top deck, immediately aft of the reactor compartment.

The reactor is controlled remotely by the reactor control and instrumentation (RCI) system. This not only controls the reactor but also monitors performance and safety parameters in order to warn of any divergences from normal. It implements independent safety and control actions; if necessary it can automatically shut down the reactor safely (scram). After a scram it can prevent further undesirable consequences of an accident for a significant time without operator intervention. The system also indicates the integrity of the reactor core, the reactor coolant system and the containment, as well as the radiological state of the NSRP. The RCI system includes the rod control gear and pressuriser heater controller (as these are the principal control vectors for the PWR and its safe operation), the remote operation of the main isolating valves and speed of the main coolant pumps. It also relies on an array of sensors to measure reactor parameters such as:

■ The temperatures of water in the primary circuits as it enters and exits the reactor
■ The pressure in the primary circuits and in the pressuriser as, if this is too high, it can cause ruptures and, if it is too low, can cause boiling in the core and cavitation of the reactor coolant pumps

1 Four hydraulic jacks for lowering and raising the SPM
2 Electric motor
3 Rotatable four-bladed pump-jet propulsor
4 Cover plate to close hull opening when the SPM is retracted

LEFT Artist's impression of the secondary propulsion motor. (Author, from information supplied by MacTaggart Scott)

■ The flow in the primary circuit, as loss of flow can reduce the cooling of the core and needs to be addressed immediately.

The RCI system fitted to Astute submarines 1 to 3 was similar to that fitted to HMS Vanguard at about the same time. This system was an updated version of the original system deployed on Vanguard class boats that had proved so reliable. However, the through-life costs of this system were increasing due to obsolescence. During building, Astute boats 4 onwards were fitted with equipment with a replacement obsolescence-tolerant RCI design. The new system is efficient and uses interchangeable printed electronic circuit boards, enabling a

BELOW Hybrid circuit demonstrator board. (Rolls-Royce)

dramatic reduction in the variety of spares. The update uses a hybrid of analogue circuitry and digital functionality. Because reliability and fail-safe operation are of paramount importance, the design uses Safety Integrity Level 3 techniques and hardware. Equipment that is certified at Safety Integrity Level 3 implies a probability of failure only once if it is operated continuously for between 10 million and 100 million hours.

The RCI system of a nuclear-powered submarine is a safety-critical system requiring design and manufacture to the highest standards. Equipment within the reactor compartment, including the sensors, has to be capable of operating in high temperatures and a harsh radiation environment.

Because of the importance of the RCI, the sensors are replicated four times and each sensor feeds into one of four identical and independent panels within the main control panel. The power for each of the four panels is supplied at all times by its dedicated static frequency inverter. Drawing power from the DC bus-bars from the main battery, the inverters convert the DC power to AC for the panels and their equipment. Under most circumstances each of the four sensors measuring a parameter will provide the same value. If, however, one

gives a different value then a voting system will use the value of three channels that agree. Excluding in exceptional operating conditions, if only two channels measure the same values then the system will shut down.

While the RCI and operating procedures will always err on the side of caution and maintain temperature and pressure within safe limits, there are instances when the on-watch engineering officer will operate the battle short switch. This switch overrides the automatic safeguards, thereby keeping the reactor online, and is used in operational circumstances where loss of propulsion power would put the boat in danger – such as when under attack or evading a torpedo. Documented examples where this was employed include the collision between HMS *Warspite* and a Russian submarine that she was tailing closely and when HMS *Conqueror* came under torpedo attack during the Falklands Conflict.

Electrical system

The electrical system is a complex arrangement of generators, interlinking cables and switches that ensure a safe and reliable source of electrical power for on-board

**BELOW Typical
nuclear submarine
turbo-generator.**
(Rolls-Royce)

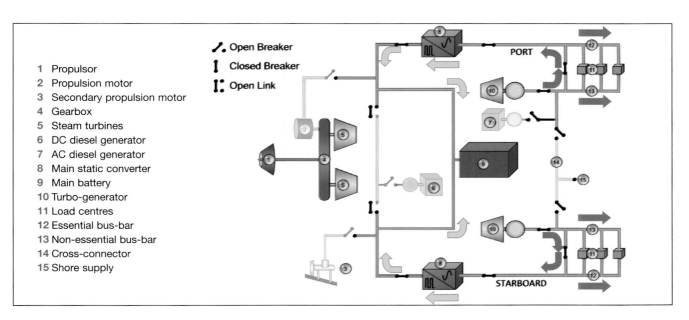

Key:

1 Propulsor
2 Propulsion motor
3 Secondary propulsion motor
4 Gearbox
5 Steam turbines
6 DC diesel generator
7 AC diesel generator
8 Main static converter
9 Main battery
10 Turbo-generator
11 Load centres
12 Essential bus-bar
13 Non-essential bus-bar
14 Cross-connector
15 Shore supply

✒ Open Breaker
❙ Closed Breaker
❙❙ Open Link

PORT

STARBOARD

equipment such as the combat sensors and weapons, lighting, heating, platform control and navigation. It also supplies power to alternative methods of propulsion should the reactor be out of action.

The principal source of electricity is two 440V three-phase AC turbo-generators (TGs) driven by steam from the NSRP. The TGs are essential equipment, converting steam from the reactor into electricity to supply all the submarine's electrical requirements. The TGs are believed to be of similar output to those fitted to the *Trafalgar* class boats (circa 4MW). Power is distributed throughout the ship from switchboards beneath the manoeuvring room. These supply major equipment directly and other equipment through distribution panels that provide 115V single phase and, through transformer rectifier units, DC supplies. Each TG has a separate distribution system, but for essential equipment there is an alternative supply from the other TG. Should there be a failure with a TG normally supplying electricity to an item of equipment, then an automatic change-over switch (or, for less urgent or vital equipment, a hand-operated change-over switch) will connect the equipment to the alternative supply. Each TG also supplies power to a main frequency converter that converts 440V AC to a nominal 280V DC for charging the boat's main battery.

Key operating parameters of submarine TGs are exceptionally low acoustic energy coupled with vibration and shock resistance. Recently, the TG hydraulic system has been replaced by a newly developed electric actuation system that offers significant weight, cost, space and maintenance savings.

In the event of the NSRP producing very little steam, the main turbines cannot turn the propulsion shaft and the TGs can produce no electrical power. Such a situation may occur when the NSRP is reduced to minimum power to lessen the transmitted acoustic signature (or even where the NSRP has been shut down because of a fault). In this event, power is drawn from the battery to supply the submarine's equipment and the DC EPM to drive the shaft. The power available from the battery is less than that available from the reactor, so the boat's speed is limited. However, if a low acoustic signature is sought, then low speed and the quiet propulsion motor both help to achieve this.

On earlier boats a 300kW reversible motor generator converted AC to DC in order to charge the battery. Should the TGs fail to generate electricity then these same motor generators could reverse their power flow and change to converting DC power from the battery to AC for the boat's important electrical equipment such as the reactor's main coolant pumps. There are disadvantages to motor generators as rotating machinery in constant operation is subject to performance degradation and their commutator brushes produce

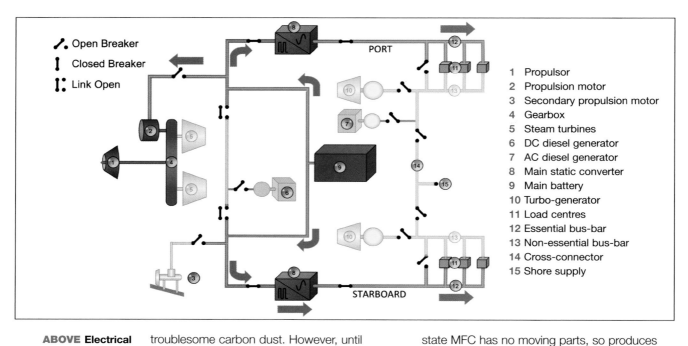

Legend (above diagram):
- Open Breaker
- Closed Breaker
- Link Open

PORT

STARBOARD

1 Propulsor
2 Propulsion motor
3 Secondary propulsion motor
4 Gearbox
5 Steam turbines
6 DC diesel generator
7 AC diesel generator
8 Main static converter
9 Main battery
10 Turbo-generator
11 Load centres
12 Essential bus-bar
13 Non-essential bus-bar
14 Cross-connector
15 Shore supply

ABOVE Electrical system schematic for battery-powered operation with reactor not providing power. *(Author)*

troublesome carbon dust. However, until recently, there were no alternatives.

Advances in power electronics such as insulated-gate bipolar transistor technology have allowed main frequency changers (MFC) to be specifically designed for *Astute* class boats to replace the motor generators. Even though the motor generators were extremely quiet, a solid

state MFC has no moving parts, so produces virtually no airborne or structure-borne acoustic energy. MFCs also require less maintenance (resulting in higher availability), occupy less space, produce less wild heat and are about 50% lighter than the motor generators.

Two diesel generators are fitted, one producing DC and the other AC. These can be used when air is available – on the surface or at periscope depth with the snort mast deployed. When air is available they can be used to charge the main battery or provide propulsive

BELOW Electrical system schematic for snorting operation on, or close to, surface with reactor not providing power. *(Author)*

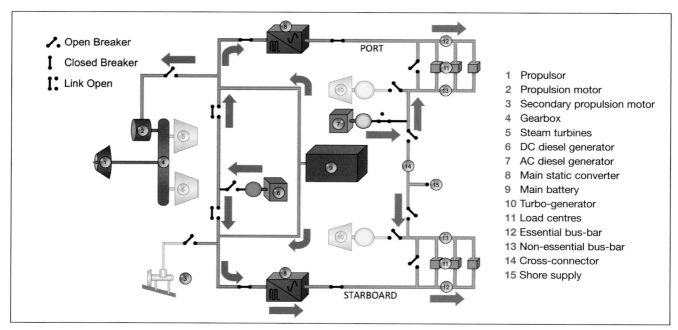

Legend (below diagram):
- Open Breaker
- Closed Breaker
- Link Open

PORT

STARBOARD

1 Propulsor
2 Propulsion motor
3 Secondary propulsion motor
4 Gearbox
5 Steam turbines
6 DC diesel generator
7 AC diesel generator
8 Main static converter
9 Main battery
10 Turbo-generator
11 Load centres
12 Essential bus-bar
13 Non-essential bus-bar
14 Cross-connector
15 Shore supply

power. However, when alongside in harbour the shore supplies (that use cables to connect the jetty supply to the submarine) are the preferred method of obtaining electricity.

Electrical storage and distribution

The submarine has two main batteries that provide an alternative high-integrity source of DC power. Each comprises 112 series-connected flooded lead-acid battery cells with a nominal voltage of 270V. The two main batteries are connected in parallel. For their size and weight, conventional lead-acid batteries store half, or even a third, less energy than modern zebra or lithium-ion batteries of the same size but the latter are between 100 and 1,000 times more expensive than lead-acid batteries. There are, however, advantages to having a large weight low in the submarine and lead-acid batteries provide dependable technology. They have a very low leakage rate so retain charge when not in heavy use and are capable of a range of discharge rates including rapid-discharge essential in emergency operation.

Submarine battery characteristics		
	Battery cell	Two batteries
Nominal voltage	2.4V	270V
Height	1.11m	1.11m
Width	360mm	7.5m
Length	450mm	50.5m
Weight	500kg	112T
5-hour rate	75Ah	16.8kAh

The battery cells have two sets of interleaved plates that form the electrodes, each with a total area of about $0.5m^2$. The positive electrode is composed of tubes arranged in a plane and filled with porous lead oxide. The negative electrode is a stretched lead/copper grid coated in porous lead. The gap between adjacent positive and negative electrodes is about 1mm and is filled with a porous spacer to prevent contact between them. As the electrolyte is sulphuric acid, the cells are located in rubber-lined troughs and sealed against water leakage. At high discharge the cells' internal resistance generates heat so each cell is water-cooled.

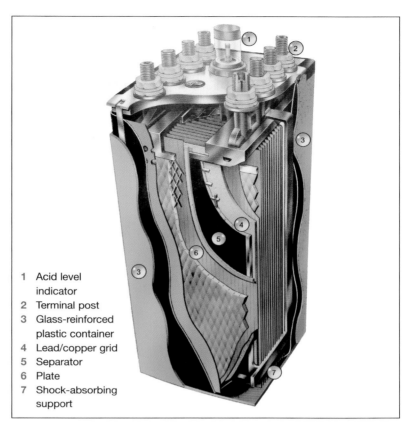

1 Acid level indicator
2 Terminal post
3 Glass-reinforced plastic container
4 Lead/copper grid
5 Separator
6 Plate
7 Shock-absorbing support

In normal operation the battery is kept charged from the MFC. Care must be taken not to overcharge the cells as this generates oxygen and hydrogen gas by electrolysis of the electrolyte. Periodic maintenance of lead-acid batteries requires inspection of the electrolyte level and replacement of any water that has been electrolysed. Ventilation systems in the battery space are designed to prevent build-up of hydrogen (which is flammable in concentrations exceeding 4%). The boat's air purification system removes hydrogen from the boat's atmosphere.

After a period, the battery's energy storage capacity begins to diminish so, at a convenient juncture, it is subjected to a conditioning discharge, during which the battery is discharged and then rapidly fully recharged. This typically takes 8–12 hours and, like all charging cycles, is undertaken in three stages:

- First the battery is charged at constant power until the cell voltage has increased to about 2.4V per cell
- Next comes a constant-voltage stage until the current drops to a very small value

ABOVE SSN lead-acid battery cell. *(Author, from Enersys)*

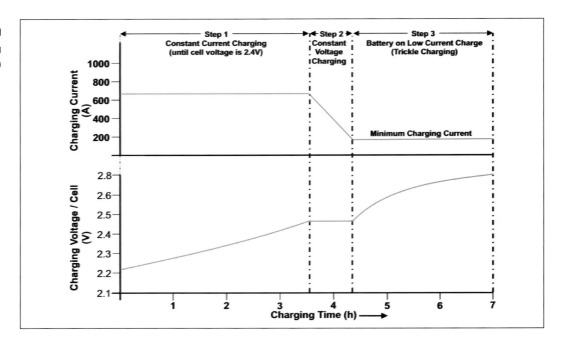

ABOVE Typical submarine Type 396 diesel generator. *(MTU)*

■ Finally a low constant-current 'trickle charge' stage with higher voltages to achieve 100% charge.

The lifetime of a submarine battery is typically five to seven years and, if possible, they are renewed every three to four years.

The large number of cells in the submarine's batteries generate considerable currents. These can cause magnetic fields, an undesirable feature in submarines. In addition, lethal voltages between the cell interconnections structure represent a hazardous working environment. As the current drawn can be significant, solid copper bus-bars are used instead of electrical power cables. The bus-bars are laminated in order to aid heat dissipation. The main switchboards are air-cooled rather than water-cooled to avoid water in the vicinity of items capable of delivering substantial power.

The boat has two 8V396 DGs that are specifically designed for submarines and are in service with several navies on both nuclear and conventional boats. When the boat is on the surface and normally aspirated, the DGs can provide their rated power. However, when snorting, flow restrictions caused by the snort pipework (resulting in high exhaust back-pressure), reduce the engine's power output. The DGs are supercharged to increase air charge and improve its power-to-weight ratio. There is potential to upgrade the DGs to the new 12-valve Type 4000 DGs that are physically similar in size, but much more powerful.

Characteristics of Type 8V396 diesel generator set	
Normal speed of rotation	1,800rpm
Output voltage	Nominal 280V DC
Dimensions DG set (L × W × H)	4.9 (engine 3.3) × 1.6 × 2.8m
Weight DG set	13T
Engine type	8-valve, supercharged, acoustically shielded

ABOVE HMS *Artful*
on the surface
during trials.
*(Crown Copyright/
CPOA(Phot) Thomas
'Tam' McDonald)*

LEFT Checking
diesels on board
HMS *Ambush* prior to
running. *(BAE Systems)*

Chapter Five

Anatomy of the combat system

The combat system principally consists of a range of sensors (such as a suite of sonars) and weapons (torpedoes and land attack missiles). The sonar suite is one of the most sensitive and advanced sonar systems known. The weapons carried are the latest Spearfish torpedoes and Tomahawk missiles.

A command team consisting of the CO, senior officers and operators controls the combat system through the command system hardware that assists the analysis of data and provides predictions of weapons trajectories.

OPPOSITE *Astute*-class submarine firing a heavyweight torpedo. *(Admiralty Model Works LLC/Tvrtko Kapetanović)*

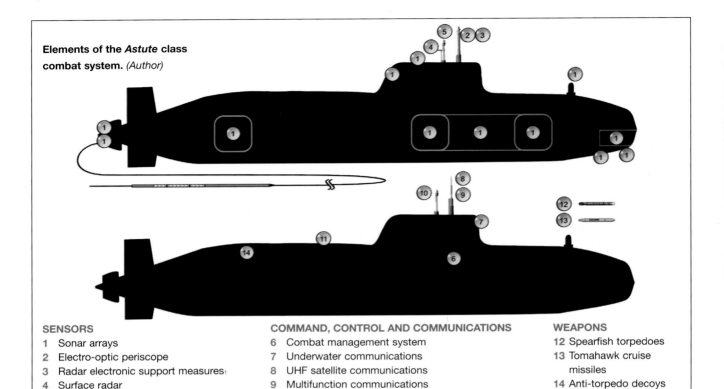

Elements of the *Astute* class combat system. *(Author)*

SENSORS	COMMAND, CONTROL AND COMMUNICATIONS	WEAPONS
1 Sonar arrays	6 Combat management system	12 Spearfish torpedoes
2 Electro-optic periscope	7 Underwater communications	13 Tomahawk cruise missiles
3 Radar electronic support measures	8 UHF satellite communications	14 Anti-torpedo decoys
4 Surface radar	9 Multifunction communications	
5 Communications electronic support measures	10 EHF/SHF satellite communications	
	11 Towed communications bodies	

Passive sonar detection of submarine by submarine.
(Author)

1 Noise emitted from target submarine
2 Propagation of acoustic (sound) waves through seawater
3 Passive detection by submarine

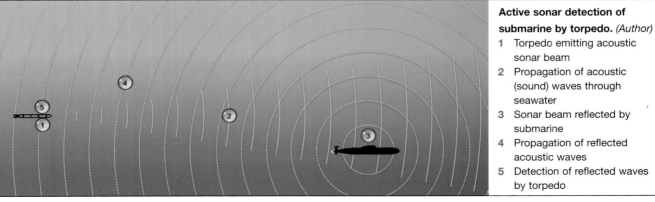

Active sonar detection of submarine by torpedo. *(Author)*

1 Torpedo emitting acoustic sonar beam
2 Propagation of acoustic (sound) waves through seawater
3 Sonar beam reflected by submarine
4 Propagation of reflected acoustic waves
5 Detection of reflected waves by torpedo

Elements of the combat system

The combat system of a submarine comprises three key elements: sensors (particularly sonars and electro-optical periscopes), weapons (torpedoes and land attack missiles) and the command, control and communications system (principally the combat management system.

A submarine's primary sensor is sonar, from which she gains awareness of her surroundings and, in particular, with which to detect underwater targets such as enemy submarines or any torpedoes that may have been launched against the boat. Like most sensors, sonars detect the energy coming from objects; in this case it is acoustic (sound) energy passing as waves through the seawater. Two techniques are used:

- *Passive detection* uses hydrophones to detect sounds being emitted by the target as acoustic waves. The hydrophones then convert the received acoustic energy into electrical signals that can be processed in the passive sonar. When passive sonars detect a signal, then the direction of the target can be determined; however, they have the disadvantage that determining the range of the target is much more difficult.
- *Active detection* employs a transducer to emit a pulse of acoustic energy. Any of the pulse's energy reflected from the target is detected and, again, converted into an electrical signal for processing. The advantage of active sonar is that the time for the pulse to return gives an indication of the distance from the target – information not available to a passive detector.

To prosecute targets *Astute* class boats have two major weapons – the Spearfish heavyweight torpedo (HWT) for use against submarines and surface ships and the TLAM that can hit, with high accuracy, land targets 1,600km away. Both weapons are discharged from the weapon launch-tubes in the bow of the submarine when the boat is submerged.

The combat management system co-ordinates all aspects of the combat system. It processes all sensor information data in order to generate a coherent overall situational awareness. The captain and his immediate staff can then develop the tactical approach and decide if, and when, to fire the weapons. When the firing command is given it is the combat management system that controls the discharge of the boat's weapons and manages their trajectory to the target.

Astute Combat Management System (ACMS)

ACMS has evolved from command systems deployed in previous UK nuclear submarines. The earlier submarine command system had a more limited scope but its design provided flexibility allowing enhancements to be implemented in an evolutionary way. Any new capability could also be successfully introduced on the *Trafalgar* class system and then, after evaluation, transferred to the ACMS. Unlike earlier systems, ACMS is procured as a single package, rather than as a collection of separately acquired systems that require integration.

ACMS combines three separate combat system requirements in a single integrated system:

- The **command system** (the command and control system) comprising new applications and new display graphics developed to update from the *Trafalgar* class. Operators can gain familiarity of the system on trainers common to both classes and from valuable experience when serving on the *Trafalgar* boats.
- The **command support system** that, unlike previous practice, is embedded in ACMS and is accessible from all console positions. It uses processed sensor data and archived information to generate the recognised maritime picture – a visual display that presents information of all tracks identified by the sensors combined with intelligence data.
- The **command workstation system**, in which the consoles are capable of displaying the recognised maritime picture and video images from the electro-optical periscope and other sources.

ACMS is a new-generation combat management system where operations are distributed across its hardware but function as a single entity. Apart

consoles display command information allowing command and tactical functions to be undertaken (one of the consoles is dedicated to the CO). The remaining two are allocated to sonar tasks – one is the sound room console and the other is the tactical picture supervisor's console. An eighth console with a single display is designated for special intelligence functions and is situated in the electronic warfare office.

While the consoles have inbuilt computers that handle local functions such as graphics processing, two identical central servers perform major processing facilities for functions such as target motion analysis and the track database. These operate in a master/slave configuration for resilience. They provide a host environment for third-party applications such as acoustic modelling and oceanography packages.

Each of the central servers contains a local area network with a switched hub. Their processor cards are variants of the SPARC2 scalable processor architecture running the Solaris 8 UNIX operating system. Duplicated fast fibre-optic Ethernet (100Mb/s) connects the two central node drawers, the seven multi-function consoles, a printer and the video server drawer of a third cabinet (support server). In addition to the local area network star-configuration connections, the central node drawer in each central cabinet is connected to weapons and external equipment through a data-bus called the tactical weapon system highway. This is also connected to the SWIM, which controls weapons launching. Tomahawk targeting is performed by a stand-alone system

ABOVE Operators at ACMS dual-screen multifunction consoles. *(BAE Systems)*

from improvements in command, control and communication functions, ACMS includes the provision of greater information, surveillance, target acquisition and reconnaissance tasks. In addition, the system interfaces with weapons data functions, as well as a normal submarine operations and management functionality. As the boats are required to conduct ever more sophisticated operational tasks, there will be a natural demand for additional functionality and the inclusion of new software applications. ACMS's open architecture and inbuilt spare capacity will enable it to handle future expansion and accommodate demands to process increasing volumes of data. Operators control the combat system from seven multifunction consoles (workstations) situated in the control room and adjacent sound room. Each has two LCDs (one above the other), a keyboard and a mouse. Five

BELOW ACMS schematic. *(Author, from BAE Systems information)*

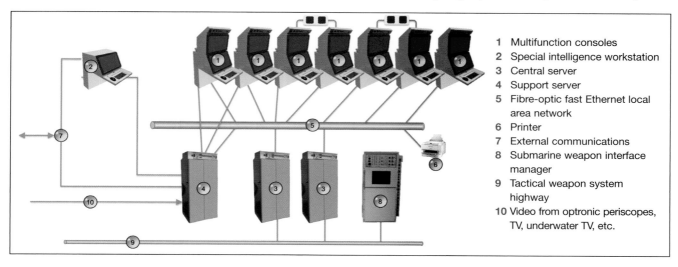

1 Multifunction consoles
2 Special intelligence workstation
3 Central server
4 Support server
5 Fibre-optic fast Ethernet local area network
6 Printer
7 External communications
8 Submarine weapon interface manager
9 Tactical weapon system highway
10 Video from optronic periscopes, TV, underwater TV, etc.

hosting the supplier's 'Tactical Tomahawk Weapon Control System' software.

A video server drawer in the support server houses video-processing cards. The cards take inputs from video sources (such as the electro-optical periscope and underwater TV) and distribute processed video to the combat management system. Its connection to the external communications system allows it to incorporate authorised data from external sources. Video is provided to two consoles by direct links. In addition to its connection to the local area network, the support server is also connected directly to two multifunction consoles: the external communications system and to the special intelligence workstation. This allows over-the-horizon data derived from the special intelligence broadcasts to be inserted into ACMS's tactical database.

While the ACMS software derives from an earlier version, there was a major change in the operating system. The submarine CMS that preceded ACMS used a Microsoft Windows operating system running on PCs. This was one of a family of Windows CMSs that were also fitted to surface ships. ACMS uses a UNIX operating system and SPARC processors – a return to the practice of much earlier submarine CMSs. The reason for the move to the Windows operating system is unclear but may have been for potential savings accruing from using a popular commercial system. The adoption of Windows was particularly contentious among the software developers who saw it as a technically retrograde step. Windows' technical shortcomings were that it was:

■ Proprietary foreign-owned technology that gave rights to Microsoft to examine the ACMS software;
■ Known to have security flaws, making it a target for cyber-attacks;
■ Not modular in structure, making it difficult to test rigorously;
■ Monolithic with redundant general-purpose commercial code (this reduces efficiency and has the potential for unwanted interactions between functions).

The developers warned that Windows could not provide a safe and secure foundation for critical engineering applications. Their opinion was ignored and several senior developers left the company – some not voluntarily.

Throughout the development of Sonar 2076 for *Trafalgar* and *Astute* classes, SPARC hardware and a UNIX operating system were adopted. This meant that the two software-intensive systems (ACMS and Sonar 2076) had common hardware and operating systems, so their integration was much more effective.

Common combat system enclosures

The *Astute* class combat system has a new common design of enclosure (the generic name for consoles, workstations and computer cabinets). Powerful COTS computing hardware is now available and has allowed the growth of sophisticated, software-driven equipment. Advances in miniaturisation have meant that greater computing capacity can be accommodated in enclosures. However, there has been a concomitant increase in the heat generated by the electronics. When the previous cabinets (bespoke equipment called naval equipment practice enclosures) were fitted with the latest processor boards, 20% of the space was left unoccupied in order to dissipate

LEFT Common enclosure cabinets used throughout the combat system.
(Aish Technologies)

heat and maintain their temperature within operating limits.

Within the new common cabinets the electronics cards are mounted horizontally, allowing the cabinets to accommodate three separate cooling circuits – each with its own air/water heat exchanger and fan assembly. Each electronics bay is cooled using an internal blown-air circuit that passes the warm air across an air-to-air heat exchanger. The bays are fully sealed to contain any toxic fumes in the event of a fire. A second blown-air circuit takes the heat away from the external part of the heat exchanger. The new cabinets can readily replace the earlier naval equipment practice cabinets as they have the same envelope, mounting points, connector panels and chilled water connections. The common cabinets contain 95% COTS equipment, so are cheaper than their predecessors. Their ability to dissipate 50% more heat means they can be fully occupied even when populated with electronics boards of much greater computing capacity. Better use of space, combined with more powerful computing, ensures that processing speed and reliability of mission-critical elements are preserved, but fewer cabinets are needed.

Like the common cabinets, the common consoles also incorporate the latest in COTS computing hardware, including quad processing power and a high-speed graphics data-bus to drive 508mm COTS displays. The desk has several versions to suit different human characteristics and layout requirements with adjustable range screen angles, screen heights and desk heights. Each console consists of two ruggedised LCDs, a peripheral component interconnect processor fitted with COTS processor, network and graphics cards. There is also a bespoke audio interface. The console operates as an X-terminal using the LINUX operating system. The console design has successfully passed trials that included shock, vibration and electromagnetic compatibility performance standards.

The common enclosures have a number of innovative features such as the ability to be easily disassembled so they can be passed through hatchways. Reassembly is equally straightforward and can be achieved without compromising safety or electromagnetic compatibility requirements. The electronic boards industry-standard form factors (physical dimensions and interfaces) mean that processing and graphics can be easily updated as technology progresses. However, each part of the enclosure that contains electronic boards is mounted on removable plates to allow new form factors and architectures to be fitted in the future.

The common enclosures are used throughout the combat system; not only on ACMS but also Sonar 2076 Stage 5, Sonar 2076 advanced integrated search and attack sonar suite, external communications system and periscope workstation.

Sonar arrays

It is claimed that the Sonar 2076 suite has 13,000 hydrophones, many times the number in previous RN sonars and probably more than any other submarine sonar. All the signals from the sonar's external arrays are processed and the resulting combined information is passed to the command system. A picture of potential threats and other vessels in the vicinity is then generated and co-ordinated with any other data.

Sonar 2076 passive and active arrays comprise:

(a) *Conformal search and attack bow array* that has hydrophones and transducers arranged in almost vertical staves. These enable it to operate both passively and actively. The hydrophones, for passive detection – the normal

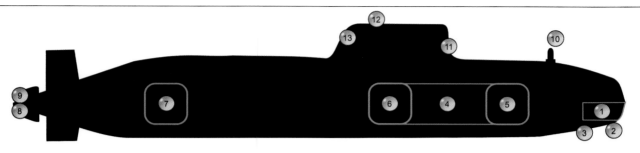

1 Conformal passive and active search and attack bow array
2 Mine detection and obstacle avoidance array
3 Under-hull echo sounder/UHF intercept array
4 Passive flank array (port and starboard)
5 Forward passive ranging patch (port and starboard)
6 Mid passive ranging patch (port and starboard)
7 Aft passive ranging patch (port and starboard)

8 Fully reelable passive towed array (starboard)
9 Clip-on passive towed array (port)
10 Main range intercept sonar
11 Forward fin intercept array and UHF communications array
12 Top intercept array
13 Aft fin intercept array and uhf communications array

mode – populate the staves with the exception of the outboard staves and the bottom two positions of each. In these positions the hydrophones are replaced by transducers that can emit beams to actively interrogate targets.

Modern signal processing has allowed the use of arrays that conform to the hull shape and allow the beam width to vary from the front to the sides of the array.

The array is 12m across and 1.8m high and weighs about 25T. It is accommodated in a forward pumpable free-flood space behind a protective bow dome that has been cast in polyurethane. The dome's surface treatment reduces the effects of radiated acoustic energy generated by turbulent flow as seawater passes over the dome at speed. The dome is transparent to sonar waves when the free-flood space contains seawater.

(b) *Horizontally directed flank arrays* down both sides of the boat comprise large panels in horizontal groups covering about a quarter of the submarine's length. The main (forward) group comprises 20 panels approximately 1m wide and over 5m high – the area of six average billboards. An aft group of four panels is used in conjunction with the forward four panels and the aft four panels of the forward group as ranging patches. These three horizontally

ABOVE Sonar 2076 arrays. *(Author)*

FAR LEFT *Astute* **awaiting the installation of the Sonar 2076 bow array.** *(BAE Systems)*

LEFT Sonar 2076 port flank array. *(Christopher Morgan-Jones)*

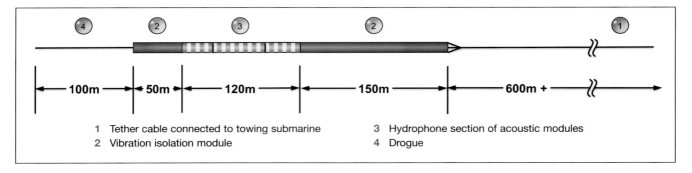

| 4 | 2 | 3 | 2 | 1 |

← 100m → ← 50m → ← 120m → ← 150m → ← 600m + →

1 Tether cable connected to towing submarine
2 Vibration isolation module
3 Hydrophone section of acoustic modules
4 Drogue

directed passive ranging patches form a long baseline and signals from these are used to determine the distance to the target (its range). All panels are composed of a piezoelectric polymer membrane, beneath a protective composite covering. The flank array is the largest acoustic sensor fitted to any submarine. Its large physical area gives it high bearing resolution and discrimination allows it to detect long-range quiet targets. Adaptive beam-forming is used to reject own-boat acoustic energy and flow acoustic energy over the array face. It can thus be used at over 28km/h (15kts) when the alternative towed-array sensors are less effective and may be constrained by the boat's manoeuvres.

(c) *Fully reelable passive towed array* – A towed-array is a line of hydrophones, contained in a flexible plastic tube, which is towed behind the submarine with its associated cables and other elements. With a fully reelable arrangement, the towed array is stored on a winch within the aft free-flood space. It offers improved operability compared with clip-on arrays, especially in shallow water and in transit. Within a few minutes the array can be automatically deployed from the winch. It is streamed through a feed pipe (supported on an A-frame above the outer hull) to ensure that it is clear of the propulsor. The towed array handling system allows the array to be smoothly and quietly deployed, positioned and recovered (involving rewinding on to the winch). The latest handling system uses a water-flushing system to provide the impetus for initial deployment of the array. As there are no mechanical systems that can damage the expensive towed arrays, the array life is extended compared with the earlier systems with capstans, cable traction or linear transfer mechanisms. Although deployment of the initial portion of the array by flushing is rather slow, when about 70–100m of array has been payed out, the array generates sufficient drag to rapidly pull out its remainder. Unfortunately, the small diameter of the winch puts a great deal of strain on the towed-array elements. This problem would be alleviated if a thinner array were used. The continued immersion of winches on *Trafalgar* class boats and maintenance difficulties reduced the reliability of the winches but an improved design is fitted to *Astute* class boats.

The length of the towed array is typically over 100m, giving it a sonar aperture greater

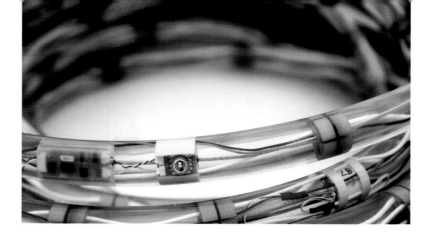

than the length of the boat. The towing cable is about 50mm in diameter and at least 600m long, so that the array streams in a straight line. It also ensures that the array is a long way from the boat's own acoustic energy sources; for instance, its machinery. A drogue at the end of the towed array helps straighten it. At either end of the hydrophone section is a vibration-isolating module to isolate the hydrophones from any vibration set up in the towing cable or drogue as they pass through the water.

The long array can detect, passively, acoustic signals at very low frequency. Sound propagation conditions at these frequencies and its isolation from acoustic energy interference enables the array to have a very long range. The signals from the hydrophone array section are passed up the tow cable where advanced adaptive beam-forming processing achieves high accuracy and discrimination in target bearing. Combined with data from other Sonar 2076 arrays, accurate information can be generated about the movement of the targets (target motion analysis).

While helping obtain accurate sonar information, the use of a towed array is not without its operational drawbacks. Streaming a towed array totalling over 1km requires skilled seamanship, especially as the array only provides reliable data if it is straight. Submarine turn rates are restricted and the array takes time to settle and become straight after a manoeuvre. Best results are obtained at low speed when there is enough motion to keep the array straight but not sufficient for flow over it to produce acoustic interference. Above about 20km/h performance deteriorates, although the towed array can remain streamed at higher speeds.

As a backup to the reelable towed array, a clip-on towed array is also carried and stored in a trough on the casing. It can be streamed at sea but, once deployed, it hampers manoeuvrability until it can be recovered; this normally requires the assistance of an auxiliary vessel.

ABOVE Array sonar elements for a thin-line towed-array. *(Systems Engineering & Assessments Ltd)*

> **JACKSPEAK**
>
> Clip-off towed array. In his book, *Secrets of the Conqueror*, Stuart Prebble describes an audacious mission of the SSN, HMS *Conqueror*. In the 1980s she was fitted with special pincers. With great skill her CO was able to covertly clip off and secure the whole of a Soviet towed array that was streamed from a spy trawler. No doubt the array provided invaluable intelligence for the West.

(d) *Intercept array* is a broadband multi-octave passive array with bearing and azimuth coverage through 360°. It provides warning of the presence of diverse targets. It has hydrophones that cover HF, MF and LF acoustic frequency bands (see Appendix 1). It detects signals emanating from surface vessels, submarines, dipping sonars, sonobuoys and

Characteristics of typical fully reelable towed array	
Bandwidth	100–1600Hz
Operational speed	7–22km/h (4–12kts)
Survival speed	46km/h (25kts)
Time for deployment/recovery	10 minutes maximum
Submarine turn rate	1.5°/sec maximum
Acoustic section diameter	90mm approx. (fat array) 50mm approx. (new thin arrays)
Acoustic section length	120m approx.
Tow cable diameter	50mm approx.
Bearing coverage	360° instrumented

ABOVE Intercept array dome on HMS *Astute*.
(Analox)

torpedoes. Mounted on the forward section of the casing it stands on a plinth beneath a free-flooding carbon fibre dome. The array (Hull Outfit 51R) derives from that used on the preceding Sonar 2019. The array comprises a replaceable array unit with several HF transducers arranged in a horizontal circle. Above these is mounted a compact array, replaceable as a unit, comprising a similar horizontal ring of smaller LF hydrophones. UHF intercept arrays mounted on the fin and on the keel beneath the launch-tubes complement the intercept array.

(e) *Fin arrays* mounted behind acoustic windows high within the leading and trailing edges of the fin are passive/active underwater communications arrays. They are cylindrical with the forward array being larger in height

BELOW Schematic of generic intercept array.
(Author)

1 Antennas feeding Ttuners in base
2 Higher frequency antenna array and base support
3 Medium frequency antenna array and base support
4 Lower frequency antenna array and base support
5 Signals from each antenna array
6 Evaluation unit (compares signals from antennas in each array)
7 Heading information from boat's navigation system
8 Signal information and direction output to command system

and diameter; both have 24 staves each with a vertical array of 8 transducers. These are available for active underwater communication with gateway buoys such as deep siren tactical paging buoys.

(f) Two *transducer arrays for deep-water echo-sounder.* The dual-frequency, dual-beam echo-sounders are completely switchable by means of two intelligent switch-boxes. One transducer is used for downward sounding while the other, facing upwards, detects the underside of sea-ice. They operate at both frequencies simultaneously with a beam width of 8° at 210kHz and of 22° at 33kHz. The unique 210kHz 19-element configuration reduces side-lobe levels and forms an excellent beam shape in both wide and narrow modes. The narrow beam width helps prevent hostile forces detecting its active transmissions. The high-precision echo-sounder can measure depth down to 10,000m. A bi-directional serial interface provides water-depth and echo-strength measurements to the CMS.

(g) A *mine detection and obstacle avoidance array* is mounted forward, beneath the conformal bow array. It can be used both actively and passively. Generally this type of sonar operates actively at LF (about 30kHz) and HF (70 kHz) to detect mines about 1km ahead. However, as a passive sonar, it can detect acoustic signals over a much wider frequency range and provide intercept data for stationary and moving objects (such as SSKs) at about three times this range. It provides short-range detection of very quiet submarines and can warn of collisions. As the sonar's beam looks forward and slightly downward, it can be used to assist navigation in shallow, confined or treacherous waters by providing bottom-mapping and a real-time visualisation of the seabed in 3-D.

The sonar's low probability of intercept waveforms ensure that other boats have a minimal chance of detecting the signal without prior knowledge of the presence of such a signal. Covertness is achieved by avoiding physical interception but, if they are intercepted, the signal appears random. Properties of the waveforms include low power, wide bandwidth, frequency agility and other stealth techniques.

(h) A main underwater telephone operates at the standard carrier frequency of 8.08kHz with transmit and receive at 10kHz. A separate Sonar 2073 emergency underwater telephone arrays are part of a multi-frequency, multi-mode system for emergency through-water communications operating at 10kHz and 37.5kHz. If the submarine is in distress, its acoustic homing beacons help rescuers locate the boat from over 7km away. It also supports secure two-way voice communications at 10kHz, 27kHz and 43kHz. Inboard equipment is located in the forward and aft escape compartments. The system's continuous endurance is 12 hours transmitting and 32 hours receiving.

Sonar array improvements

The installation of the bow array of the fourth boat, *Audacious*, was achieved in a fraction of the time of those fitted to the first three boats. On the earlier boats, hundreds of hydrophones and transducers had to be individually assembled to create the bow array and were wired using many hundreds of cables. A new modular approach embedded all the array components into eleven composite material panels that, thanks to digital techniques, could now be connected by only 34 cables. The massive reduction of cabling cuts down the complexity of setting the array to work, reducing the amount of cable checking and avoiding rework. The success of this installation technique has been achieved with no effect on performance but with an additional benefit of a 30% weight saving. The change is not visible from outside the boat because the bow dome covers the panels.

It was reported in early 2011 that HMS *Tireless* had just completed the test and trials of the new flank array using polyvinylidene difluoride technology. The new installation aimed to establish the suitability and viability of the technology for the Sonar 2076 suite. The existing flank array was heavy, expensive and costly to install. On HMS *Audacious* a new thin flank array was fitted, while the earlier boats will be back-fitted with these arrays. The improved acoustic materials have a depth of less than 70mm, which affords a significant reduction in the weight of the

array without sacrificing performance. The panels are not only much easier to install but, when subjected to the pressure at DDD, they compress less than the earlier panels.

The UK is also exploring thin-line towed-array solutions for the Sonar 2076 integrated suite. Use of lightweight thin-line technology offers improved handling and a more compact winch installation that, in turn, allows the deployment of longer arrays. Lightweight thin-line towed arrays are ideally suited to operations in restricted shallow waters.

Sonar 2076 Stage 4 equipment (boats 1–3)

The range of passive and active arrays mentioned above are fully incorporated and integrated into the federated submarine Sonar 2076 sonar suite that provides sensors for the boat's search and attack capability. The suite passes signals to the submarine's CMS to enable the command team to access comprehensive situational awareness information.

Development of Sonar 2076 began in 1994 and has progressed through stages from a series of stand-alone sonars to a fully integrated system that incorporated new arrays. The five stages represented waypoints on the sonar's planned evolutionary path.

The first three *Astute* class boats were initially fitted with Sonar 2076 Stage 4 that entered service in 2003 on HMS *Trenchant*. This stage included large flank arrays on the side of the hull that increased sensitivity and passive-ranging capability. Rather than having operators and processors dedicated to specific sonar frequency bands and arrays, Stage 4 was highly integrated. However, the display system was based on technology and experience of at least a decade earlier that made it difficult to exploit all the information generated. This problem was addressed with the next, Stage 5, update.

With any sonar, signals from the various arrays pass through a number of processes to develop the below-water picture and allow the situation to be comprehended. First, the signals are amplified within a receiver before passing to a beam-former. The beam-former essentially combines the signals in a number of ways to determine the direction of the source of the signals; this requires a large number of computations and can only be performed by a powerful bank of computers. The data then undergoes signal and data processing before it is ready to be sent to the operators' terminals. The computing for these processes is carried out in the sonar cabinet space forward of the command deck using dedicated proprietary hardware based upon high-performance SHARC digital signal processor arrays with more than 2,000 processors (equivalent of that of 60,000 PCs). The system uses specialist operating systems and a proprietary fibre-distributed data interface network.

The sonar terminals in the sound room – the forward part of the command deck – convert the data into graphical forms and merge signals from the multiple arrays into a single picture. The sonar operators are presented with the information on display consoles that, as part of the drive to converge on a uniform console design within submarines, have many design elements in common with other combat system consoles. Inboard equipment was housed in seven naval equipment practice processing cabinets.

Sonar 2076 Stage 5 inboard replacement (Stage 5 IR)

Having provided the boats with a comprehensive system of sonar arrays, the latest in a series of developments of Sonar 2076 was to improve the capability, efficiency and through-life cost of the system. Stage 5 IR succeeded in these aims through improvements to the electronics systems on board, achieved by the insertion of new hardware, software functionality and new algorithms. It allows the data gathered to be effectively processed as well as making the sonar more adaptable to changing mission requirements. Stage 5 is the build-fit for *Audacious* onward and will be retro-fitted to earlier boats.

In 2006 the Stage 5 IR began development to provide, initially, three sets for: the Shore Integration Facility at the SSISC; an industrial reference set; and a full boat fit. Harbour and sea trials, comprising a retrofit of inboard equipment, were completed on HMS *Talent* in 2010. The USN's Acoustics-Rapid COTS Insertion programme was included to introduce software processing and data management to impart existing hardware with improved operational effectiveness.

The first boat fitted with Stage 5, HMS *Trenchant*, re-entered operational service in 2011.

Stage 5 incorporates a modular open systems architecture for software and hardware and is based on a hierarchical structure of seven specified layers. Rigorous procedures ensure that the interfaces between modules are consistent, coherent and complete, and that there are common standards for interactions between the layers. This ensures that there is well-defined cohesion within the elements of the overall Sonar 2076, while allowing for a high degree of flexibility. The advantage is that the hardware solution can readily change to adapt to advances in technology and overcome obsolescence by the use of COTS equipment. The progressive replacement of legacy processing architecture with COTS products will enable the future insertion of new software functionality, new processing and new data management over a further 30 years.

The use of a modular open systems architecture also has the benefit of a high degree of commonality across all the submarines in the fleet. In the past the *Vanguard*, *Trafalgar* and *Astute* classes have had different array fits and have had bespoke software. Even among the same class the progressive introduction of improvements have militated against commonality. The Stage 5 architecture will promote common

design patterns and interfaces. The subsequent greater commonality will have attendant logistics, repair and training advantages.

Thanks to improvements in notebook-computer technology, the use of COTS computing was practical, enabling Stage 5 to introduce significant enhancements in processing power and reduced space. Its new embedded computer boards using 200 Intel Core Duo computer chips require less power and less cooling than earlier proprietary ones. Stage 5 adopted the same common cabinets as ACMS. The improved heat management and powerful processors reduced the seven Stage 4 cabinets to six. In total the system houses 15Gb of real-time data and runs 10 million lines of code over an Ethernet 10Gbps network. Approximately 400 open-architecture application modules with in excess of 1,500 open interfaces allow the software to process about 100 sonar functional chains.

Stage 5 has an improved interface for the operators and supports 29 human–computer interface roles that give operators the flexibility to combine complex acoustic energy patterns from different arrays in various ways. The operator can use the on-screen dashboard to select relevant information, reduce clutter and build up the signal. During development, the interface was refined through the use of eye-tracking and motion sensors.

The *Astute* class has also seen changes to other elements of the combat system that are not directly associated with Sonar 2076, such as a new tactical weapon system highway (that incorporates an on-board centralised data recording system to log all mission and system data on the highway) and an upgrade to the rationalised internal communications equipment – RICE 10. This is the latest incarnation of a range of equipment used as an internal voice telephone communication system. Built around a distributed switch network and audio-user terminals, it provides all internal communications (intercom, alarms, sound-powered telephones and wireless communications). It is also used for broadcasts to keep the crew informed of any emergency or messages of general interest. In harbour, there is a link to the shore exchange to provide telephone communication.

Tactical Environmental Data Acquisition System (TEDAS)

TEDAS (Sonar 2115) is an oceanographic sensor system that provides detailed ocean environmental data such as the temperature of the ocean from the surface to the depths. This enhances the boat's situational awareness and provides valuable data to the Sonar 2076 system in determining the paths of sonar waves. The robust, high-precision sensors incorporate novel built-in test technologies to extend calibration intervals and decrease maintenance costs. The system combines the outboard oceanographic sensors, expendable bathythermograph system and acoustic modelling tools.

Non-hull-penetrating electro-optical periscope CM010

Since the first submarine was accepted into service over a century ago, the primary above-water sensor for both tactical data-gathering and safety has been traditional direct-view optical periscopes. These use a complex optical system that relies on two small prisms at each end of a vertical tube to direct light from the surface to an eyepiece at the bottom. The predecessors of HMS *Astute* were supplied with both a 250mm-diameter search periscope and a 75mm-diameter attack periscope. These allowed the command-deck staff to view the surface situation without the boat surfacing – provided it was just below the surface at periscope depth. When the boat was dived, the optical periscope was stowed in a deep well. As the boat approached the surface the periscope was raised so that the commanding officer could visually assess the situation. He could rotate the periscope to gain a 360° view of surface ships nearby. Red lighting was used at night in the control room in order to maintain the night vision of those using the periscope. Submarines were particularly vulnerable to detection when a periscope was raised. Although the probability of detection

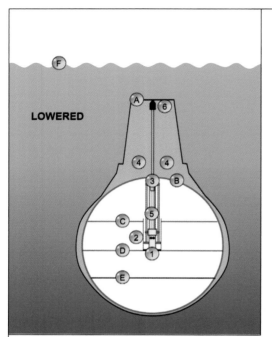

1	Stool and buffer	**5**	Circular steel mast	**C**	Command deck
2	Mast well	**6**	Optical head	**D**	Number 2 deck
3	Hull insert	**A**	Top of fin	**E**	Number 3 deck
4	Two hydraulic lifting rams	**B**	Top of pressure hull	**F**	Sea's surface

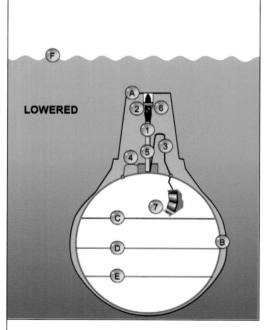
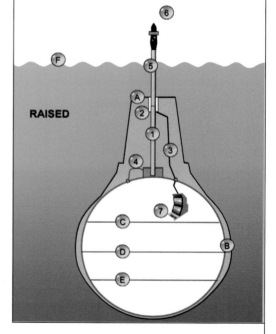

1	Double-acting hydraulic cylinder	**5**	GRP fairing	**C**	Command deck
2	Fin bearing	**6**	Electro-optical sensor	**D**	Number 2 deck
3	Electrical and data cables	**7**	Periscope console	**E**	Number 3 deck
4	Hydraulic pipes	**A**	Top of fin	**F**	Sea's surface
		B	Pressure hull		

can be reduced if the periscope is above the surface for short periods, this conflicts with the need to provide sufficient time to assess the situation and make appropriate decisions. The reliability of the direct-view periscopes was vital as, without it, the submarine was blind.

The holes in the hull for the direct-view optical periscopes were always a potential structural weak-point because of their size. Furthermore, maintaining a watertight seal that allows the periscope to be easily raised, lowered and rotated is also difficult, especially as it must be able to withstand the pressure at DDD. In addition, the position of the control room and the well for the periscopes are predicated by the periscope's location. The electro-optical periscope requires only small hull penetrations for service supplies: a hydraulic connection for the mast-raising equipment, a data connection for the image data and an electrical supply for the sensor head unit (SHU) electronics and the azimuth drive module that rotates the unit.

The *Astute* class boats are fitted with a completely new type of sensor – two almost identical electro-optical periscopes. Each has an advanced CM010 above-water electro-optical (optronic) sensor system that has significantly greater capabilities than optical periscopes. The electro-optical periscopes, like the direct-view periscopes, are highly reliable but the ability to fit two almost identical masts provides additional redundancy in the unlikely event of failure of one mast.

The electro-optical periscopes use modern electronic technology to capture images and display them on a control room console. The masts do not penetrate the hull. The top of the mast is a SHU and, when dived, the whole periscope is housed within the fin beneath a protective shutter. Close to periscope depth the shutter can be opened; the mast can be raised hydraulically by about 6m giving the SHU a good view while the boat remains below the surface. The SHU can rapidly perform a 360° scan of the surface; blur-free imagery at high-speed is ensured by a high-performance three-axis stabilisation system, after which it can be lowered. Unworried about the risk of detection, the boat's command can give due attention to analysing the high-quality images in detail and have adequate time for decisions.

LEFT **Single electro-optical periscope raised on HMS *Astute*.** *(Crown Copyright/ WO(Phot) Ian Arthur)*

Other members of the command team can also, where time is not critical, perform a more detailed evaluation.

The SHU is a pressure proof, electro-optical assembly that contains a true high-definition colour TV camera, an image intensifier (or a high-performance 3–5μm thermal camera), environmental sensors, an electronic support measures antenna (covering both radar and communications frequencies), a laser rangefinder and a GPS antenna. A single window provides a common line of sight for both TV and thermal imaging. The two periscopes not only provide resilience but also extend the capabilities as one provides infrared images and the other low-light images. The SHU is designed to withstand a nearby explosion and to function in temperatures ranging from -15°C to more than 60°C. The head has a reduced radar signature and a special fairing on the water-cutting section that gives a better wake and plume performance than even a traditional direct-view small attack periscope.

A difficulty with the earlier direct-view periscope was that, in rough weather, the boat's motion prevented a clear image from

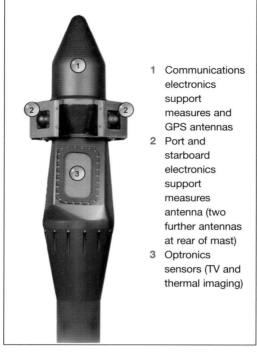

1 Communications electronics support measures and GPS antennas
2 Port and starboard electronics support measures antenna (two further antennas at rear of mast)
3 Optronics sensors (TV and thermal imaging)

being seen. Clear images are critical to mission success, so, with the electro-optical periscope, all images are stabilised in three axes to compensate for the effects of the boat's movement. The stabilisation is complicated by the motion of the sensors' azimuth drive that rotates them about the mast centreline – often at high speed. Consequently, the deterministic, high-standard servo-controlled stabilisation system is linked to the azimuth drive.

Within the submarine's control room there is a dedicated dual-screen periscope workstation and three main electronic units:

- The optronic processing unit that undertakes video capture, manipulation and storage for presentation on the workstation;
- The power supply unit that converts and controls boat's power for the SHU;
- The mast control unit that co-ordinates mast activity, communicates with the submarine's tactical, data and combat systems, as well as controlling and monitoring the built-in test equipment.

The workstation's two high-resolution screens allow both general viewing and periscope with operation simultaneously. On both screens the sensor image is displayed above a data bar. On the upper screen the bar displays sensor image and mast data, while on the lower screen sensor image, orientation and control data is shown. A bearing strip, an artificial horizon and cross-hairs are overlaid on to the image of both screens. An LCD alongside the screens shows sensor selection, magnification and status.

The operator's primary control is a rigidly mounted control stick but a combination of keys and on-screen buttons also control a wide variety of tasks. The operator can use the control stick to rapidly slew the mast to any point and adjust its height. To reduce activation times, functions that are frequently used are assigned specific hard keys. On-screen buttons on the lower screen's data bar control more complex operations including:

- Selecting the sensor to be displayed (high-definition colour TV or thermal imager);
- Selecting the magnification (low, high or extra-high);
- Moving the line of sight in azimuth and elevation;
- Initiating a programmable mode.

The programmable modes provide functionality significantly more advanced than a direct-view periscope. Even with the mast fully lowered the operator can select a mode to carry out the predefined set of operations automatically. There are three main modes whose parameters can be pre-selected:

- In *quick look round* mode, the mast raises and starts to spin at high speed over a pre-

defined arc. The images are digitally captured and stored. The stabilisation and special step-stare techniques ensure a rock-steady full-resolution image even in the roughest sea. A 360° sweep of the horizon takes only a few seconds of periscope exposure. The high-definition colour TV and thermal images are aligned in magnification and position to allow direct comparisons.

- The *snap shot* mode is similar to quick look round but a sequence of individual frames are captured.
- Whereas both quick look round and snap shot modes minimise the mast exposure, in non-threat environments *continuous-view* mode can be employed. This scans automatically over a series of azimuth and elevation arcs with magnification and rotation changing as appropriate.

The operator can select images to be digitally recorded and those to be immediately printed in high-resolution colour. A stadiometric system can be used to measure the angle subtended by objects on detected ships. A database of the dimensions of such objects gives fast and accurate ranging.

The electro-optical periscope is a mission-critical application and its software runs on an Ada operating system in order to provide the essential reliability. The application controls the stabilisation system, video, the thermal and high-definition colour TV cameras, as well as all of the mechanisms and motors in the SHU. It also manages communication between the SHU and the in-hull systems.

The original digital signal processor has been replaced by a general-purpose platform (a quad PowerPC 7410 AltiVec board) in a significant step towards a standard, open-architecture approach. This will have the advantage of increasing the efficiency of future upgrades, particularly in allowing the developer to use a common toolset and software architecture across projects wherever possible.

On HMS *Astute*'s first deployment, the electro-optical periscope proved particularly effective in the dark, enabling her to perform complex manoeuvres even in the dead of night.

Radar Electronic Support Measures (RESM)

The RESM specified for the first batch of three *Astute*-class submarines was Outfit UAP(4). This was based on versions of the UAP family of RESMs fitted to earlier submarines. Four UAP(4) antennas are mounted on each periscope alongside the electro-optical sensors and below a communications electronic support measures (CESM) antenna in order that all the key sensors can be deployed while exposing only a single mast. RESM fulfils the four principal functions of self-protection, surveillance, data gathering and over-the-horizon targeting. Importantly, at periscope depth it provides the command with a warning of potential threats by sensing radar transmissions that could detect the submarine's masts (such as radars used by ships and aircraft). Its output indicates power of received emission, approximate bearing and, by comparing the characteristics with a database of known radars, a classification of the threat. High-accuracy direction finding for targeting over-the-horizon is undertaken using the separate antennas on the AZE mast rather than the RESM.

UAP(4) covers the electromagnetic frequency bands from 1 to 40GHz with omnidirectional coverage and automatic warning of threat radars. Direction-finding capability covers the I- and J-bands and its four ports provide an accuracy of at least 5°. A frequency extension capability has been applied to cater for current-generation requirements. While still operationally effective, UAP(4) suffered from increasing component obsolescence. An upgraded version, designated outfit UAA4, introduces COTS components so reduces through-life costs while enhancing performance. In addition, the inboard architecture embraces advances made for the equivalent surface ship RESM equipment, Outfit UAT(16).

UAA4 was first fitted to *Vanguard* class boats and features new signal processing and emitter identification technology. The pulse train of detected radars is analysed by a Minerva de-interleaver with an error rate significantly lower than earlier versions. Minerva uses the vast computing power of a neural net of 1,000 parallel processors to test a large number of ways of associating the pulses before selecting the most appropriate one. This technique gives a high detection rate and great fidelity. By comparing these characteristics to those in its database, the system can distinguish the radar type, so determining if it is likely to be a hostile or friendly asset. The inboard hardware was reduced to a single cabinet with two main cardframes; one for the receivers and the other for processing.

Communications Electronic Support Measures (CESM)

The small CESM antennas mounted on top of the periscopes complement the new CESM/RESM capability on the Type AZE Eddystone mast that is included as the baseline fit for *Audacious* onwards as part of the *Astute* Capability Sustainment Programme. It senses electromagnetic signals in three groups from HF to radar D-band.

Eddystone is a fully integrated RESM and CESM system combining intelligence gathering with threat warning that supports targeting with accurate bearings. It uses its integrated submarine communications receiving system, communications acquisition system and direction finding system to detect and analyse the communications groups as well as many other types of signal, including those from mobile networks and low probability of intercept signals. Eddystone is based on COTS technology and hosted on a modular, scalable open architecture, enabling regular technology insertion and capability upgrades. The software incorporates advances in computing, digitisation, data movement and signal capture that both enhances operator efficiency and system automation.

Underwater communications

Radio communication with a submerged submarine has always been a technical challenge as electromagnetic waves are highly attenuated by seawater. Generally communication is receive-only, as any attempt to respond has the danger of disclosing the submarine's precise location. When surfaced (or at periscope depth) submarines can transmit using Satcom. The extremely high data rates at Satcom frequencies allow complex transmissions to be sent in a brief burst. In addition, Satcom's highly directional antenna produces a beam that is difficult to

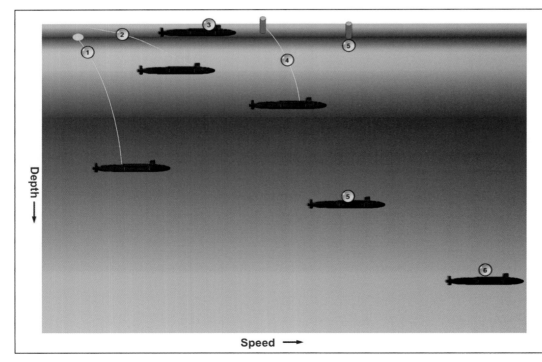

1 Towed communications buoy (VLF)*
2 High-speed buoyant cable antenna (VLF)*
3 Mast-mounted antennas at periscope depth (VLF/HF/UHF/EHF)
4 Tethered expendable communications buoy (VHF/UHF)
5 Expendable communications buoy (VHF/UHF)
6 Deep antenna (ELF)
* Suitable for use under ice

intercept. The use of expendable buoys and gateway buoys also disguise the position of submarine transmissions.

Communication with a nuclear submarine that remains submerged for very long periods is challenging because electromagnetic waves only penetrate seawater to a depth of a few wavelengths. The longest wavelengths, penetrating to a depth of over 150m, are those of ELF, reception of which requires long antennas. A tethered buoyant wire antenna streamed from the upper aft part of the fin is used for ELF reception. ELF signals have a very low data rate, so take minutes to transmit a few characters. Their use, however, is to transmit launch codes to SSBNs travelling at depth and speed and to alert SSNs to the need to come closer to the surface to use higher data-rate communications systems.

SSNs can receive VLF transmissions while submerged but have to sacrifice depth and speed for the ability to benefit from these higher data-rate signals. When a boat is near the surface, the tethered buoyant wire antenna, floating close to the surface, can receive the VLF signals. The alternative, a towed buoy, can be deployed from greater depth as the buoys' hydrodynamic form forces it up towards the surface to depths similar to the buoyant wire antenna. However, the resistance of the buoy, which puts inordinate strain on the towing cable when being towed fast, restricts the submarine's speed. Both the wire antenna and towed buoys can operate under ice.

To operate covertly, submarines cannot transmit electromagnetic signals without betraying their position. Sending signals using expendable communications buoys avoids detection. A buoy, with the message preloaded on board, is launched using the submerged signal and decoy ejector (SSDE) and, having floated to the surface, transmits the message once the submarine has had time to clear the area. Having sent its message, the buoy scuttles.

These traditional forms of communication have their shortcomings in modern operations that not only require submarines to work in concert with surface forces (and even friendly submarines) but also to operate at depth and speed. Recent developments linking above-water electromagnetic communications with underwater acoustic communications are showing promise and will change not only submarine communications techniques but also submarine operational tactics.

Deep Siren Tactical Paging (DSTP) communication system

The DSTP system provides long-range submarine communications using expendable gateway buoys to link underwater acoustic communications with a constellation of communication satellites that have worldwide coverage, such as Iridium low earth-orbiting satellites. This system is generically known as acoustic to radio frequency (A2RF) communications.

DSTP was developed as part of the US Communications at Speed and Depth programme that led to buoys that can be deployed by surface ships, aircraft and submarines. The submarines require acoustic transducer arrays such as those on HMS Astute's fin. Signals from headquarters, surface ships or aircraft are sent to the satellite and thence to the buoy. The buoy then emits low-frequency acoustic transmissions that can be detected by submerged submarines up to 350km away, even if it is at depth. Such paging (one-way) signals can be used to alert submarines to evolving situations, changes to rules of engagement and to request the establishment of two-way communications.

If the submarine's operational profile allows it to transmit low-frequency acoustic signals, then it may respond with a similar acoustic transmission. The buoy forwards the transmission to the satellite in order to establish direct connectivity with headquarters and own forces while remaining stealthy. Messages to and from the submarine are encoded prior to transmission and decoded upon receipt so are difficult to usurp. They also have a high resistance to interference from jamming. The system is capable of operation in a wide range of acoustic environments and, because it has high tolerance to Doppler effects, it can be used to communicate with submarines

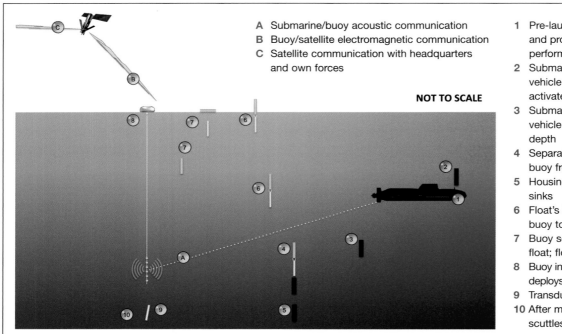

A Submarine/buoy acoustic communication
B Buoy/satellite electromagnetic communication
C Satellite communication with headquarters and own forces

NOT TO SCALE

1 Pre-launch checks and programming performed
2 Submarine launch vehicle released and activated
3 Submarine launch vehicle descends to depth
4 Separation of float and buoy from housing
5 Housing scuttles and sinks
6 Float's buoyancy takes buoy to sea's surface
7 Buoy separates from float; float sinks
8 Buoy inflates and deploys transducer array
9 Transducer casing sinks
10 After mission, buoy scuttles and sinks

ABOVE Deployment of DSTP expendable buoy from a submarine. *(Author, using Raytheon/Ultra Electronics information)*

travelling at speed. Because the two-way transmission is almost in real time, it allows adaptive underwater battlespace management, co-operative anti-submarine warfare and closer support to Special Forces.

The submarine-launched version of DSTP is based on the A-size sonobuoy container encased with a float within a submarine launch vehicle.

Before DSTP is deployed from a submarine it undergoes pre-launch checks and programming. When the submarine launch vehicle is ejected from the SSDE a release sequence is activated during which the vehicle descends to depth while the submarine begins to leave the launch area. When DSTP has reached its pre-programmed depth, the submarine launch vehicle releases the float and buoy. The empty submarine launch vehicle casing sinks to the bottom while the float delivers the buoy to the surface. At the surface the buoy inflates and separates from the float that brought it to the surface (which then sinks). After a pre-programmed delay that permits the submarine to move well away from the buoy's position, the buoy's array of transducers is lowered beneath it. The buoy then establishes a radio link to the satellite while its array begins acoustic transmissions to the submarine. Any acoustic signals received from the boat are relayed to the satellite for onward transmission.

DSTP can operate for up to 72 hours, after which it scuttles.

In 2009 an evaluation took place on *Trafalgar* class submarines.

Characteristics of submarine-launched Deep Siren buoy		
	Submarine launch vehicle	Buoy system alone (A-size)
Diameter	214mm	124mm
Length	1,006mm	914mm
Weight	28kg	14kg
Depth capability	240m	
Payload	Active acoustic transmit array GPS positioning	
Acoustic communication	Low-frequency acoustic spectrum	
Satellite communications	Iridium Commercial Constellation	
Modes	Paging and active anti-submarine warfare	
On-station time	72 hours (on lithium batteries)	

The US Communications at Speed and Depth programme also developed two new tethered buoys that could be towed at speed from a deep-dived submarine. The tow was long so as not to betray the boat's exact position when transmitting to a satellite.

Naval Extremely/Super High-Frequency (Satcom) Terminal (NEST)

As part of the *Astute* Capability Sustainment Programme, *Audacious* will be launched with NEST, a new antenna to provide wide-bandwidth survivable Satcom. NEST provides dual-band terminals, able to operate at super high-frequency (SHF) communications (uplink and downlink) using British Skynet 5 satellites. They can also use extremely high-frequency (EHF) uplink/SHF downlink using the American Advanced EHF satellite constellation. Skynet 5 satellites use transparent transponders, often referred to as a 'bent pipe', because the signal from and to the earth terminals is simply amplified and retransmitted.

Weapons Handling and Launch System (WHLS)

The WHLS is a major mechanical system designed to perform the complex tasks associated with the safe embarkation and disembarkation of weapons as well as the safe loading and unloading of the weapon launch-tubes. It ensures that the weapons can be safely stowed and protects them from submarine movement and shock. Within the confined space of the weapons stowage compartment it can reposition stowed weapons. It handles a mixture of torpedoes and missiles. If necessary it could also accommodate mines designed for submarine launch-tubes, but the UK no longer holds war-stock mines. Until recently the Stonefish mine was manufactured in the UK and was supplied to foreign navies for their submarines, but the mine is no longer in production.

The WHLS uses a modular approach to provide the highest packing density of tube-launched weapons, enabling HMS *Astute* to carry 32 weapons within its weapons stowage compartment. The weapons are stowed in three-tier-high racks either side of a central access space. Semi-automated operation reduces both the manpower required and time to handle the weapons when compared with earlier systems. If the boat went to sea with weapons in all the tubes, then a total of 38 weapons could be

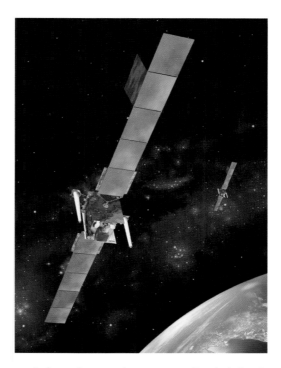

carried – an increase in weapon outload of about 50% compared with previous SSNs.

Weapons are embarked when the submarine is alongside using a temporary handling platform attached to the forward part of the deck. Each weapon in turn is attached to a temporary rail system that is rigged from the deck to the hatch. Once the weapon is struck

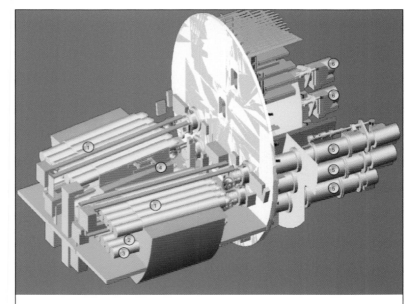

1	Top storage tier (Tier 1)	4	Centre-line lift
2	Middle storage tier (Tier 2)	5	Starboard launch-tubes
3	Lower storage tier (Tier 3)	6	Port launch-tubes

ABOVE **A weapon being loaded into submarine.** *(BAE Systems)*

JACKSPEAK

The weapons stowage compartment is known as 'the bombshop'.

down through the weapons embarkation hatch, it transfers to a permanent rail fitted within the boat. This rail is at about 30° to the horizontal as it enters the boat, but swings to a horizontal orientation once the weapon reaches the central passageway within the weapons stowage compartment. The weapon can then be hydraulically traversed inboard or outboard on to an adjacent rack or moved up or down between tiers using a lift on the centreline.

RIGHT **Sequence of embarking weapon using the weapons handling and launch system.** *(Author, from Babcock International Group information)*

BELOW **Artist's impression of weapons stowage compartment.** *(BAE Systems)*

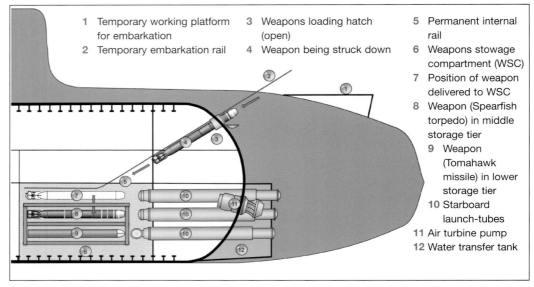

1   Temporary working platform for embarkation
2   Temporary embarkation rail
3   Weapons loading hatch (open)
4   Weapon being struck down
5   Permanent internal rail
6   Weapons stowage compartment (WSC)
7   Position of weapon delivered to WSC
8   Weapon (Spearfish torpedo) in middle storage tier
9   Weapon (Tomahawk missile) in lower storage tier
10 Starboard launch-tubes
11 Air turbine pump
12 Water transfer tank

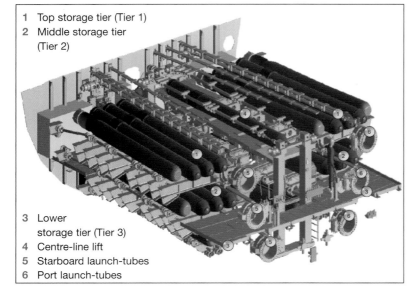

1   Top storage tier (Tier 1)
2   Middle storage tier (Tier 2)

3   Lower storage tier (Tier 3)
4   Centre-line lift
5   Starboard launch-tubes
6   Port launch-tubes

BELOW **X-mount shock-protection fitting.** *(Stop-Choc)*

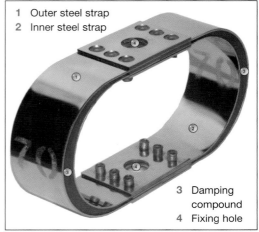

1   Outer steel strap
2   Inner steel strap

3   Damping compound
4   Fixing hole

LEFT **Weapon being prepared in the 'bombshop'.** *(Babcock International Group)*

Weapons stored in each tier are protected from the effects of underwater explosions by flexible shock-absorbing X-mounts. These provide adaptable protection according to the number of weapons stored on each stowage tier, which increases safety and improves the ability of the weapons to function following a shock event.

Very tight tolerances are required especially when loading weapons into the launch-tubes. The system compensates for any misalignments caused by compression of the hull, flexing of the deck and varying weapon load weights on the stowage racks. Vertical alignment is measured optically and presented to the operator at a central control position to ensure that, once the weapon is readied, it can smoothly be slid into the launch-tube.

The launch-tubes external diameter is nearly 1m in diameter and each weighs 3T. The entire main tube section is manufactured from a single forging to provide material integrity. Each launch-tube has an inner (breech) door within the weapons stowage compartment and a further, outer (muzzle) door at the outboard end of the tube, outside the pressure hull. There are interlocks to prevent both doors being opened at the same time. With the breech door open, the weapon is slid into the tube. Necessary connections are made (such as the connection of the Spearfish guidance wire) and the door secured. Forward of the launch-tube muzzle door is a free-flooded tube, along which the weapon travels towards the outer submarine hull. This tube is covered with a shutter that maintains the smooth shape of the hull until the boat is ready to discharge its weapon. Before firing the muzzle door and the shutter are opened.

The system uses a multi-tube air turbine pump to launch torpedoes and missiles. HP air at 13.8MPa drives the turbine blades that suck in seawater to pressurise the water transfer tank. To eject a weapon, this water is forced into the selected launch-tube delivering significant power. This provides the initial

JACKSPEAK

Torpedo tubes. Before the Second World War, the size of heavyweight torpedoes fired from submarines had standard diameters of 21in (533mm). Subsequently, all tube-launched devices have also been this diameter, be they torpedoes, missiles, mines or unmanned underwater vehicles. Although often still referred to as 'torpedo tubes', a more accurate term is 'launch-tube'.

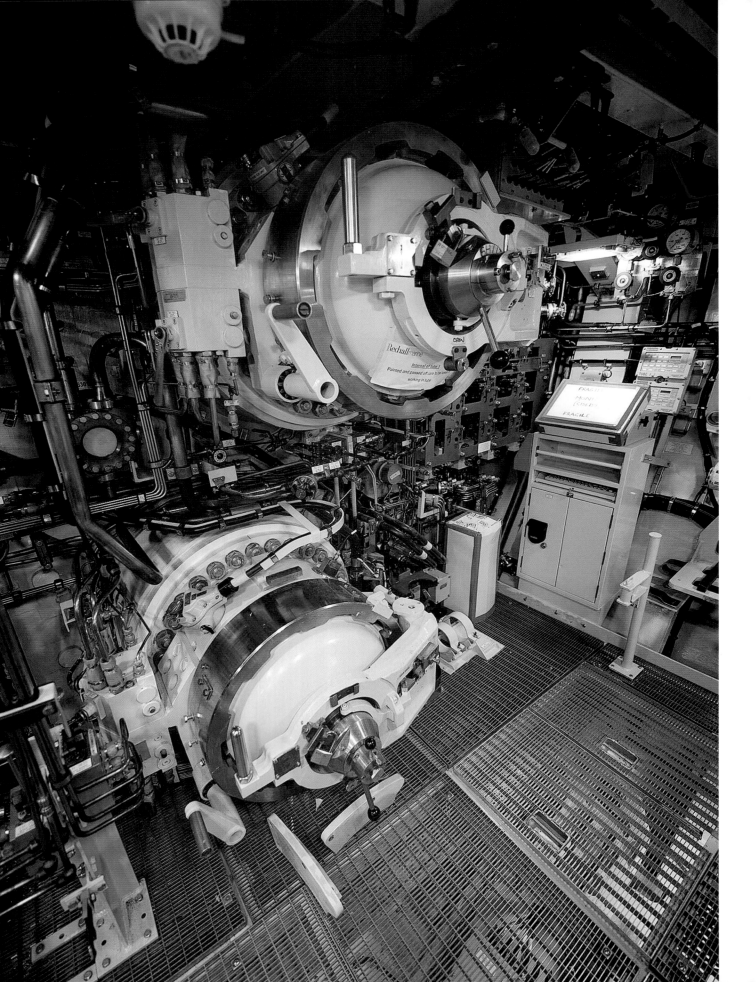

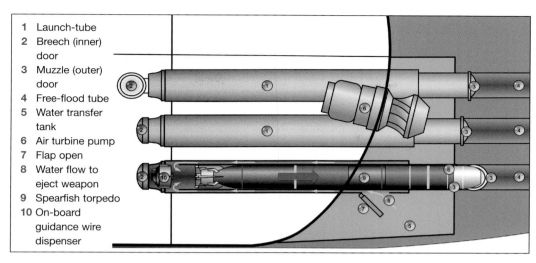

1 Launch-tube
2 Breech (inner) door
3 Muzzle (outer) door
4 Free-flood tube
5 Water transfer tank
6 Air turbine pump
7 Flap open
8 Water flow to eject weapon
9 Spearfish torpedo
10 On-board guidance wire dispenser

LEFT Weapon launch-tube operation. *(Author)*

acceleration to launch the weapon so that it clears the tube. For Spearfish the torpedo's motor then propels it forward, but in the case of Tomahawk, natural buoyancy and a booster takes the missile to the surface. The optimum power needed to launch a weapon depends on a range of variables including weapon type, submarine speed and depth. The air turbine pump's programmable firing valve precisely matches power delivered to the weapon's firing profile. The turbine discharge technique uses substantially less operating air than earlier air-ram systems, has a much lower acoustic signature (so reducing the probability that enemy submarines will detect the discharge of a weapon) and benefits from an extended operational life cycle.

Submarine Weapon Interface Manager (SWIM)

SWIM, developed specifically for the *Astute* class, manages and monitors command and control signals between the various elements of the combat and tactical weapons systems.

SWIM provides the interfaces between ACMS, the Tomahawk tactical weapon command system, the air turbine pump and tube-launched weapons (Spearfish and Tomahawk). It is used throughout the preparation, launching and control of these weapons. SWIM consists of two identical cabinets; one designated for the weapons in the

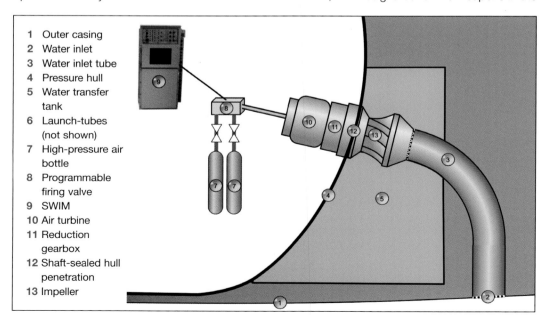

1 Outer casing
2 Water inlet
3 Water inlet tube
4 Pressure hull
5 Water transfer tank
6 Launch-tubes (not shown)
7 High-pressure air bottle
8 Programmable firing valve
9 SWIM
10 Air turbine
11 Reduction gearbox
12 Shaft-sealed hull penetration
13 Impeller

LEFT Operation of air turbine pump. *(Author)*

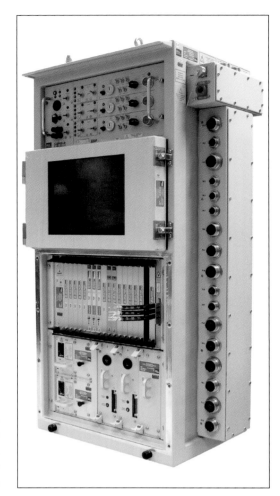

RIGHT Submarine Weapon Interface Manager. *(Ultra Electronics)*

BELOW 100mm submerged signal and decoy ejector. *(Babcock International Group)*

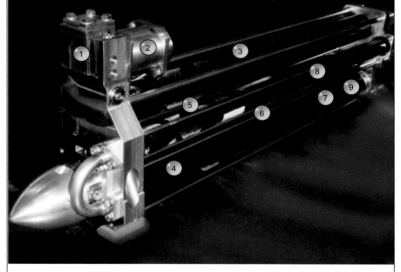

1	Manifold	5	Firing piston	8	Firing tube
2	Trigger mechanism	6	Rope	9	Rear flood
3	Air reservoir	7	Discharge ram		chamber
4	Decoy				

three port tubes and the other for the starboard tubes. Cabling and safety interconnect systems pass weapons data and power from SWIM to the tube-launched weapon through a high-integrity component fitted into the wall of the launch-tube. High system safety, reliability and availability are vital for such a weapons firing system, so SWIM includes redundancy features such as backup circuitry. In addition, each cabinet has a 'traffic light' monitoring facility to determine the state of the fire-control solution and weapon launch process. This facility also gives an in-depth diagnosis of faults that can be cleared using the built-in spares provided. A 'casualty' firing mode is available.

Submerged Signal and Decoy Ejector (SSDE) Systems

HMS *Astute* is fitted with two internal, reloadable Mk 11 SSDEs. They are mounted close to the escape hatches for use in escape and rescue and are used to release emergency indicator smoke candles, grenades and signal buoys. The forward ejector is capable of manual use but the aft ejector is operated automatically from a remote location (although local and manual operation are also possible). The ejectors in manual mode can also be used to accept into the submarine mini-pods containing emergency stores from rescuers. The ejectors are capable of launching a range of cylindrical stores that meet the NATO standard of 100mm in diameter and up to 1m in length. Removable cylindrical reducing sleeves can be used to deploy smaller stores of the standard 75mm diameter, such as communications buoys, measurement buoys (*eg* bathythermographs) and anti-torpedo decoys. The current decoys are the Type 2066 (Bandfish) submarine countermeasure acoustic decoy device that, after ejection, remains suspended in the water emitting pulses to confuse active homing torpedoes. This decoy, commercially known as SCAD 102, is 100mm in diameter and 1,000mm long and weighs 12kg.

Many countermeasures are pre-programmable but the SSDE can also be used with countermeasures requiring data links. They are also suitable for bathythermographs that relay data to the boat using an attached umbilical cord.

External to the pressure hull, mounted athwartships beneath the casing port and starboard are multiple-tube submarine decoy launchers. These fire the 127mm-diameter SCAD 101, also known as Type 2071. The countermeasure has acoustic multi-mode capability and is completely programmable by the user. Communications with the store, including mission programming, is available until the device is launched. The tubes of these launchers are permanently loaded so that a decoy may be fired within seconds of an incoming torpedo being detected, thereby giving the decoy the maximum chance of persuading the torpedo to follow it rather than the decoy's parent boat.

Before launching the decoy, the command system can select one of eight programmes that are stored in the decoy's digital signal generator. The signals drive a hydrosounder that emits, repeatedly, a pre-recorded signal emulating the signature of the boat. The signal generator can also simultaneously produce 11 signals such as single tones, swept tones, bands of random acoustic energy, modulated

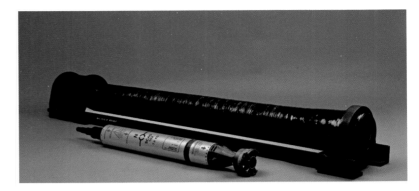

acoustic energy and pulses, all of which are intended to confuse and decoy the torpedo's homing function. Having executed its mission, the countermeasure scuttles.

Spearfish HWT Mod 0

The Spearfish torpedo is the RN's submarine-launched HWT. Principally intended as an anti-submarine weapon, it also has a capability against surface ships. Spearfish Mod 0 was accepted into service in January 2001 and, by 2004, had replaced the unreliable Mk 24 Tigerfish HWT. It is believed that the RN has an inventory of around 400 war-shot Spearfish torpedoes that could remain in service until 2025. Spearfish was designed to destroy faster, quieter and deeper-diving submarines

ABOVE Submarine countermeasures acoustic decoy SCAD 101 protected for under-casing use and the smaller SCAD 102. *(Ultra Electronics)*

BELOW Cutaway of Spearfish HWT Mod 0. *(Author, from BAE Systems information)*

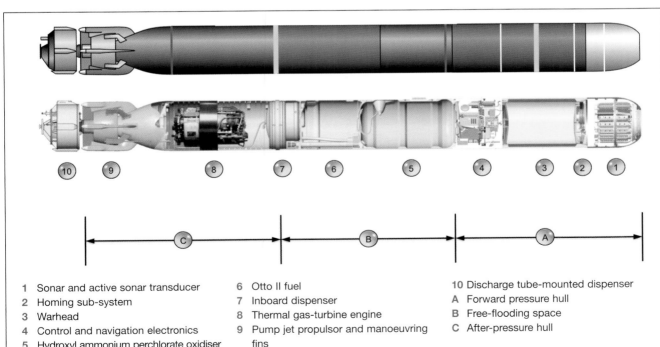

1 Sonar and active sonar transducer	6 Otto II fuel	10 Discharge tube-mounted dispenser
2 Homing sub-system	7 Inboard dispenser	A Forward pressure hull
3 Warhead	8 Thermal gas-turbine engine	B Free-flooding space
4 Control and navigation electronics	9 Pump jet propulsor and manoeuvring fins	C After-pressure hull
5 Hydroxyl ammonium perchlorate oxidiser		

Characteristics of Spearfish HWT Mod 0	
Length overall	7.0m
Diameter	533mm
Launch weight	1.85T
Propulsion motor	Sundstrand 21TP01 gas-turbine engine
Fuel/oxidant	Otto II/Aqueous hydroxylammonium perchlorate (HAP)
Propulsor	Ducted pump jet
Propulsion power	746kW
Maximum speed	Autonomously set with maximum of 130km/h (70kts)
Maximum range	23.2km at 111km/h (60kts) 54km at low speed
Maximum depth	900m (estimated, not confirmed)
Control	Autonomous with wire-guided option
Homing	Autonomous passive, broadband, frequency agile sonar with active terminal homing sonar
Warhead	300kg high-explosive
Fuze	Contact (anti-submarine) or proximity (anti-ship)

than previous torpedoes. Like its predecessor, it has an under-ice capability; however, Spearfish has the advantage of being able to operate in the shallow waters of the littoral.

Spearfish has the shape of a tube with a blunt fore-end and tapered tail. It comprises two pressure-tight sections and a central mid-body free-flooding area. At the front of the forward pressure hull are the sonar transducers. This array and its associated electronic equipment use a combination of active and passive homing techniques to acquire, identify and prosecute the target. Although primarily used passively, when the sonar emits in the active mode, its transducers are frequency-agile to reduce the effectiveness of countermeasures and to distinguish the torpedo's own returns from those of other Spearfish torpedoes. Powerful beam-forming techniques are employed to optimise performance in all environments. These features allow the firing of torpedo salvos, as each torpedo will only detect the returns of its own sonar beam. The sonar interfaces with the homing subsystem electronics immediately behind it.

The majority of the torpedo's forward pressure hull contains a 300kg warhead that is highly lethal against the strong hulls of deep-diving or double-hulled submarines as well as surface ships.

To the rear of the warhead, located in the mid-body of the torpedo, is the guidance section that contains tactical computers controlling all functions from propulsion to homing. In search, detection and attack modes it is able to autonomously select the optimal transmission, classify the signal returns and decide on appropriate tactics. The controller's ability to classify, track and overcome countermeasures and decoys gives a high probability of a strike although, if necessary, it can initiate re-attacks. The torpedo's capability can be enhanced by software updates as target and countermeasure characteristics evolve in future.

The control electronics includes a sensor unit incorporating a strap-down INS that measures the acceleration and attitude changes from its launch location to determine position and converts the data into speed, course and depth measurements for the tactical computer.

The propulsion system, mounted in the aft pressure hull, is a thermal turbine open-cycle variable-speed engine driving a pump-jet propulsor. The system has been designed to be very quiet to protect the firing submarine; if the launch of torpedoes is detected then a subsequent counter-attack is invited. Spearfish has a greater speed, endurance and diving depth than other HWT – double that of the less efficient electrically-propelled HWTs.

JACKSPEAK

Torpedoes are referred to as 'tin fish' or simply 'fish'.

The turbine engine is powered by Otto II fuel and oxidant, the two components being contained in separate tanks in the mid-body free-flood space. The fuel is a reddish-orange, oily liquid consisting of a mixture of three synthetic chemicals. An oxidant is not essential but increases combustion efficiency, giving Spearfish high speed and great range when compared to other HWTs. It also reduces to a minimum any insoluble waste products in the torpedo's wake that can divulge its presence. Otto II does not emit any volatile gases and is extremely stable, so ideal for use in a weapon on board a submarine; however, the oxidant requires special handling measures.

The pump-jet propulsor is based on that used for the Sting Ray lightweight torpedo. This design avoids the need for a gearbox, thereby saving weight and space as well as reducing self-generated acoustic energy. Four fins support the pump jet and extend aft to pods that contain hydraulic actuators for four control surfaces. Opposing control surfaces in the efflux of the pump jet operate together to control azimuth and pitch, as well as reducing roll. Such an arrangement of control surfaces makes the torpedo extremely agile.

Spearfish HWT Mod 1

By 2010 it was evident that Spearfish was becoming inadequate against emerging threats in the littoral environment and against advanced countermeasures. In addition, neither the blast warhead nor Otto/HAP fuel were compliant with the latest standards. That year work began to develop a mid-life upgrade package to adapt the existing hull and thermal propulsion system to improve capability and on-board safety. The latter involved replacing the Otto/HAP engine with a single-fuel Otto II cell and substituting a new insensitive munition warhead using APBX (aluminised polymer-bonded explosive).

With the removal of HAP, the 500mm-diameter Otto fuel tank now occupies the space of the two previous tanks – a length of 1,200mm. It is manufactured from electron-beam welded high-strength titanium forgings and has an integral internal rubber bag to provide the primary sealing of the fuel.

Capability was improved by introducing fully digital weapon architecture (hardware and software) into the firing, tactical and navigational computing sections. The architecture also applied to the sonar, signal processing and homing electronics to improve its capability against very quiet submarines in very shallow (15m) littoral waters. The digital, broadband, frequency-agile sonar gained multiple passive and active detection modes with high-power active transmissions for long range to improve quiet target detection and countermeasures resistance. An improvement in the accuracy of the navigation system aided precise targeting, countermeasure resistance and provided high-performance dynamic control.

Adaptive beam-forming provided between 10 and 20dB improvement in performance. The new electronics hardware replaced obsolescent components and this, combined with the ability to more easily upgrade the software, reduced through-life costs. The communications wire was also changed to a small-diameter fibre-optic cable with high bandwidth. This increased the amount of data that can be exchanged between the CMS and the torpedo and reduced data latency of the signals. The highly reliable tube-mounted dispenser unit was retained.

Since December 2014 current Spearfish Mod 0 weapon stocks have been in the process of being changed to incorporate some of these Mod 1 improvements.

Initial deliveries of Spearfish Mod 1 are scheduled to start in 2020, with the remanufacture programme continuing through

BELOW Changes incorporated into Spearfish Mod 1. *(Author, from BAE Systems information)*

| 1 Fully digital frequency-agile homing head | 3 High-accuracy navigation | 5 High-efficiency gas-turbine engine |
| 2 Insensitive munition blast warhead | 4 Single large Otto II fuel tank | 6 High-capacity fibre-optic telemetry link |

to 2024. This will extend the life of Spearfish beyond 2050. A prototype of Spearfish Mod 1 torpedo was launched from a chute frame at the BUTEC range on the west coast of Scotland in 2015. This first in-water trial was successful in demonstrating control of a range of manoeuvres and the new capabilities.

Characteristics of the Royal Navy's TLAM (Derived from US Navy Tomahawk fact file)		
	TLAM-C Block III	TLAM-E Block IV
US designation	UGM-109C	UGM-109E
Length overall	6.25m (including 0.7m booster)	
Capsule diameter	533mm	
Missile diameter	518mm	
Wings/wingspan	1m × 360mm/2.62m	
Fins	4	3
Weight	1,510kg (including booster)	
Speed	880km/h (0.72Mach)	
Maximum range	1,300km	1,600km
Warhead	450kg Unitary warhead	
Cruise turbo-fan engine	F107-WR-402	
Booster	ARC/CSD solid-fuel	
Guidance	INS, TERCOM, DSMAC, GPS	

TLAM Block IV

Tomahawk missiles are a family of American long-range cruise missiles for striking high-value or heavily defended tactical land targets with precision. They can be launched from aircraft and surface warships as well as submarines. They are designed to fly at extremely low altitudes and at high subsonic speeds. Controlled by several mission-tailored guidance systems they follow evasive routes. The first Tomahawk missiles were intended for submarine launch and the USN achieved this in 1978. All versions of the missile have the same dimensions, including the diameter that was determined by the internal diameter of submarine launch-tubes. Since its introduction, Tomahawk has undergone a series of modernisations and improvements. The latest evolution, Block IV, is the fourth major upgrade. Submarine versions of Tomahawk are unique in having a chine nose and a tapering tail.

Submarine-launched Tomahawk, termed TLAM by the UK MoD, has been in service with the RN since 1998. In that year the RN fired its

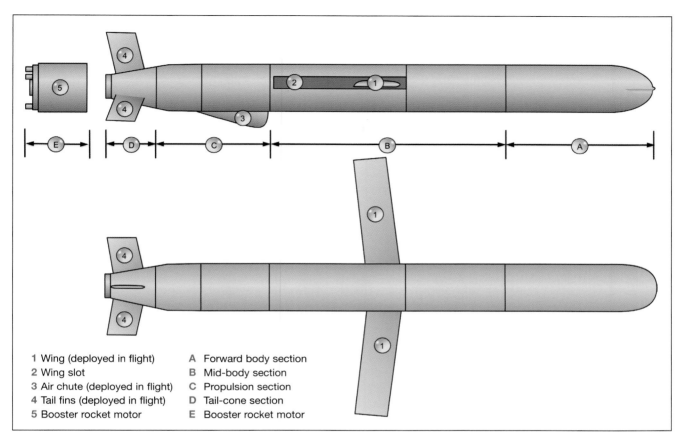

1 Wing (deployed in flight)
2 Wing slot
3 Air chute (deployed in flight)
4 Tail fins (deployed in flight)
5 Booster rocket motor
A Forward body section
B Mid-body section
C Propulsion section
D Tail-cone section
E Booster rocket motor

first TLAM, a Block III version, in anger as part of Operation Allied Force. It has been reported that a total of 20 TLAMs were fired during this Serbian conflict, with further missiles being expended in subsequent conflicts.

It is believed that most, if not all, of the initial RN buy of Block III missiles have been expended. In late 2004 HMS *Trafalgar* was the first RN boat to be fitted with the later Block IV TLAM. The first, unsuccessful, firing trial took place in June 2005. A second firing in

May 2006 was also unsuccessful, however, HMS *Trenchant* subsequently achieved a successful launch in June 2007, the missile hitting its target after a flight of 1,200km. Block IV missiles entered operational service with the RN in March 2008 in HMS *Torbay*, and have subsequently been supplied to the *Astute* class.

The Block IV missile not only has a greater range than its predecessor but also can be directed, through two-way SatCom, to alter course in mid-flight, to loiter over a target area

ABOVE Block IV TLAM. *(Author, based on dimensions in US Navy fact file)*

BELOW Block IV TLAM main internal components. *(Author, based on cutaway in Jane's Weapons:* Naval *2014–15)*

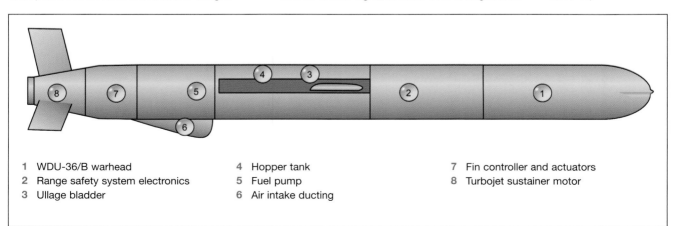

1 WDU-36/B warhead
2 Range safety system electronics
3 Ullage bladder
4 Hopper tank
5 Fuel pump
6 Air intake ducting
7 Fin controller and actuators
8 Turbojet sustainer motor

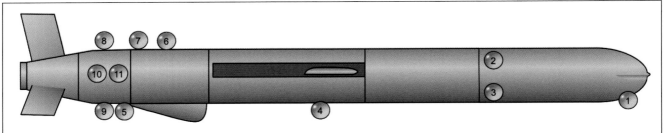

1 Nose-cone electro-optical sensor	**5** Digital scene-matching area correlation (DSMAC) IV camera	**8** Satellite data-link terminal
2 Inertial measurement unit	**6** Anti-jam global positioning system antenna and receiver	**9** Missile radar altimeter transmitter
3 Digital scene-matching area correlation (DSMAC) IV illuminator (strobe)	**7** Satellite data-link antenna	**10** Navigation processor including terrain contour matching (TerCom) system
4 Missile radar altimeter antenna		**11** Guidance electronics unit

ABOVE Block IV TLAM sensors. *(Author, based on cutaway in* Jane's Weapons: Naval *2014–15)*

or attack any pre-programmed alternative targets. This enables it to respond to emerging or moving targets and to time its strike to coincide with other assets. The SatCom can also redirect the missile to any GPS target co-ordinates. It also features an on-board camera to record battle damage that can be sent back to the launch platform.

For many years the world-renowned reference publication *Jane's Weapons: Naval* has described the evolution of Tomahawk missiles. Much of the information related to TLAM in this publication derives from this unofficial source. Jane's explains that, internally, the missile is divided into sections. From forward to aft, these are described by open sources as:

Forward-body section. The forward body section consists of the nose and conventional high-explosive warhead.

Mid-body section. The mid-body section contains a pair of slim, rectangular wings that are folded back into wing slots for launch but deploy during flight.

Propulsion and tail-cone sections containing the fins, turbofan engine, air chute inlet and the majority of the electronic processors for the missile. TLAM Block IV has three delta-shaped fins to provide stability and control in flight. While these are folded initially, in flight a pneumatic actuator swings them into position.

The turbofan engine sustains the missile in 'cruise' flight from the end of the boost phase until it reaches its target. The latest turbofan engine is smaller and lighter than previous versions. The turbofan engine also drives an internal alternator to provide power for the on-board electronics.

The lower half of the aft-body contains the moulded GRP air chute inlet that is deployed in flight to provide air to the turbofan engine.

Booster rocket motor connected to the tail-cone section. The booster propels the missile using a single fixed nozzle but four vanes are attached to the nozzle to provide thrust vector control that steers the missile during the boost phase.

TLAM Block IV has a number of sensors and electronic devices that provide it with positional information. *Jane's* lists these as:

■ An *inertial navigational system* (INS) that is located close to the centre of rotation of the missile (within the mid-body). Generally any INS comprises three orthogonally arranged gyros to measure rotational angular rates, and three orthogonally arranged accelerometers to measure linear acceleration. This positional information relative to its launch point allows the missile to determine its attitude and position when there are no reference features below it, for instance, during its initial flight over sea.

■ A *radar altimeter* underneath the missile comprises a (rear) transmitter antenna to beam radar pulses to the surface and an identical (forward) receiver antenna to detect the returned pulse. This radar signal is essential for the missile to maintain the correct altitude over sea and later over land.

■ A *terrain contour-matching device* (TerCom) confirms landfall and periodically corrects and updates the guidance system. The elevation readings supplied by the missile radar altimeter are compared with a set of stored digital maps of the ground to maintain the missile on its flight path to the target. TerCom has been used in cruise missiles since the 1950s. It greatly improves the accuracy of navigation when compared to INS alone, as TerCom is updated upon reaching each waypoint. Since distance travelled is measured from the last waypoint (rather than the launch point) terminal accuracy is enhanced. TerCom has the advantage of being relatively insensitive to weather, season and ground cover.

■ A *digital scene-matching area correlator* (DSMAC) is an optical system used as an adjunct to TerCom. Used in a range of missiles, DSMAC has an optical sensor mounted underneath the missile that captures digital greyscale images of ground features and compares them with stored digitised images. Although some care must be taken to program the processor to recognise unique and unchanging features, accuracy is potentially extremely high.

■ A *global positioning system* (GPS). TLAM Block IV receives signals from military GPS satellites, processes the signals and provides navigational data. This data can be used in lieu of, or in combination with, TerCom/DSMAC fixes to provide more flexibility and higher reliability in accomplishing mission objectives.

■ A *satellite communications* (SatCom) *data link terminal* mounted on the top of the missile uses encrypted data communications so that the missile can receive operational updates from the missile controller beamed through satellites. In addition, it is reported that data and images can be sent to the missile controller by using a satellite data-link antenna (mounted just forward of the SatCom terminal) that transmits and receives the UHF signals.

Submarine tube-launched Tomahawk missiles are protected during storage, transit and on-board stowage by their submarine horizontal-launch missile capsules. The capsule is watertight and completely encloses the TLAM. It comprises a barrel that is closed by a conical shell at the nose of the missile and a flat circular back-plate at the rear (breech end) of the missile.

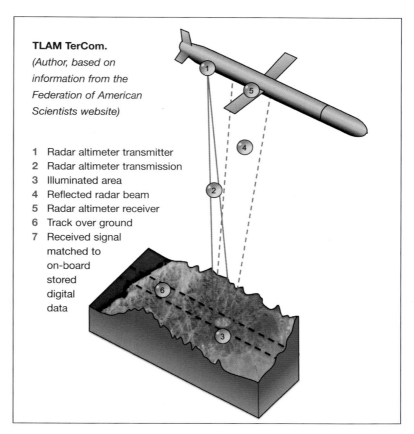

TLAM TerCom.
(Author, based on information from the Federation of American Scientists website)

1 Radar altimeter transmitter
2 Radar altimeter transmission
3 Illuminated area
4 Reflected radar beam
5 Radar altimeter receiver
6 Track over ground
7 Received signal matched to on-board stored digital data

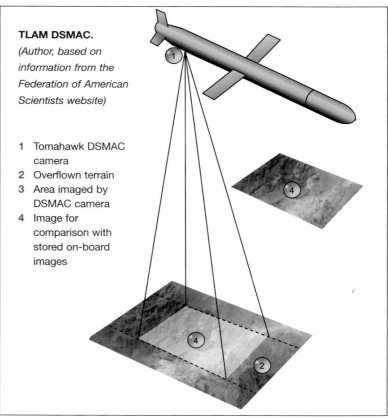

TLAM DSMAC.
(Author, based on information from the Federation of American Scientists website)

1 Tomahawk DSMAC camera
2 Overflown terrain
3 Area imaged by DSMAC camera
4 Image for comparison with stored on-board images

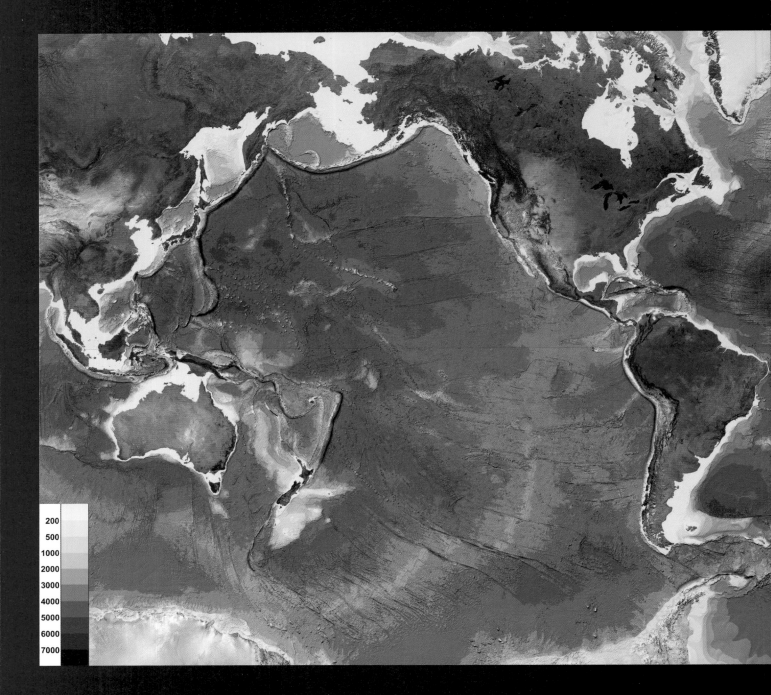

200	
500	
1000	
2000	
3000	
4000	
5000	
6000	
7000	

Chapter Six

Into the deep: operation of *Astute* class submarines

Astute class submarines have a major role in ensuring that SSBNs are not followed in peacetime and are protected in wartime. They are also responsible for tracking enemy SSBNs and neutralising them in times of war. Secondary roles include surveillance and the insertion of Special Forces. During peacetime the boats are continually undertaking exercises to prepare for the eventuality that they would have to deploy, in anger, their Tomahawk and Spearfish weapons.

OPPOSITE General bathymetric chart of the oceans (GEBCO) with coloured depth contours in metres. *(Image reproduced with permission from the GEBCO world map 2014, www.gebco.net)*

159

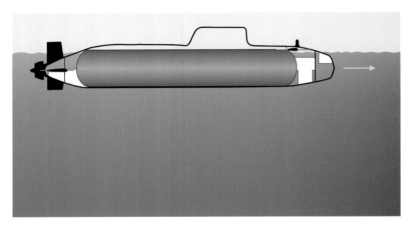

ABOVE On surface, preparing to dive. *(Author)*

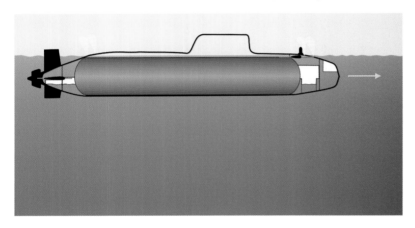

ABOVE Main vents open, ballast tanks filling. *(Author)*

BELOW Hydroplanes set to dive. *(Author)*

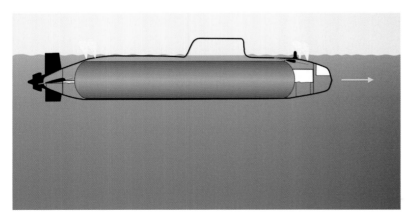

The *Astute* class has already proved to be a remarkably powerful and flexible tool of power projection, largely thanks to the enduring characteristics of all nuclear-powered submarines. First, their sustained speed and endurance enable the boats to rapidly deploy to any ocean and to remain covertly poised for action for long periods. They avoid escalating tensions by not committing the forces to offensive action. Nevertheless, their independence of in-theatre support and their flexibility allows them to respond to a range of new tasks without delay. Secondly, their stealth characteristics allow them to remain undetected and take full advantage of surprise, thereby enabling them to maintain a tactical advantage. Thirdly, they can launch a strike from enduring cover with access to 80% of the population of the planet. The value of the *Astute* class submarines is likely to grow as the strategic horizons change with the concomitant need for them to carry out ever more complex missions.

Diving: submerging, manoeuvring and resurfacing

As might be expected, there is a set procedure to prepare for diving that ensures all the relevant personnel are at their duty stations, the hatches are closed and the ballast tank valves are aligned ('opened up for diving'). On the surface, the ballast tanks are filled with air, but the surrounding free-flood space aft is filled with water and the space forward almost flooded with water; the casing and fin are still above the waterline.

To dive, the main vents are opened, allowing water to displace the air in the main ballast tanks, increasing the weight of the submarine and allowing it to sink.

The hydroplanes are then set to dive, which has the effect of forcing the boat below the surface and pitching it downward, complementing the effect of increasing weight (losing buoyancy) as the tanks flood. If the submarine is progressing at a modest speed before it dives, the helmsman sets the forward hydroplane to tilt downwards and the aft hydroplane upwards. However, if the boat is fast-moving before the dive, then, because of the shift in hydrodynamic forces at high speed, the aft hydroplanes will be set in the opposite direction.

Once the main ballast tanks are flooded, the boat will continue to be driven downwards by the propulsion system.

The angle of dive will continue to increase until the hydroplanes are set to level. It will then maintain its dive at a constant angle.

As the submarine approaches the required depth, the hydroplanes are set to rise to bring the boat to a level attitude.

Once the boat is horizontal the hydroplanes are again set to their neutral (horizontal) position. When the submarine is submerged the hydroplanes are used to control the attitude (roll, pitch and yaw). The trim tanks and ballast tanks are used to maintain correct trim and buoyancy as the submarine moves vertically within the ocean. At high speeds the motion of the boat is increasingly sensitive to any

movement of the forward hydroplanes. As a consequence, during high-speed transits only the aft hydroplanes are used.

When it is necessary to surface HP air is pumped into the main ballast tanks in order to displace the water, thereby increasing the

ABOVE Artist's impression of HMS Astute operating at depth. (Admiralty Model Works LLC/Tvrtko Kapetanović)

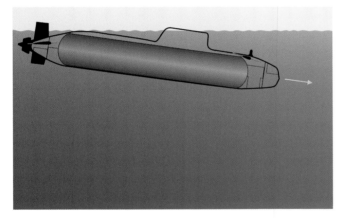

ABOVE Main ballast tanks flooded. (Author)

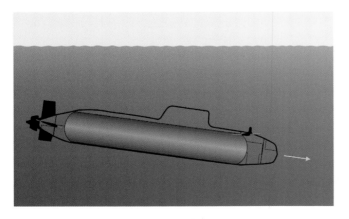

BELOW Hydroplanes to rise. (Author)

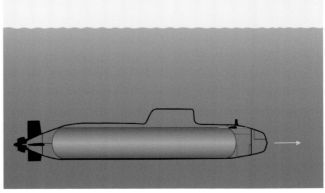

ABOVE Hydroplanes level, main vents shut. (Author)

BELOW Straight and level. (Author)

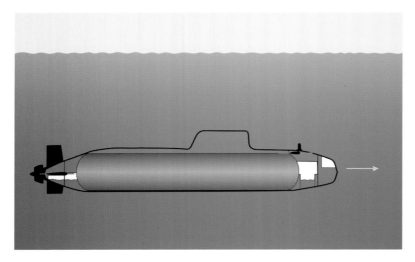

ABOVE Initiation of surfacing manoeuvre: hydroplanes to rise, blow main ballast tanks. *(Author)*

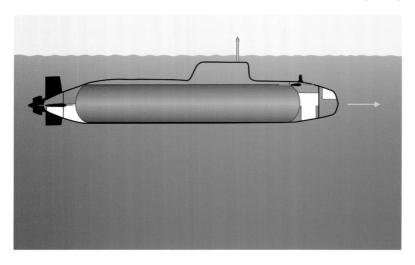

ABOVE At periscope depth deploying electro-optical periscope. *(Author)*

BELOW On the surface. *(Author)*

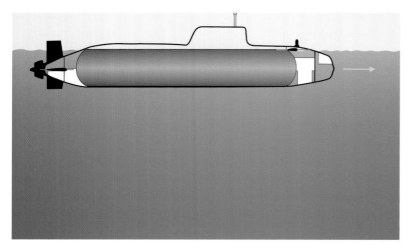

JACKSPEAK

A submarine at the sea's surface is said to be 'on the roof'.

submarine's buoyancy. The hydrodynamic forces from the water flowing over the hydroplanes, combined with the hydrostatic forces from the loss of weight, causes the boat to rise towards the surface.

Care must be taken when approaching the surface to ensure that there are no surface ships in the immediate area. When the water has been displaced from the main ballast tanks and the submarine approaches the surface, the hydroplanes are used to bring the boat to a level attitude beneath the surface. Once periscope depth is reached the periscope can be raised to survey the surface situation.

Once the submarine is on the surface, the blower brings the boat to full buoyancy by blowing further air from inside the boat into the ballast tanks.

Deep-water Anti-Submarine Warfare (ASW)

The traditional role of SSNs has been to locate and then trail enemy submarines, particularly SSBNs armed with nuclear weapons. In times of war, they would then be able to destroy enemy submarines. As a consequence, they were referred to as 'hunter-killer submarines'. Modern SSNs such as the *Astute* class have gained additional roles, such as land-attack with missiles, so they now have the soubriquet 'fleet submarines'. Nevertheless, ASW remains important. The submarine versus submarine engagement is fought in three dimensions with imprecise information. It continues to be one of the most challenging of underwater warfare skill sets.

As they can detect each other using sonar, it is paramount that a submarine remains aware of other submarines without itself being detected. This ability is termed sonar range advantage and is a combination of the sensitivity of each boat's sonar and the degree to which their own acoustic emissions have been suppressed. A very quiet boat with a responsive sonar will be able to detect a noisy boat and a less sensitive sonar long before the adversary is aware of the quieter boat's presence. The propagation conditions of sonar waves in seawater and the efficacy of any torpedo fired also affect the success of any engagement.

Acoustic energy emitted by the combatants propagates at the speed of sound in seawater and this is affected by the properties of the seawater – mainly its temperature, but also pressure and salinity. In the deep ocean, the speed of sound close to the surface is determined principally by the temperature of the surface layer. As depth increases, the speed of sound increases but then begins to decrease. The temperature in deep water varies little with depth but the speed of sound continues to decrease with depth until it once more begins to rise, largely as a result of the increasing pressure in the deep isothermal layer. The depth of the surface variation depends on the degree to which the surface of the sea is warmed or cooled by the sun and air temperature. While it is of constant depth in equatorial regions, in higher latitudes it depends on the seasons and varies from 50m to 150m deep.

If the oceans were totally homogeneous, acoustic energy would spread out in all directions, declining in energy by the cube law (doubling the distance travelled results in a decrease in energy of eight times). However, the

1 Seasonal thermocline
2 Main thermocline
3 Deep isothermal layer
4 Sea's surface
5 Surface duct
6 Deep sound channel

500m
1000m
Depth
2000m

Speed of Sound ⟶

inhomogeneous nature of seawater has major impacts on propagation. The surface layer will diffract (bend) the acoustic waves as they propagate and, when they reach the surface, they are reflected. The result is that some sonar waves will be trapped in the surface duct and can propagate long distances. Beneath the surface duct is another layer where acoustic energy may propagate largely isolated from the surface duct – the deep sound channel. Here acoustic waves are also diffracted, making it difficult for any sonar to determine the direction of the source of the signal.

A further constraint on the propagation of acoustic energy is the presence of oceanic

ABOVE Propagation of acoustic energy in deep water is related to the speed of sound in seawater. *(Author)*

BELOW Sonar propagation in ducts. *(Author)*

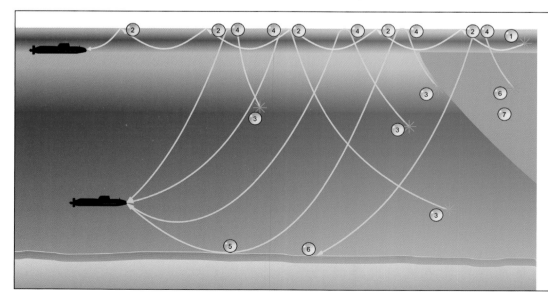

1 Noise source detected in surface duct
2 Reflected sound wave
3 Noise source detected in deep sound channel
4 Refracted sound wave
5 Bottom grazing ray
6 Noise source undetected in either sound channel
7 Shadow zone where threat submarines are undetected

fronts – features that occur at the boundaries of ocean currents. At these junctures there is a rapid change in temperature and a consequent change in the speed of sound. This acts like a reflective surface to acoustic waves and blocks their propagation. The fronts may be over 1km deep but less than 100m wide. Depending on the nature of the currents associated with the fronts, their position may be fixed or vary significantly over time.

Interference in the form of acoustic noise also affects whether a submarine can be detected against the background. Interference is produced by physical events (waves breaking and rain striking the sea's surface), biological sources (the calls of whales and the effects produced by large shoals of fish) and man-made noises (shipping).

The vagaries of sonar propagation in the deep ocean make hunting for submarines extremely challenging for surface ships or other submarines. There are many ways that a submarine's CO can make a submarine all but disappear.

Discovering a submarine in the vastness of the ocean is extremely difficult – the area covered by the northern North Atlantic Ocean, for instance, is over 40,000,000km^2. It, and the Arctic Ocean, covers over 10% of the earth's surface. One tactic is to try to detect a submarine as it leaves its base on patrol and trail it. However, submarine COs are aware of this and one of the roles assigned to SSNs is to make sure that SSBNs are not followed as this would jeopardise the nation's continuous at-sea deterrent.

Areas where submarines may be detected are 'choke points' – relatively narrow regions that submarines have to transit in order to reach their more extensive operational areas. One example is the Greenland–Iceland–UK gap that during the Cold War was of strategic importance, as Soviet submarines trying to break out to the open Atlantic Ocean had to traverse this area. With the increase in Russian

submarine activity this choke point is, once more, gaining in importance.

During the Cold War a cat-and-mouse game was played between NATO (US and UK) submarines and Warsaw Pact (Soviet) submarines. Each side attempted to shadow the other's SSBNs to ensure that they were in position to eliminate the potential source of a nuclear attack should this be necessary. The role of SSNs was not only to trail Soviet SSBNs, but also to disrupt any Soviet SSNs attempting to follow NATO submarines. Sonar is least effective over the stern arcs where the powerful bow sonars are blind, so submarines regularly undertake manoeuvres to check if they are being followed.

Conventional submarines cannot safely operate beneath sea-ice because it is difficult to guarantee regular and reliable access to the air that they need. Nuclear submarines do not have these constraints and any SSBNs lurking below could launch ballistic missiles once they broke through the ice covering. Consequently, during the Cold War, the vast area under the Arctic sea-ice was a continuation of the area of nuclear-powered submarine operations. SSNs stalking SSBNs beneath sea-ice also have to be able to penetrate it for safety reasons and so that they may establish temporary operational bases on the ice. This is a challenge for submarine designers as ice is as strong as concrete. The *Astute* class, like her predecessors, can penetrate ice, but a modern submarine can only surface where ice cover is less than 2m thick, and it takes tens of minutes to surface.

Operations to trail Soviet submarines did not cease with the end of the Cold War but there was diminution of activity when Russia adopted the Soviet mantle. After an accident that killed two sailors, the RN ceased under-ice operations in 2007. However, this capability is once more an operational priority.

The resurgence of ASW activities has once again highlighted the importance of the Arctic. In addition, as climate change is causing the Arctic ice coverage to shrink, and with subsequent increases in international military and commercial maritime activities, the area is likely to become a key theatre for other SSN roles. In particular, Russia is vying with other northern nations for control of potentially vast supplies of oil and gas under the Arctic Sea.

Whether trailing an SSBN or following an SSN, having detected a submarine it is necessary to establish its track. The passive sonar will indicate the direction of the target submarine but it takes time to establish its range, course and speed. During this time both boats are manoeuvring and it requires complex calculations to unravel the parameters of the target boat's motion. The target boat may be trailed for days, during which time the sensors may identify thousands of potential targets. Target motion analysis algorithms allow maximum use to be made of the sensor information, developing an accurate picture of contact position, course and speed, as well as characteristics that allow the potential target's classification and identification to be established.

Should it be necessary to attack a submarine then *Astute* class submarines would usually launch a salvo of two Spearfish torpedoes.

Spearfish engagement

Once Spearfish is loaded into the launch-tube a two-way communications link is established between ACMS and Spearfish using the copper/cadmium communications wire wound on the dispenser at the rear of the launch-tube. This, in turn, connects to the torpedo's mid-body dispenser. ACMS provides the torpedo with updated command data about the target (position, speed, heading and uncertainty volume), the environmental conditions (seabed, sea-state and water temperature layers) and the submarine's position and attitude. Spearfish provides data about its position, speed and heading as well as the engagement status and the track of the target.

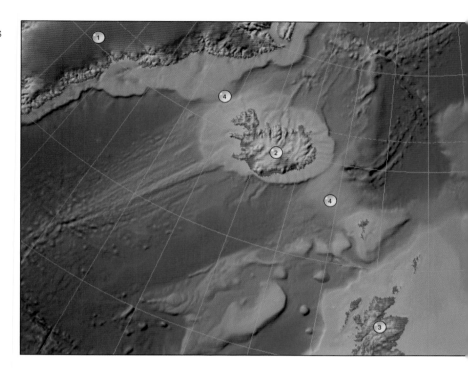

Although Spearfish can operate autonomously from the time of launch, the operator can use the wire to take control at any time.

After firing, the communications wire (that is less than 2mm in diameter) is payed out simultaneously from the two dispensers. They resemble a large version of the reel that

ABOVE Greenland–Iceland–UK gap choke point. *(Author, map NOAA)*

1 Greenland
2 Iceland
3 United Kingdom (UK)
4 Greenland–Iceland–UK gap.

LEFT Closing the breech launch-tube door. *(Crown Copyright/ PO(Phot) Owen Cooban)*

1 Tube-mounted
   dispenser
2 Torpedo-mounted
   dispenser
3 Heavy 'hose-pipe'
4 Light 'hose-pipe'
5 Guidance wire

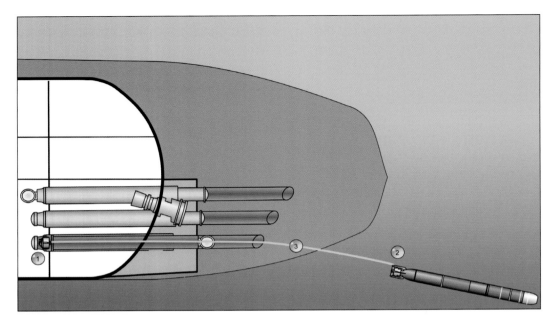

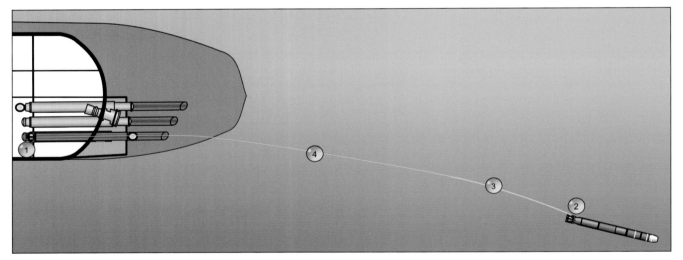

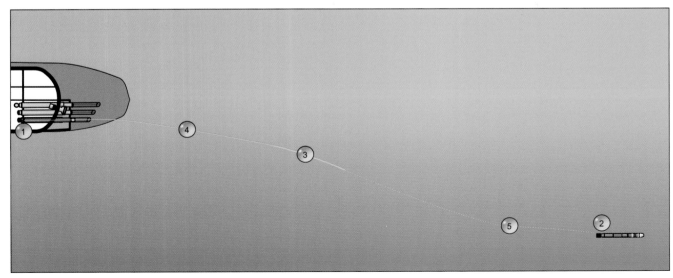

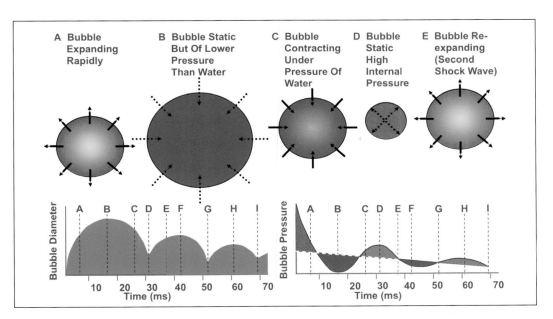

Within the figure:

A Bubble Expanding Rapidly

B Bubble Static But Of Lower Pressure Than Water

C Bubble Contracting Under Pressure Of Water

D Bubble Static High Internal Pressure

E Bubble Re-expanding (Second Shock Wave)

Bubble Diameter | A B C D E F G H I | Time (ms) 10 20 30 40 50 60 70

Bubble Pressure | A B C D E F G H I | Time (ms) 10 20 30 40 50 60 70

LEFT Pulsating bubble produced by blast of an HWT. *(Author)*

dispenses fishing line on a rod. By discharging the wire from both ends, the strain on the wire is reduced, allowing the submarine to manoeuvre during the torpedo's engagement without breaking it. Typically the length of wire on the dispenser within the launch-tube is 10km and, in the torpedo dispenser, 20km. The wire from the launch-tube is contained within protective flexible 30m hosepipe-like tubes that are also payed out from the launch-tube dispenser. The hosepipe closest to the boat is termed the 'heavy hosepipe' and that further from the boat the 'light hosepipe'. These provide further protection against snagging by the boat during post-firing manoeuvres and are only needed to protect the wire close to the boat. When the torpedo approaches its target, the communications wire is no longer needed and it is jettisoned.

Spearfish is capable of variable speeds across the entire performance envelope. At low speed it is very quiet, which is suited to its passive search capability. In a typical engagement, Spearfish will run to the general vicinity of the target and then conduct a covert passive search. The high-capacity wire link system, specifically designed to match Spearfish's manoeuvre and speed envelope, provides two-way data exchange between the torpedo and the launch submarine. This allows the submarine to pass to Spearfish information about the target obtained since launch by the submarine's sonar and to control the torpedo's trajectory. Conversely, Spearfish relays target data to the submarine. If the

guidance wire connection is lost, then Spearfish's on-board electronics can autonomously detect, locate and attack its target.

Against a very quiet target Spearfish may be forced to operate in active mode. Even when it approaches in the passive sonar mode, Spearfish will switch to active mode close to the target. Spearfish also attains an exceptional sprint speed in this terminal stage of an attack. High-power active transmissions and sophisticated signal processing enable it to accurately discriminate targets from background acoustic energy, to distinguish, and reject, countermeasures, decoys or evasive manoeuvres. The homing system guides the torpedo to the optimum impact point on the target submarine's hull.

Surface ship attack

There are occasions when submarines are required to attack surface ships, for instance to enforce a blockade. Blockades seek to prevent access to facilities or impose area denial to commercial shipping or military forces. The only time that a British nuclear-powered submarine has fired a torpedo in anger was during the Falklands Conflict when HMS *Conqueror* sank the Argentinian cruiser ARA *General Belgrano*.

Once a submarine has fired a torpedo, it has declared its presence. However, nuclear-powered submarines, such as HMS *Astute*,

ASTUTE CLASS NUCLEAR SUBMARINE MANUAL

OPPOSITE PAGE AND RIGHT

HMAS *Farncomb* sinks a surface ship with a HWT.

(Commonwealth of Australia/POPH Scott Connolly)

A Surface ship target acquired.
B Torpedo strikes target forcing up the centre of the ship.
C Explosion forces up the centre of the ship.
D A plume of water is forced upward by the water bubble.
E Plume reaches its maximum height.
F Aftermath – the ship broken in two.
G Stern detaches and sinks.
H Main part of ship begins to founder.
I Ship destroyed.

have the speed to depart rapidly to avoid detection. Because of their stealth they remain a perceived threat to the enemy's surface units even if they have left the area.

When attacking surface targets the torpedo passes underneath the target and is detonated by an acoustic proximity fuze. The explosion generates a large, hot bubble of detonation gases that expands rapidly. The bubble continues to expand to a size where its pressure is lower than the surrounding water and it then begins to collapse. Eventually, the bubble contracts to a size where its pressure is greater than the seawater and the cycle begins again. This pulsating bubble will have a whipping effect that breaks the back of the surface ship.

Should Spearfish fail to come close enough to the target on its first attack, the tactical software automatically selects an appropriate re-attack mode to successfully conclude the engagement or select a new, more viable target.

Tomahawk land-attack operations

*A*stute class submarines' TLAM Block IV missiles are carried to provide a strike capability at long range against precisely defined land targets. Tomahawk is also deployed on aircraft and surface ships but submarines have the benefit of providing an undetectable launch platform.

The Tactical Tomahawk Weapons Control System that controls the firing and mission of TLAM missiles is integrated with HMS *Astute*'s navigation, communication, situational awareness and launch systems. The control system computes the missile's route to strike targets and

also allows new missions to be planned aboard the submarine before (and during) the missile's flight, and then communicates with TLAM to rapidly retarget and redirect the missiles.

Open sources such as *Jane's* describe the typical TLAM mission as being divided into six phases: loading, launch, boost, transition to cruise, cruise and terminal phase:

Loading phase. During this phase the missile is moved from the weapons handling racks into the launch-tubes. Before launching a TLAM missile, the submarine must adopt an almost

BELOW Tomahawk missile being prepared for the launch-tube. *(Crown Copyright/ PO(Phot) Paul Punter)*

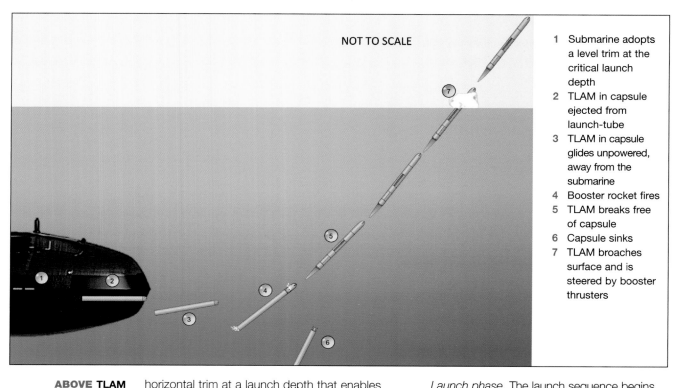

1 Submarine adopts a level trim at the critical launch depth
2 TLAM in capsule ejected from launch-tube
3 TLAM in capsule glides unpowered, away from the submarine
4 Booster rocket fires
5 TLAM breaks free of capsule
6 Capsule sinks
7 TLAM broaches surface and is steered by booster thrusters

ABOVE TLAM underwater launch and boost phase. *(Author, based on information from IHS Jane's Weapons:* Naval 2014–15*)*

horizontal trim at a launch depth that enables the missile to reach the surface smoothly. To prevent the capsule from being crushed by the external pressure when the launch-tube is flooded, the capsule is pressurised before tube flooding. Once the launch-tube pressure reaches that of the external water pressure, the muzzle door can be opened.

Launch phase. The launch sequence begins upon transmission of the launch command from the submarine's command system to the missile.

A pulse of water delivered by the air-turbine pump into the launch-tube ejects the missile in its capsule. The capsule is able to protect the missile from harsh environmental abuses, such as launch-tube flooding, water impulses that

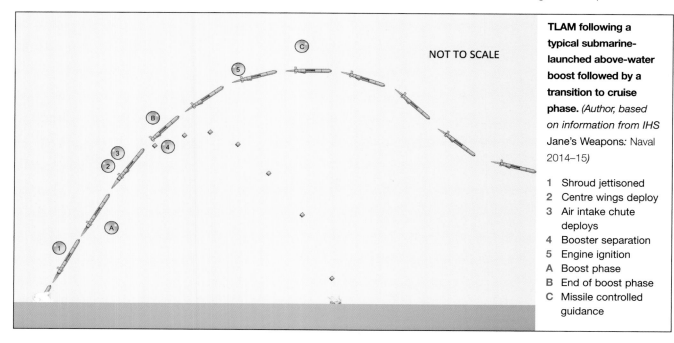

TLAM following a typical submarine-launched above-water boost followed by a transition to cruise phase. *(Author, based on information from IHS Jane's Weapons:* Naval 2014–15*)*

1 Shroud jettisoned
2 Centre wings deploy
3 Air intake chute deploys
4 Booster separation
5 Engine ignition
A Boost phase
B End of boost phase
C Missile controlled guidance

NOT TO SCALE

eject the weapon from the launch-tube and damage caused by impact with surfaces during ejection. The force imparted to the capsule and missile is such that they continue to travel away from the submarine to a safe distance. The capsule and missile together have negative buoyancy, so begin to sink slightly but also to pitch upwards because of the relationship of the centre of buoyancy to the centre of gravity. When the guidance system determines that the missile is at the right attitude, it ignites the booster solid-rocket motor.

Boost phase. After booster ignition, the burning propulsion gases from the rocket motor produce a sudden overpressure within the capsule. The immediate result is that the back-plate is blown free allowing the gases to vent. The overpressure within the capsule is also sufficient to tear open the nose-cone, allowing the missile to leave the capsule.

The capsule sinks as the booster propels the missile towards the sea's surface. The booster burns for about 12 seconds in water and then in air, after which the booster thrust decays.

Once the missile is in the air, it jettisons the shroud between missile and booster, as well as the covers from the turbofan engine inlet and the folded wing slots. As the missile leaves the sea it is controlled for a few seconds by the four vanes in the booster rocket exhaust. With the missile now 335–400m above the water, the fins are deployed to roll the missile, first by 180° to open the wings, and then back to a horizontal attitude. As the wings pop open while the booster is still firing, they can generate lift, so the missile can move to a flatter trajectory to avoid detection. The missile is already difficult to detect on radar because of its small size and the application of radar-absorbing materials on projecting parts like the air inlet. Furthermore, its small engine has a low infrared signature.

With the missile having cleared the tube, the muzzle door can be closed and the launch-tube drained so that it can be reloaded.

Transition to cruise flight phase. When the booster burns out it is jettisoned and falls away. The turbofan air inlet then pops open and the sustainer engine is started.

Cruise phase. Once the missile has achieved the correct altitude and speed, it cruises at constant speed and height. The missile's

LEFT TLAM broaches the sea's surface and discards the shroud that streamlines the missile/booster interface. *(USN photo)*

BELOW TLAM fired by HMS *Astute* streaks towards Eglin Air Force Base. *(Crown Copyright/Lt Tim Allen RN)*

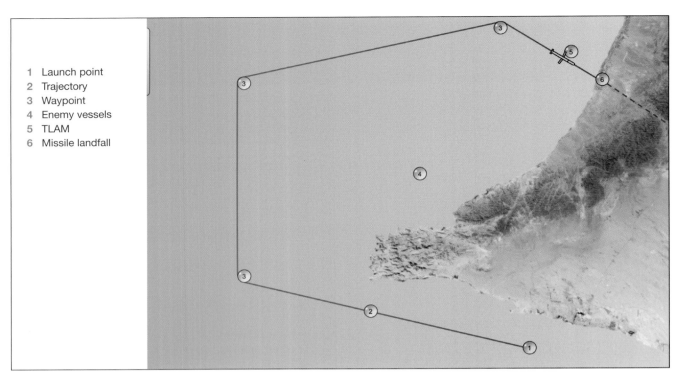

1 Launch point
2 Trajectory
3 Waypoint
4 Enemy vessels
5 TLAM
6 Missile landfall

ABOVE TLAM navigating at sea using pre-programmed waypoints. *(Author)*

BELOW TLAM over-sea profiles. *(Author, based on US General Accounting Office/ National Security & International Affairs Division 95-116 (1995))*

electronics hold details of waypoints along its programmed path and digital TerCom maps of landfall sites, as well as information relating to its main and alternative targets. While over sea it relies on INS combined with GPS to guide it between waypoints.

When TLAM makes landfall, it compares data collected by the radar altimeter with its stored digital TerCom maps to confirm its position and to adjust the altitude. The missile typically adopts a low-altitude trajectory, hugging the ground using terrain-following radar. The altitude along the selected flight path depends on the roughness of the terrain and any evasive manoeuvres required to avoid enemy defences. Overland it continues to navigate between programmed mission waypoints with a combination of INS and GPS. However, it can now perform mid-course position fixes using TerCom maps.

Once in flight, TLAM can receive various directives through the in-flight mission modification messages transmitted by the missile controller, such as updates to the target's aim-point co-ordinates, orders to loiter or commands to strike any of its pre-programmed alternative targets.

1 Launch
2 Trajectory
3 Track over ocean
4 Landfall TerCom field

A Launch and boost phase
B Transition to cruise phase
C Cruise phase

NOT TO SCALE

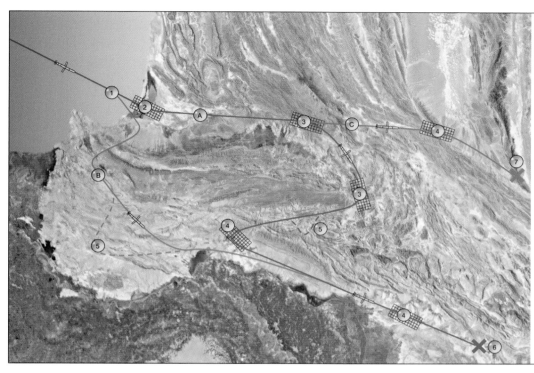

1 Pre-planned waypoint
2 Landfall TerCom field
3 TerCom fields
4 DSMAC IIA digital maps
5 Diversion to delay time of arrival
6 Main target
7 Reassigned/ alternate target

A Block III-type navigation
B GPS navigation
C GPS navigation to alternate target

TLAM terminal phase. As the missile approaches the target, DSMAC will match the target scene to its internally stored images to guide the missile towards the target. If, however, a message during the mission redirects it to a target that is not one of its pre-programmed targets then terminal phase navigation will be controlled by GPS.

Diving at a steep angle reduces targeting errors, so is appropriate against hard targets (*eg* bunkers) or where precision is paramount. The missile detonates on impact.

Near the end of the mission, the missile can transmit a battle damage indication – messages that contain its estimate of navigation error as it approaches the target. In addition, the TLAM Block IV can transmit compressed images taken by the DSMAC sensor as part of a health and status message.

ABOVE TLAM over-land features. *(Author, based on US General Accounting Office/ National Security & International Affairs Division 95-116 (1995))*

BELOW LEFT TLAM variable-angle dive terminal manoeuvre as it approaches its target. *(USN photo)*

BELOW TLAM detonation at having impacted the target. *(USN photo)*

ASTUTE CLASS NUCLEAR SUBMARINE MANUAL

Strategic intelligence, surveillance and reconnaissance

One of the traditional roles undertaken by submarines is the gathering of information about potential or actual adversaries, in peacetime and during hostilities. HMS *Astute* can gather timely strategic intelligence by monitoring radar and communications traffic (including the intercept of mobile phone communications) using its ESM equipment when the masts are deployed at periscope depth. The electro-optical periscope also collects information in the form of infrared and visual images. The submarine may also carry out surveillance – the systematic observations of an adversary's activities for a specific period – or reconnaissance – harvesting mission-specific data, usually for a short duration.

Much of the intelligence gathering has to be carried out covertly, close to the adversary's coast, for which submarines are ideally suited. HMS *Astute* has the advantage of being able to stay on task in littoral waters for long periods. When embarked on HMS *Astute*, Special Forces can significantly increase the quality, quantity and range of intelligence gathered by landing covertly on the shore and moving inland. Of course, in time of war, their mission may include activities such as sabotage.

Special Forces

When HMS *Astute* is surfaced, Special Forces can be put ashore in kayaks or small inflatable raiding boats to perform clandestine missions. Divers may also be deployed for tasks in shallow water.

Astute class boats can be fitted with Special Forces payload bay (SFPB), a cylindrical chamber from which Special Forces are able to carry out covert missions. The SFPB is carried on the submarine's deck immediately aft of the fin. The aft section of the fin beneath the underwater telephone sonar array can be removed and replaced by a fairing that mates the fin and the SFPB.

Special Forces equipment is highly classified and rarely disclosed. While there is no official

OPPOSITE *Astute* **class submarine fitted with a SFPB at Z Berth, HMNB Gibraltar.**
(Moshi J. Anahory)

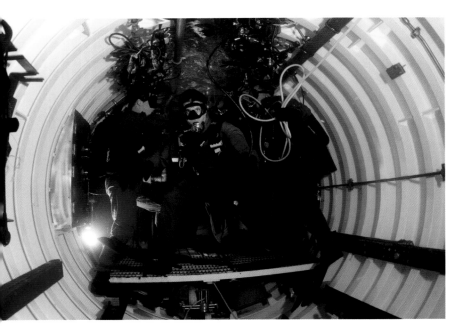

ABOVE **The midget submarine hangar compartment of the dry deck shelter believed to be identical to the SFPB.** *(USN photo/CPM (Diver) Andrew McKaskle)*

information from the MoD, the supposition in the specialist press is that the SFPB is probably the latest version of a USN dry deck shelter (DDS). The SFPB appears to be a similar size to the DDS (about 13m long and 3m in diameter). The DDS comprises three watertight chambers made from HY-80 steel within a GRP fairing. The spherical forward chamber is a hyperbaric chamber for divers to reacclimatise following deep and long dives. The aft chamber, the hangar, has a full-diameter door that allows a midget submarine or raiding boats to be launched. The latest USN DDS has a remotely operated door. It is reported that up to 20 divers can use the aft chamber as a lock-in/lock-out compartment for a surge deployment. The DDS can be pressurised too, so that personnel can exit or enter it in 40m of water. The SFPB is a portable fixture that can be fitted to any *Astute* class boat that is heading to a crisis zone where Special Forces may be required to covertly approach a hostile or denied shore. If the SFPB were to carry a midget submarine, there would be a means for the stand-off insertion while the SSN is dived. Surface warships and helicopters

provide an alternative means of deploying midget submarines, but they are much easier to detect.

The current midget submarine is reported unofficially to be similar to that deployed by the USN – the electrically propelled Swimmer Delivery Vehicle Mk 8 that was updated to the Mod 1 version in the 1990s. This vehicle is a chariot for divers wearing self-contained underwater breathing apparatus. The SFPB appears to be larger than those photographed on *Swiftsure* class boats. This accords with US statements that their larger Shallow-Water Combat Submersible will replace the obsolescent SDV in both the USN and RN. It weighs approximately 3.5T and its pilot and navigator will transport six commandos across several kilometres near the surface.

Unlike the SDV, the USN's Shallow-Water Combat Submersible is likely to feature an electro-optical periscope, Doppler sonar array and an advanced INS so that the craft will be able to carry out its missions without surfacing to take GPS bearings. Quiet electronic motors, passive sonar and a sound-absorbing GRP hull will give the vessels a degree of stealth.

Valedictory comments

Nuclear-powered submarines are some of the most challenging and complex engineering projects in design, production and operation. The programme to produce HMS *Astute* and her sister ships suffered many setbacks and had to overcome several technical problems – a common feature of any large project with a high level of state-of-the art innovation. Now in service, HMS *Astute* and other submarines of the class are proving to be powerful and highly effective additions to the fleet. They benefit from a reactor fuel core that removes the need for refuelling in the life of the submarine, thereby significantly reducing through-life costs. The boats entered service with some innovative technology, increased weapons capacity and a new Special Forces fit. These allow a submarine originally specified at the end of the Cold War to be well suited to modern operations.

To meet evolving threats and new adversaries, HMS *Astute*'s capabilities will have to develop.

JACKSPEAK

Using a DDS is considered as a perilous evolution and has given rise to its nickname of 'the caravan of death'.

LEFT The midget submarine SDV Mk 8 Mod 1 leaving the DDS. (USN photo/ CPM (Diver) Andrew McKaskle)

Equipment programmes are already in place to capitalise on the open architecture of the *Astute* class computer-based systems that allow rapid upgrades of combat and control equipment. Studies of future operations have suggested that HMS *Astute* will be able to evolve to fulfil its roles for the foreseeable future, a testament to her enduring utility and flexibility. Future strategic challenges will predicate a greater requirement for HMS *Astute*'s inherent qualities – known as the 'seven deadly virtues' – of flexibility, mobility, endurance, reach, autonomy, stealth and punch.

The living standards on HMS *Astute*, while still austere, set a new, higher standard for the Submarine Service. The service needs to attract high-calibre individuals, as submarines are complex vessels and their operations require highly trained and motivated personnel. Improved living conditions will go some way to attracting and retaining submariners. Nevertheless the boat's complement can be confined for months at a time in close company. This life consequently requires exceptional individuals who can cope with such mental, physical and emotional demands. The rewards come from being a member of a highly professional team operating one of the most complex vehicles ever built as it battles an inhospitable environment. They must train hard to overcome life-threatening scenarios in both peacetime and wartime. Such a tight-knit team functions on mutual trust in their comrades' expertise. This camaraderie often leads to close and lifelong friendships.

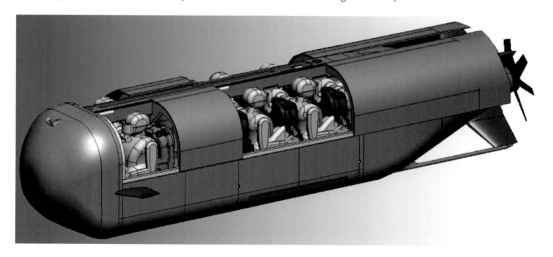

LEFT USN's Shallow-Water Combat Submersible. (Teledyne Brown)

Acoustic and electromagnetic frequencies

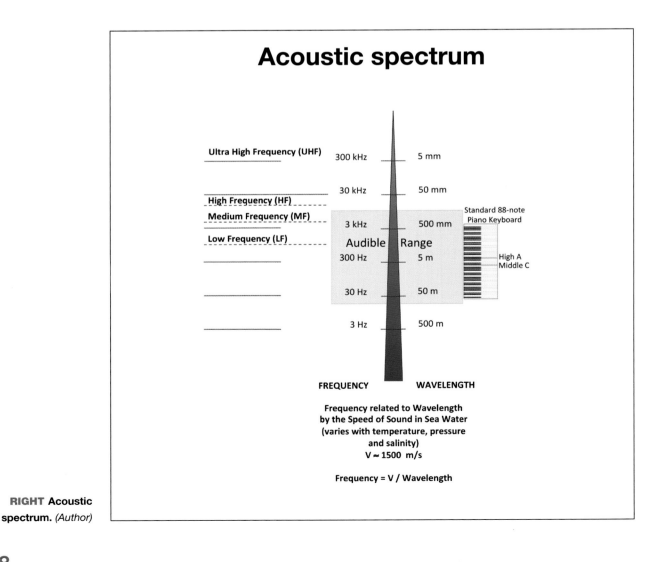

RIGHT Acoustic spectrum. *(Author)*

Electromagnetic spectrum

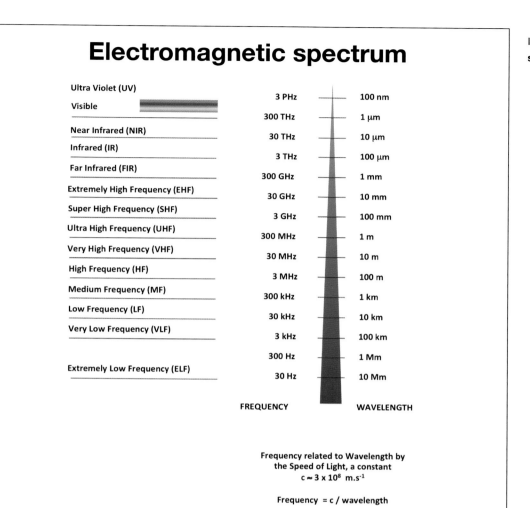

Ultra Violet (UV)
Visible
Near Infrared (NIR)
Infrared (IR)
Far Infrared (FIR)
Extremely High Frequency (EHF)
Super High Frequency (SHF)
Ultra High Frequency (UHF)
Very High Frequency (VHF)
High Frequency (HF)
Medium Frequency (MF)
Low Frequency (LF)
Very Low Frequency (VLF)
Extremely Low Frequency (ELF)

FREQUENCY	WAVELENGTH
3 PHz	100 nm
300 THz	1 µm
30 THz	10 µm
3 THz	100 µm
300 GHz	1 mm
30 GHz	10 mm
3 GHz	100 mm
300 MHz	1 m
30 MHz	10 m
3 MHz	100 m
300 kHz	1 km
30 kHz	10 km
3 kHz	100 km
300 Hz	1 Mm
30 Hz	10 Mm

Frequency related to Wavelength by
the Speed of Light, a constant
$$c \approx 3 \times 10^8 \text{ m.s}^{-1}$$

Frequency = c / wavelength

Radar designations

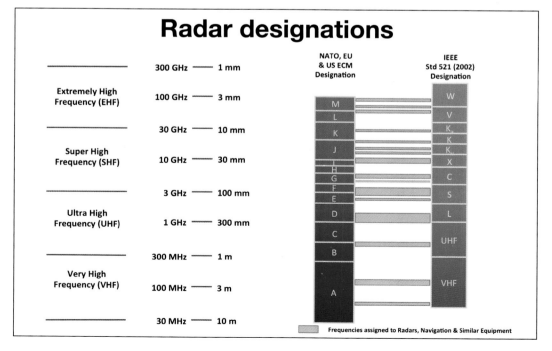

Frequencies assigned to Radars, Navigation & Similar Equipment

Appendix 2

Glossary of naval and shipwright terms

Aft Towards the stern of the submarine.

Athwartships Orientated across the submarine.

Attitude An indication of the angle of roll, pitch and yaw (see image on page 84).

Ballast Water taken into the MTB to decrease the buoyancy of the submarine when diving. This is blown out by compressed air when the submarine wishes to surface. Also solid material used to ensure stability.

Bib cock A tap whose nozzle is a horizontal pipe that is then bent downwards.

Bollard A short, thick post (originally a short tree trunk) used for securing ropes and **hawsers** (q.v.).

Bow The forward part of the submarine, generally meaning the forward free-flood space.

Breech The rear part of the barrel of a gun or weapon tube, especially the opening and associated mechanism that allows the loading of a weapon.

Broach To break the sea's surface.

Bulkheads Vertical partitions.

Butts Prefabricated units that fit together but do not overlap, so may be welded together to form a larger unit.

Cabins Sleeping accommodation of up to six bunks. Spaces with more than six bunks are termed **bunk spaces** or, if general-purpose living spaces, **messes**.

Capstan Rotating machine to haul in anchor chains, **hawsers** and the like.

Calorifier An electric water heater.

Captain The commanding officer of a warship is informally called captain even though he or she may not hold that rank. Most nuclear submarine COs hold the rank of commander.

Closed boat The shipbuilding term for a submarine where the hull has been completely welded together so any activities such as final outfitting and testing have to be carried out using only the normal accesses.

Commission (*verb*) The process of exhaustive testing to ensure that any equipment or system, having been constructed or modified, is verified to be in accordance with design and will correctly and safely operate. A submarine undergoes a similar process after which it is accepted by the RN and is formally commissioned with the award of the prefix HMS.

Compartment A generic term for a space between decks whose sides are bulkheads and, possibly, the submarine's pressure hull.

Con The action of directing the steering of the ship; this responsibility is passed to another officer with the phrase 'You have the con'.

Decks Horizontal surfaces.

Defects Any item that does not meet the design intent (however minor). May range from a faulty pump to a scratch on paintwork.

Draught When the submarine is on the surface, the vertical distance between the waterline and the bottom of the hull.

Dress (*verb*) To grind a weld in order to remove the cap of excess material and produce a smooth finish that is flush with the surrounding steel plate.

Drop anchor Lowering the anchor to the seabed to secure the submarine.

Escape compartment Watertight compartment bounded by pressure hull and bulkheads to provide a safe haven for personnel to await rescue. Contains, or is connected to, an escape tower.

Evolution A task, often to effect a new arrangement or disposition, requiring co-ordinated action for its successful completion.

Fairlead A ring-like structure on the deck to guide cables or hawsers.

Fighting the ship A term relating to the

performance of offensive and defensive evolutions dating from a period when such military duties were distinct from those of mariners who were responsible for 'sailing the ship'.

Fleet (*verb*) To move smoothly into a confined space.

Fore/forward Towards the front of the submarine.

Free-flood space The volume between the outer hull and the pressure hull that floods with water when the submarine submerges.

Fuze A device to initiate the detonation of an explosive and not to be confused with an electrical **fuse** that prevents high currents from causing damage.

Galley An area for the preparation of food (equivalent to a kitchen ashore).

Gash Rubbish or refuse, hence also something 'surplus to requirements' or useless.

General arrangement (GA) A diagram (generally printed A0 size) showing a plan of every deck and an elevation of the vessel showing compartments. Although designers now use 3-D models for their work, the GA is still a useful summary of the vessel's layout.

Hatch An opening in a deck allowing access to a lower deck by means of a companionway.

Hawser A thick rope for mooring or towing.

Heads Toilets.

Hold-point A point in the commissioning or operation of the reactor beyond which progress is prohibited without the consent of the relevant authority.

Hot-work Any construction activity involving heat such as welding or removal of material through burning.

Hydroplane A fin-like attachment, normally horizontal, that can be angled about a horizontal axis to control the submarine to rise or fall in the water.

Intelligent customer An organisation capable of specifying requirements, supervising work and technically reviewing the output before, during and after implementation.

Intelligent supplier A supplier which has in-depth knowledge and experience of submarines in terms of the technical solutions available, the context in which they are operated and the techniques available for their construction.

Littoral The area of sea close to the coast.

Masts Tall, narrow structures named in recognition of the masts that carry the sails of sailing ships.

Module A construction assembly that is pre-outfitted with equipment and systems so that it may be tested before it is slid into place within the appropriate construction unit of the submarine's hull.

Mouse (*verb*) To tie-wrap loose equipment,

ABOVE HMS *Astute* leaving HMNB Clyde. *(Crown Copyright/ LA(Phot) A.J.MacLeod)* such as clips or chain, to prevent rattling.

Muzzle The part of the barrel of a gun or weapon tube from which ordnance or the weapon appears when discharged.

Noise Acoustic energy.

Pay out (*verb*) To allow a cable or wire to be dispensed.

Pennant number (originally pendant) Letter and numbers identifying the type and unique number of a submarine; HMS *Astute*'s pendant number is S119, where S indicates that it is a submarine. Later boats of the class will have the identifiers S120 to S125 in the order that they are laid down.

Periscope depth The depth of dived submarine that is sufficiently close to the surface to operate her periscope.

Pitch Up and down movement of the bow and stern about the horizontal axis (see image on page 84).

Plummer block A bearing used to support a propeller shaft.

Port The left-hand sides of the submarine *when facing forward*.

Pressure hull The central structure of the submarine occupied by the submarine's complement and maintained at approximately atmospheric (surface) pressure.

Redundant Components that are normally not required until the principal components fail,

RIGHT Sailors standing proudly on the casing of HMS *Astute*. *(Crown Copyright/LA(Phot) Stuart 'Stu' Hill)*

in which event they automatically take on the functions of the failed item. **Dual redundant** means that there is one fall-back item and **triple redundant** have two fall-backs.

Roll Movement from side to side about the longitudinal axis (see image on page 84).

Scupper Any cunningly contrived orifice for the speedy removal of excess moisture – an opening, especially on the casing, that enables water to drain over the sides.

Scuttle To deliberately sink.

Ship-wise During building, the description of a part of the ship that is in the correct orientation – for instance, a unit that has been fabricated vertically for ease of working is then turned horizontally, 'ship-wise', to the orientation where it can be welded in place on the boat.

Shipwright Someone whose occupation is to design, construct and repair ships; originally a hewer of wood.

Sickbay The place on board where a sailor can receive medical attention. In the days of sail sick-berths were located in the rounded stern that is in the shape of a bay, so sick-berths became sickbays.

Skeg (in the case of a submarine) Projecting section beneath the rudder.

Snort When on the surface or at periscope depth, to draw air into the submarine through the snort mast (and expel used air through the exhaust mast).

Sonobuoy A disposable sonar device dropped by helicopters searching for submarines; its cylindrical main body floats on the sea's surface for a few hours, during which time it sends data back to the helicopter.

Soundings Measurements of the depth of water beneath the ship; now achieved by sonar, these were originally done by 'heaving (or swinging) the lead'.

Starboard The right-hand side of the submarine *when facing forward*.

Stern The back, or aft, part of the submarine.

Stowage Space for storage; stowing implies storing in a neat and compact way.

Tankside valves Spring-loaded non-return valves used to supply air to exterior tanks; they shut off the supply line at the pressure hull to prevent water from entering the air line when the tanks are flooded.

Transverse activities Design factors that must be tackled on a whole-boat level. They have contributions from many of the systems and complex interactions between these systems must be taken into account. Examples are safety, survivability and ship power and cooling.

Trim To adjust the overall buoyancy balance of the submarine.

Victuals (pronounced 'vittles') Food supplies and provisions for the submarine's company, hence 'to victual' (take food on board the ship) and 'victualling' (supply of food).

Wardroom The compartment where the officers eat and relax.

To weigh an anchor Raising an anchor from the seabed and pulling it up to its stowed position within the free-flood space in the bow. The term derives from the time before mechanisation when sailors raised anchors by using their weight to turn a capstan.

Yaw A movement from side to side about the vertical axis (see image on page 84).

ABOVE *Audacious*, the fourth *Astute* class submarine, is rolled out onto the ship-lift in Barrow-in-Furness. *(BAE Systems)*

OVERLEAF HMS *Astute* at sea in Scottish waters, from the stern. *(Crown Copyright/LA(Phot) Will Haigh)*

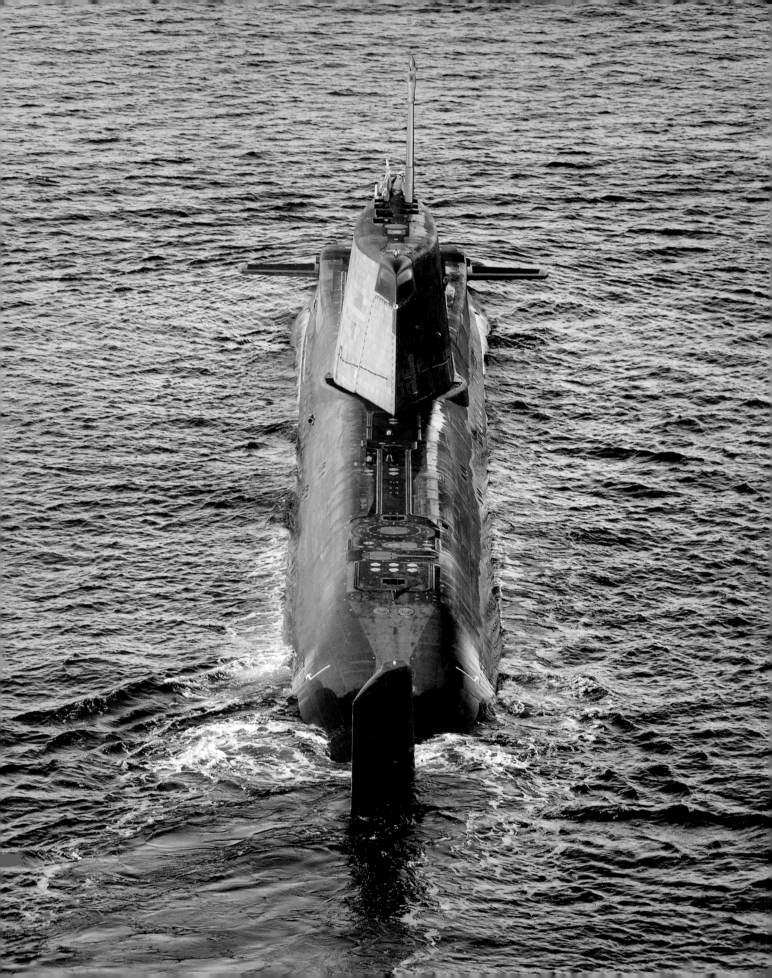

Appendix 3

Abbreviations

AC	alternating current
ACMS	*Astute* combat management system
ALARP	as low as reasonably practicable
AMM	auxiliary machinery module
AUTEC	Atlantic Underwater Test and Evaluation Center
B2TC	Batch 2 *Trafalgar* class
BAe	British Aerospace
BAE	BAE Systems
BUTEC	British Underwater Test and Evaluation Centre
CAD	computer-aided design
CDM	command deck module
CESM	communications electronic support measures
CH_4	methane
Cl_2	chlorine
CO	commanding officer
CO	carbon monoxide
CO_2	carbon dioxide
COTS	commercial off-the-shelf
CST	contractor's sea trials
DC	direct current
DDD	deep diving depth
DDH	Devonshire Dock Hall
DDS	dry deck shelter
DG	diesel generator
DSMAC	digital scene-matching area correlation
DSTP	deep siren tactical paging
ECG	emergency cylinder group
EHF	extra high-frequency
ELF	extra low-frequency
EPM	emergency propulsion motor
EVM	earned value management
FERM	forward engine room module
FET	forward escape trunk
FOSSN	follow-on SSN
FRTAS	fully reelable towed array sonar
GPS	global positioning system
GRP	glass-reinforced plastic
H_2	hydrogen
HAP	hydroxylammonium perchlorate
HF	high-frequency
HMCS	Her Majesty's Canadian Ship
HMNB	Her Majesty's Naval Base
HMS	Her Majesty's Ship

HP	high-pressure
HWT	heavyweight torpedo
INS	inertial navigation system
IPMS	integrated platform management system
KUR	Key user requirements
LAN	local area network
LCDs	liquid crystal displays
LP	low-pressure
MBG	main bottle group
MBT	main ballast tank
MCP	main coolant pump
MFC	multifunction console
Mk	mark
MMC	Monopolies and Mergers Commission
MoD	Ministry of Defence
MOD	modification
MP	medium-pressure
MPMP	main propulsion machinery package
MRM	manoeuvring room module
MSC	main static converter
N_2	nitrogen
NAS	New Assembly Shop
NBF	Nuclear Build Facility
NDE	non-destructive examination
NEST	naval EHF/SHF (Satcom) terminal
NOAA	National Oceanic and Atmospheric Administration
NSRP	nuclear steam-raising plant
O_2	oxygen
PC	personal computer
PCI	peripheral component interconnect
PCO	Prime Contract Office
PFAS	planar flank array sonar
PWR	pressurised water reactor
RCI	reactor control and instrumentation (system)
RESM	radar electronic support measures
RICE	rationalised internal communication equipment
RLG	ring-laser gyrocompass
RM	Royal Marines
RN	Royal Navy
RPV	reactor pressure vessel

SO_2	sulphur dioxide
S&T	*Swiftsure*- and *Trafalgar*-class submarines
Satcom	satellite communications
SCAD	submarine/sonar counter-measures acoustic decoy
SFPB	Special Forces payload bay
SHF	super high-frequency
SHU	sensor head unit
SMCC	submarine command course
SMITE	Submarine Machinery Installation and Test Establishment
SPM	secondary propulsion motor
SSBN	(designation for) ballistic missile armed submarine
SSDE	submerged signal and decoy ejector
SSISC	Submarine Systems Integration and Support Centre
SSK	(designation for) conventional submarine
SSN	(designation for) nuclear fleet submarine
SSN20	(designation for) first design for a *Trafalgar*-class replacement
SSN0Z	original designation of *Astute*-class design
SWCS	Shallow-Water Combat Submersible
SWIM	submarine weapon interface manager
TEDAS	tactical environmental data acquisition system
TerCom	terrain contour-matching
TG	turbo-generator
TLAM	Tomahawk land-attack missile
TTWCS	tactical Tomahawk weapons control system
UHF	ultra high-frequency
UK	United Kingdom
USN	United States Navy
USS	United States Ship/Submarine
VLF	very low-frequency
VSEL	Vickers Shipbuilding and Engineering Ltd
WHLS	weapons handling and launch system

Index

electronic product model 24
equipment procurement specifications 24
expertise lost 19
flaws 53
Initial Certificate of Design 24
provenance of elements 15
'requirement creep' 15
responsibility 18
shortage of designers 21, 49, 55
Diesel fuel tanks 31
Diving 8, 42, 47, 64, 68, 73, 82, 84, 86
angle 161
characteristics 40
collapse depth 64
deep diving depth (DDD) 63-64, 73, 76, 139
'submarine equation' 12
Dounreay Shore Test Facility 110-111
HMS *Vulcan* Naval Reactor Test Establishment 110-111

Electric Boat company 21
Electrical systems and supply 40, 80, 100, 113, 118-122
diesel generators (DGs) 36, 120, 122-123
schematics 119-120
secondary circuit 113
shore supply 121
turbo-generators (TGs) 33, 100, 113, 118-119
Electronic system 57
Elements 101-104
nuclear structure 101
Entry into service 7
Escape systems 40, 63, 150-151
submerged signal &decoy ejector system (SSDE) 150-151
Exercise Fellowship 52-53

Falklands Conflict 11, 118, 167
Fin 36-37, 69-70, 72, 175
Free-flood spaces 68-69, 160, 162
aft 65
equipment 64
forward 64
sonar array dome 134
Fuelling 15, 24, 42-43, 100, 109, 176

Gauss, Carl 83
GEC 16
GEC-Marconi 14, 16-17, 20, 55
GEC-Marine 17-19
General Bathymetric Chart of the Oceans (GEBCO) 159
GIANT2 sea-going vessel 110
Greenert USN, Admiral Jonathan 52-53
Greenland-Iceland-UK gap 164-165

Handover to RN 46, 53-55
Health & Safety Executive
Office of Nuclear Regulation 37
HRH Camilla, the Duchess of Rothesay 39, 50
Hull 60-65, 80-82
acoustic tiles 29, 36-37, 78, 80-82
aft machinery space 116
bulkheads 61-62
casing equipment 68
construction units 27-30, 57
damage control doorway 62
domes (forward and aft) 31, 61
holes and penetrations 63, 139
installed items 12
midget submarine hangar compartment 176
nuclear reactor compartment 61-62
outer 61, 64-65, 68-69, 80

outfitting 36, 57
painting 36
passageways 93
pressurised 16, 21, 27, 29, 35, 61, 63, 78, 92; aft 116
reactor compartment 62, 111-112
sacrificial cathodic protection 83-84
Special Forces payload bay (SFPB) 53, 70, 175-177
testing 49
Unit 1 stem dome 31
Units 4 36; 4/5 32; 5 37; 5/6 36; 6/7 31, 35; 7/8 36
watertight doors 75
Hydraulic systems 40, 68, 73-75, 78, 139
Hydrogen 88

Incidents and accidents 48-49
collision with a tug 49
groundings 48, 74
HMS *Warspite* and Russian submarine collision 118
junior rating gun rampage 48
under-ice 164-165
In-service date 17-18, 21
Integrated Logistic Support 18
Integrated Platform Management System (IPMS) 78-80, 84
Iraq 11

Jane's Weapons: Naval 156, 169

Keel-laying ceremony 30
Kings Bay submarine base, USA 50-51
Magnetic Silencing Facility 50-51, 82
Kockums 16

Launches and celebrations 36, 39-40, 42
Laundry machines 91
Laying-down ceremony 20
Libya 11
Life cycle 12, 15
Lister RN, Rear Admiral Simon 49
Lloyds Register 19
Loch Goil 48
Lockheed-Martin 16

Magnetic signature 82-84
degaussing 82-83
electromagnetic signature 83, 178
flash deperming 51, 82
induced signature 82-83
Main bottle group 68
Manoeuvring 160
limitation diagram 74-75
Manufacturing staff 24
shortages 21, 55
Marx, Karl 17-18
Masts 57, 69-71
AZE CESM 72, 142
AZL 72-73
communications electronic support measures (CESM) 73
fin 72
Naval EHF/SHF satcom terminal 72
navigation 70, 72
quiet modular 71
raising equipment 139
Snort and diesel exhaust 72, 120, 123
UHF satcom communications 72
Midget submarines 176-177
Swimmer Delivery Vehicle Mk 8 176-177

MoD (Ministry of Defence) 15-18, 21, 109
Defence Nuclear Safety Regulator 37
design team 13
Naval Overseeing Service 21
project team 14-15
Modules 21, 31-35, 57
Command Deck Module (CDM) 33-36
Forward Engine Room Module (FERM) 32-33
installation 31-36
Main Propulsion Machinery Package (MPMP) 31, 33
Manoeuvring Room Module (MRM) 32, 80, 117
sequence 32
Molyneux RN, Lt Cdr Ian 48
Monopolies and Mergers Commission 17

Naming 39, 50
National Grid 33
NATO 53, 164
Navigation aids 84-85
attitude and heading reference systems 85
gyrocompasses 85; fibre-optic (FOG) 85
inertial navigation system (INS) 84-85
motion sensors 84
Navigation lights 72-73
Navigation positions 70, 72
North Atlantic Ocean 84, 164
North Pole 9
Nuclear deterrent 9-10, 13, 25, 164
Nuclear fission 101-104
configuration of fuel bundles 105
nuclear chain reaction 104
Nuclear reactors 9, 12, 15-16, 19, 31, 42, 82, 99, 176
output 114
PWR (pressurised water reactor) 10, 13, 15, 37, 42, 100, 104-107
reactor control and instrumentation (RCI) 117-118
battle short switch 118
second PWR (PWR2) 13, 15, 26, 42, 109-111
prototype plant 109-110
shielding 107-108
testing and commissioning 37
Nuclear safety regulations 56
Nuclear steam raising plant (NSRP) 100, 109, 111-113, 117, 119

Operation Allied Force 155
Operational deployment and procedures 8, 11-12, 47, 49, 53-55, 63, 143
anti-submarine warfare exercises 54
Astute's first deployment 141
future 177
land attack 162, 169-173
long patrols 96
night-time 141
special forces insertion 11, 53, 65, 70, 175-176
equipment 175-176
inflatable raiding raft 65, 175
strategic intelligence, surveillance and reconnaissance 175
surface ship attack 167-169
Oxygen supply 63, 86-87

Performance 16, 160
Periscopes 63, 72-73, 137-141
direct-view 138-139
electro-optical non-hull-penetrating (CM010) 137-141, 162
workstation 140
Pipe and cables 24, 32-33, 36, 82
Platform control system 19